This book is a lifeline of hope when you are drowning in sorrow. In forty years of pastoring, I have never seen a family grieve the loss of a child so thoroughly and transparently or with such faith. I urged September to share her story for those of us who need to find a better way to grieve. You will be marked by her journey—and its ultimate message of joy.

BILL HYBELS
Founder and senior pastor, Willow Creek Community Church

I need to know, deep in the sinews of my soul, that death doesn't have the final word. I try to ignore death—my own—but I am even more committed to hiding from the potential loss of those I desperately love. September Vaudrey and her family suffered a loss most of us can't imagine. She enters it with intense honesty and writes with the lyric power of a poet. She invites us to sing hope in the minor key. I could not read her stunning and beautiful prose without believing even more that death doesn't win. I wish you the courage to read this holy labor and prize the radical hope it will call you to hold.

DAN B. ALLENDER, PhD
Professor of counseling psychology and founding president, The Seattle School of Theology & Psychology

Agonizing and heartrending and poignant as grief, grateful and faithful and tender as new love, these words and this story have in them the power to name what cannot be named and to bring life where it seems life could not be again.

JOHN ORTBERG
Senior pastor, Menlo Church; author of *All the Places to Go*

May 31, 2008, changed everything for everyone who knew and loved Katie Vaudrey. *Colors of Goodbye* brings you into the precious, raw, honest, defining journey of the soul as uninvited, irreversible, and horrific circumstances invade the Vaudrey family—and they begin the trek to rebuild their lives. I see and love Jesus more deeply today because of this story. You will too.

SANTIAGO "JIMMY" MELLADO
President and CEO, Compassion International

I was scared to open this book because I knew that its pages held the story of a mother who was living my worst nightmare: the loss of a child. But once I started reading, I was swept into a captivating, hopeful, and exquisitely written story. I could not put it down. *Colors of Goodbye* is a deeply moving memoir that will inspire you and awaken your heart to the goodness of God, even in the midst of your darkest hour.

JENNIFER DUKES LEE
Author of *Love Idol*

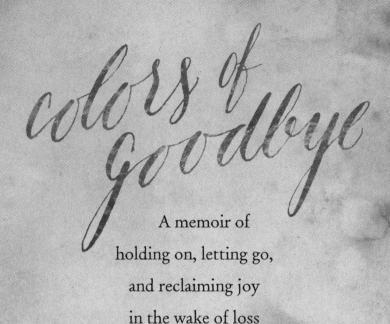

colors of goodbye

A memoir of
holding on, letting go,
and reclaiming joy
in the wake of loss

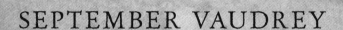

SEPTEMBER VAUDREY

TYNDALE
MOMENTUM

An Imprint of
Tyndale House Publishers, Inc.

Visit Tyndale online at www.tyndale.com.

Visit Tyndale Momentum online at www.tyndalemomentum.com.

Tyndale Momentum and the Tyndale Momentum logo are registered trademarks of Tyndale House Publishers, Inc. Tyndale Momentum is an imprint of Tyndale House Publishers, Inc., Carol Stream, Illinois.

Cover designed by Mark Anthony Lane II

Interior designed by Julie Chen

Published in association with Christopher Ferebee, attorney and literary agent, www.christopherferebee.com.

All Scripture quotations are taken from the Holy Bible, *New International Version*,® *NIV*.® Copyright © 1973, 1978, 1984, 2011 by Biblica, Inc.® Used by permission. All rights reserved worldwide.

The names of some individuals and institutions have been changed to honor their privacy. Conversations have been recreated to the best of the author's memory.

Library of Congress Cataloging-in-Publication Data
Names: Vaudrey, September, author.
Title: Colors of goodbye : a memoir of holding on, letting go, and reclaiming joy in the wake of loss / September Vaudrey.
Description: Carol Stream, IL : Tyndale House Publishers, Inc., 2016.
Identifiers: LCCN 2015042661 | ISBN 9781496408174 (sc)
Subjects: LCSH: Vaudrey, September, author. | Children—Death—Religious aspects—Christianity. | Mother and child—Religious aspects—Christianity. | Vaudrey, Katie, -2008.
Classification: LCC BV4907 .V38 2016 | DDC 248.8/66092—dc23 LC record available at http://lccn.loc.gov/2015042661

Printed in the United States of America

22   21   20   19   18   17   16
7   6   5   4   3   2   1

For Scott,

whose wisdom, strength, and selflessness are soil for my soul,

and whose relentless encouragement brought these pages to be.

For Tember, Sam, Bethany, Andrea, and Matt,

who live each day with unflinching kindness and undaunted joy.

And for Katie,

who left ripples as she'd hoped,

and who never will be forgotten.

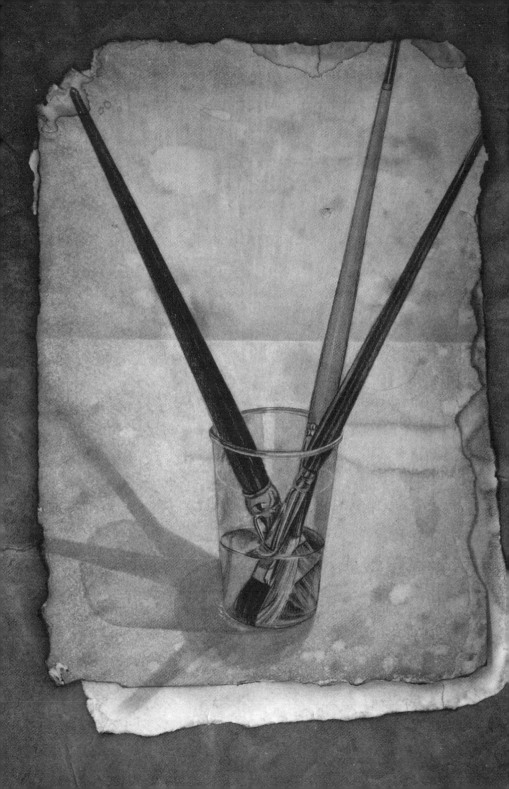

CONTENTS

"But One"

A pile of heavy winter boots
Makes puddles by the kitchen door,
And icy mittens, hats, and coats
Reflect the snowy day's explore.
The day was rich and fast and fun,
And all the beds are filled, but one.

Now suppertime has come and gone,
The table full, each belly fed.
The conversation lingered on
Till weary, we climbed into bed.
The sun has set, the day is done,
And all the heads are kissed, but one.

We lie alone, with grateful hearts
And memories that will not fade.
But slow and long, these years apart—
Oh, how I wish our girl had stayed.
Another Christmas come and gone,
And memories made with all, but one.

But just beyond these lovely days,
Alongside streets of brilliant gold,
Our daughter dances, laughs, and plays
And paints in brushstrokes bright and bold.
Here, all the dreads of earth are gone,
And Son shines brighter than the sun,
And death has lost its sting at last,
And beds are filled, and life begun.

—S. L. V., December 2013

Foreword

by Shauna Niequist

Bestselling author of Savor *and* Bread and Wine

THE FIRST TIME LOSS RIPPED THROUGH MY LIFE, it left me deeply disoriented. I felt profoundly alone, like the first person on the planet to experience such grief. That's how it is, isn't it? Grief sends us to outer space, lost and isolated.

And then someone reaches out to us, pulls us close, whispers their own story. And it changes everything.

We live in a culture that doesn't grieve well—we shut down, close our hearts, pretend, pretend, pretend. This book is a vision for another way, a better way, a more whole and wholehearted way of living with a broken heart. The exact circumstances of what has broken your heart do not matter; September's story will call out to you, a much-needed voice in the silence that so often comes with loss.

My friend September is, simply put, one of the best moms I know. And I'm not the only one who thinks so. My friends and I—moms of young kids, babies, rookies—have been watching September and her family for years, taking notes, asking questions.

September and Scott have raised the kind of family you want your family to be—not perfect, but real and warm and smart and funny and totally imperfect in such lovely and endearing ways. Long before that terrible May day, that terrible phone call, that terrible everything, September was a mom we all wanted to be like.

And then in the midst of all the terrible, right there in the middle of it, September was still a mom we wanted to be like: She was devastated and yet faithful, howling and yet praying in alternating moments. If we'd been watching her before, we were watching all the more closely now as she walked through what is commonly known as every parent's worst nightmare: losing a child.

What we saw in those days and months was such honesty and bravery. Some people run away from grief. September didn't. Some people transform into grief itself. September didn't. We watched her raise five beautiful, funny kids, and then we watched her bury one extraordinary daughter, and the way she did that blew our minds.

Because, frankly, sometimes I don't think it can be done. Sometimes I think when pain like that slices through your life, you just fold. You drink first thing in the morning, maybe, or you numb yourself a million different ways. You escape into the past or a fantasy life or . . . I don't even know what the other options are. But September presented us with a new one: You live. You live fully and with a broken heart, and some days are a mess and some are better, and you just keep living. I can't describe to you how astonishing it was to watch her do this.

And now, several years later, we're still watching September. She continues to teach us, giving us a vision for the moms we can be. This is a story about one amazing daughter, but it's also a story about an extraordinary mother, a very special family, and a legacy of love and laughter and honesty and resilience that has affected thousands of people throughout the years.

This book is a love letter, but it's also a map: *Here is a way through.* Not around the grief, not hiding from the pain, but right on through the center of the journey—loss, heartbreak, joy, new life, memories, mistakes, celebrations—all of it. This book is a map for many of us who have been lost in the wilderness of grief of one kind or another. This beautiful book is a hand reaching into the darkness, a voice whispering, *I know the way home.*

vermillion

[ver-'mil-yuhn] / a brilliant, scarlet red

The shocking, retina-searing red

forces its way into our eyes.

We cannot bear to look—

but we cannot look away.

All we have to decide is what to do
with the time that is given us.

GANDALF, *THE FELLOWSHIP OF THE RING*,
BY J. R. R. TOLKIEN

I want to leave ripples in the lives I leave behind.

KATIE VAUDREY, 15

1

2:50 P.M., SATURDAY, MAY 31, 2008

Katie races down the stairs and into the kitchen, where I am cutting brownies into squares.

"Mom! Where are my keys?" she asks, pulling on her black flats as she scans the room. "It's ten to three! I'm gonna be late!"

Even flustered, our nineteen-year-old daughter looks electric, her brown eyes sparkling with excitement about her first day as a summer waitress at Bandito Barney's, a sports bar fifteen minutes from our home in the northwest suburbs of Chicago. Setting the brownie pan aside, I turn and help her scour countertops and tables piled high with desserts for the party we've been hosting since nine this morning—an end-of-year celebration for our church's drama team. Katie's sixteen-year-old brother, Sam, and fourteen-year-old sister, September (Tember for short), are members of the team. My friend Deanna, the team's director, continues to fill platters as I join Katie in her search.

"I can't believe I'm late!" Katie says, rifling through the key basket next to the fridge. "I've just been hanging out here all day long, waiting to go to work, but then at the last minute I got distracted and forgot to leave! *Where are my keys?*"

Katie rarely screws up like this. She's the creative type, to be sure— she's a painter majoring in studio art with a respectable portfolio already under her belt. But Katie's artsy personality has a heavy dollop of responsibility mixed in, which usually keeps lapses like this at bay. All morning, she helped me direct party details in the kitchen, which has been overflowing with the laughter and bustle of dozens of thespians, young and old.

Cohosting this event with Katie—our middle child, a month home from her freshman year at Azusa Pacific University—has filled me up. Once things quieted after lunch, she retreated to her bedroom to check Facebook and write messages to friends as she waited to leave for work. She lost track of time, and now she's going to be late.

I search through her purse—no keys—and then sling its strap over her shoulder. Katie checks her pants pockets for the keys, and then she rummages again through the key basket, digging deeper this time.

"Aha!" She raises her keys triumphantly from the basket. "Victory! Right where they belong! Okay, I'm off!"

She flashes an impish grin and rushes for the back door, past her dad who has come into the kitchen to see what the commotion is about. As she hurries by, Katie takes his hand, lifts it over her head, and does a quick pirouette.

"Bye, Daddy!" she calls.

"Bye, Bug," Scott replies, using her childhood nickname, Katiebug—Bug, for short. I follow to see her off.

I am struck by how especially terrific Katie looks today. *What a beauty, inside and out.* She's sporting a crisp, white blouse; jean capris; and a blue plaid men's tie she picked up at a thrift store, knotted loosely around her neck. She has her own hippie-esque sense of fashion and consistently looks adorable, whether in sweats or a skirt. But today, for some reason, I take note. Hair, makeup, the men's necktie—everything works.

"Thanks for all your help with the party, Katie. Have a great first day. You'll be fantastic!"

"Thanks, Mom! Bye!" she says, closing the door behind her. As I walk back toward the kitchen, I hear the door pop open again. "Aagh!" Katie says, her voice sharp, her eyes flashing. "Someone's car is blocking me in!" My daughter's world is either hot or cold—rarely in-between.

"All right already, Katie," I say. "Settle down."

"That's my car," Deanna says, looking out the back door at where Katie's Taurus is parked. "I'll move it!" She grabs her purse and hurries outside.

"Katie, don't take out your frustrations on others," I say. "It's no one's fault but your own that you're running late."

"I'm just so *irritated*!"

"No excuse for rudeness."

"*Fine.*"

Deanna reenters the kitchen. "All set!" she says, grinning and bowing melodramatically. "Your path is clear!"

"Thanks, Deanna!" Katie says, sunny once again. "Thanks so much!"

I walk my daughter to her car—a '94 gold Ford Taurus she bought from a family friend. She climbs in, starts the engine, backs down the driveway, and pulls onto the street. I wave goodbye, but she is focused on the road ahead and doesn't notice. I stand there watching as she drives away. I wave again in case she looks in her rearview mirror, which she does not. Her Taurus pulls around the bend and out of sight.

It's almost three o'clock. With a fifteen-minute drive to her new job, she will indeed be late. I know she feels bad for losing track of the time—and on her first day, to boot. *But they'll forgive her.* Katie's genuine joy and playfulness have a way of winning people over, even new bosses who have every right to be angry.

Before I head back inside, I take a pass through the backyard. Deanna and her assistant, Brooke, have gathered everyone in a semi-circle for their closing ceremony. They are presenting trophies—not for Best Actor and such, but for important character traits and effort. How rich to have this community of people in my kids' lives. It's been a picture-perfect day.

❧

Five minutes later, Katie calls from her cell phone.

"Mom! I need to tell my boss I'm going to be late. Can you find Bandito Barney's phone number? It's on my desk."

"Sure, no problem." I run upstairs to her room, find the number, and read it aloud to her.

"Thanks, Mom. You're a lifesaver! I still can't believe I'm going to be late on my very first day!" She moans but then laughs. In her world, making low-cost mistakes is good story fodder—an opportunity to poke fun at herself later, once the crisis is averted.

"Don't speed, baby," I say. "They'll know you'll be late."

"I won't. Love you, Mama!"

"I love you, too."

The party ends, and I spend the next hour saying goodbye to the team. Only a few of Sam and Tember's friends remain.

My husband, Scott—the introvert—has been working from the sanctuary of our bedroom all day, reading, thinking, and avoiding the crowd. Formerly an attending emergency medicine physician in our hometown of Spokane, Washington, he left medicine six years ago to attend seminary. Now he is a pastor at Willow Creek Community Church, a large nondenominational church just outside Chicago. Days off are his chance to savor another good book and see if it sparks any new ideas he can employ at work or in his own life. And today is his kind of day—sunny, blue skies, warm breeze, and three of our kids at home. Sensing the coast is clear, he reappears in the kitchen.

"Need any help?" he asks, pouring himself a Diet Coke over ice.

"Nope, I think we've got it," I say. "But thanks." Book and soda in hand, he heads to our screened back porch, the Bug Room—no connection to Katie's nickname, but named, rather ironically, for being a refuge from Midwest mosquitoes.

❧

Deanna and Brooke are helping to clean up in the kitchen. Sam is moving chairs, and Tember stands at the kitchen counter, cutting up lemons to make some fresh lemonade as she chats with one of her girlfriends. The phone rings again, and I pick up. "Hello?"

"Mrs. Vaudrey?"

"Yes."

"This is Nancy, the nurse administrator at Kane County Hospital. Your daughter has been brought in to the emergency department, and I need you to come down right away."

Her polite directness catches me off guard. I try to untangle her words. Daughter? Which daughter? I have three. Tember is here at the counter. Our oldest daughter, Bethany, twenty-one, and her brother Matt, twenty-three, are away at college in California. *Is she talking about Katie? Kane County Hospital? That's not far. It must be Katie. Yes, Katie.*

From my years as the wife of an emergency department physician, I know exactly what it means when an ER nurse calls the family and tells them only "come down right away." It means she has news that should not be shared over the phone. My mouth goes dry. It's against procedure for a nurse to give answers over the phone to the rapid-fire questions now surging into my mind. *What happened? Is Katie badly hurt? Is she conscious? Is she . . . alive?*

I try to collect my thoughts. The bustle in the kitchen ceases, and all eyes turn to me. I glance at the clock—4:10 p.m. I spoke to Katie on her cell around three. Whatever has happened, it has taken more than an hour to get her to the hospital and notify her family. Not a good sign.

"Mrs. Vaudrey? Will you come?"

"Oh. Yes. Okay, we'll be right down."

"Thank you, Mrs. Vaudrey."

"Wait—Nancy?"

"Yes?"

"Was it a car accident?"

She hesitates. "Yes."

"We're on our way." I hang up the phone.

My body goes numb. I become small, and my skin turns cold. My tongue is thick and tingly, as if I'd stood up too fast and might pass out.

At that moment, at some core level, I know.

2

OCTOBER 1993

The autumn sun and azure sky couldn't mask the crisp bite in the air. In the garden, a few late raspberries clung to withering brambles. Out in the pasture, the brittle alfalfa stubble meant shoes were once again a necessity. Barefoot season was over. Autumn had come.

Big sister Bethany, six, and her school friend Mary had spent the afternoon exploring the fields that surround our house. They now wandered toward the large, deserted doghouse next to the garage—the perfect spot for a secret fort.

Little sister Katie played nearby, far enough away to honor her big sister's playtime with a friend but near enough to eavesdrop on their "big girl" conversations. She was wearing—as always—a dress with matching ribbons on her pigtails. Her love of girlish fashion outweighed her certainty that fresh scratches on her unprotected legs would sting in the bathtub later that night.

Scott was reading on the back deck and I was rinsing dishes at the kitchen sink when Bethany's shrill, panicky cries pierced the afternoon calm. I dropped my sponge and bolted toward her screams. Scott was one step ahead of me. By the time we crossed the lawn and rounded the garage, the three girls were racing toward us.

"What's the matter? What happened?" I asked, pulling Bethany close and searching for cuts or bruises.

"Bees! I got attacked by bees!" she said. Angry red welts were already rising on her tear-streaked face and trembling hands. Scott scooped her into his arms, and we hurried to the house where he could inspect her more closely. Beestings in large quantity on a young child were no small matter. Once inside, I pulled the Benadryl from the bathroom cupboard and checked on newborn Tember, swaddled and asleep on the sofa, oblivious.

In the calm of the kitchen—with Mary, Katie, eight-year-old Matt, and little brother Sam looking on—Bethany recounted her ordeal.

"We were playing in the doghouse, and all of a sudden these bees just started attacking me! They went under my shirt and in my hair!" Bethany turned and looked squarely at her little sister. "But Katie killed them all!" she said proudly.

All eyes turned to Katie, her hair ribbons still daintily in place, her dress unmussed. She smiled and looked down.

"Mary just stood there," Bethany said, a hint of betrayal in her voice. Poor Mary grinned awkwardly. "But Katie came running and just started swatting the bees. They were flying everywhere! But she kept swatting my head and my shirt until she killed all the bees!"

Upon inspection, Scott counted half a dozen welts on Bethany, and he pulled seven dead yellow jackets out of her hair—and even more from under her shirt.

But Katie hadn't been stung—not even once.

In the moment of crisis, Bethany had screamed in pain. Mary had frozen. But Katie had charged in, systematically defending her sister by swatting and killing more than a dozen yellow jackets with her bare hands.

Katie was four years old.

3

4:12 P.M., SATURDAY, MAY 31

I steady myself against the counter by the kitchen phone. I blink, straighten my back, and turn to face the kids. Sam and Tember stare, motionless. Deanna and I lock eyes.

"What's the matter?" Tember asks, setting down a lemon and her knife. Sam and Tember step closer.

I don't want to believe what my gut is telling me. And without more information about Katie's condition, I don't want to overreact and freak out the kids. Perhaps Katie is fine and Nurse Administrator Nancy is an idiot at protocol. So I choose my words carefully.

"Katie's been in a car accident," I say, "and the hospital would like us to come down right away." I pray Deanna will interpret the unspoken meaning behind these words.

She gets it. "You go. I'll take care of things here. Go!"

Sam's face turns white. Tember's eyes catch mine and fill with tears. Afraid my face will betray my attempts at nonchalance, I avert my gaze.

"C'mon, kids," Deanna says. "Let's gather up and pray for Katie." She and Brooke begin circling everyone together.

I walk past them toward the French doors that separate our family room from the Bug Room. Through the glass, I see Scott rocking in his favorite chair, reading, enjoying the beautiful day, at peace. I grasp the cool brass door handle, but pause. We are in two different worlds separated by these doors. I twist the handle, crashing into his world so I can drag him into mine.

Scott looks up, dark eyes blinking and brow furrowed as he reins in his thoughts from his book and turns to me.

"Kane County Hospital just called," I say. "Katie's been brought in. Car accident. They want us to come down right away." Without moving his eyes from mine, Scott sets down his book. I keep my voice steady. Perhaps I am overreacting. I don't want to sway the jury with what I'm about to say next: "The nurse gave me no details. Just 'Come down.'"

The color drains from his face.

For a brief second, we look at each other in silence, aware that with one phone call, our lives may have changed forever. How many times as an ER physician had Scott asked a nurse to make such a phone call to another person's family as he worked to save their loved one? Now he is on the receiving end of such a message. He, too, interprets the nurse's glaring omission of details as an ominous sign. She offered no "She's stable," no "Her injuries are not life threatening"—not even a "She's being taken to surgery." Just "You need to come down right away."

Scott closes his eyes, motionless, and then I see a slight flinch in his jaw. *He understands.*

He stands to his feet, steps past me, and pushes through the French doors.

Tember meets him. "Can Sam and I come?" she asks, pleading in her voice.

"No." He heads to our bedroom for his shoes.

Okay, then. I'd be inclined to bring the kids with us and keep everyone together, whatever this afternoon might hold. But a hospital ER is Scott's world. He knows better than I do what we may be facing.

"You guys stay put," I say, trying to sound upbeat as I grab my purse. "We'll call you as soon as we know more."

"We'll take care of everything here," Deanna reassures me.

Scott returns to the kitchen, grabs his keys from the basket, picks up his cell phone, and feels his back pocket for his wallet. Sam and Tember stare, silent.

"Go," says Deanna.

I kiss the top of Tember's silky head and squeeze Sam's arm. Then Scott and I walk out the door. Seconds later, we are en route to the hospital—a thirty-minute drive.

Out of earshot of the kids, I want to hear it straight from Scott. Am I overreacting? Have I misinterpreted Nancy's silence?

"What does it mean, that the ER nurse didn't tell us anything?" I ask. "That's not good, right? Do you think she just forgot to tell us how Katie is doing? Could she be all right?"

Scott is rocking forward and back in the driver's seat, one hand on the wheel, one hand rubbing his forehead. "No, honey. It's not good. Not good."

"Should we have brought Sam and Tember?"

"When we get to the ER, we'll need to focus on Katie. If this turns out badly, I don't want Sam and Tember sitting off to the side somewhere by themselves. At least at home they'll have Deanna and Brooke."

"Should I call the big kids?" Bethany and our oldest son, Matt, and his wife, Andrea—"the big kids"—live in Southern California, where they attend college and grad school, respectively.

"Let's wait until we get to the hospital and know more," he says, continuing to rock.

"Agreed. They will feel helpless being so far away." And I am hoping against logic to have good news for them once we see Katie. "Dear God, please-please-please help Katie be okay," I pray aloud. Our family is rooted in the Christian faith, strengthened over the years by finding God more than trustworthy to see us through some of our darker days. So my reflex response in crisis is to pray. "Please, God. Please."

I am helpless in the passenger's seat as the miles tick by. All I can think to do is to get other people praying. I scroll through my cell phone and begin calling our friends. "Katie's been in an accident. Please pray— and spread the word," I say again and again to our friends. I leave voice messages with those who don't pick up. I call my best friend, Sandy, in Spokane, but it goes straight to voice mail. When I hear the familiar sound of her voice on the recording, I get choked up and leave her a semifrantic message.

4

WE FIND THE HOSPITAL, park on the street, and enter through the ambulance bay. A nurse sees us and approaches.

"I'm Nancy, the nurse administrator," she says.

"We're Katie Vaudrey's parents. Is she alive?" I blurt out.

She pauses before responding. "She is alive. But she is unconscious."

"What happened?"

"Evidently her car swerved into oncoming traffic, and another driver struck her on the passenger side. Let me bring you to her."

"Was anyone else hurt—in the other car?" I ask.

"No. The other driver walked away with only a few scratches on his cheek from his air bags."

"Thank goodness."

Nancy leads us into the trauma room and pulls back the curtain. There lies Katie, laid out on a gurney with tubes up her nose and down her throat. Gone are her plaid men's necktie, white dress shirt, and capris. She is draped in nothing but a white sheet. Monitor wires and IV lines link her body to a host of blinking, beeping machines. A stiff neck brace holds her head in place. Yet in spite of the violent car crash, there's not a scratch on her. Not a cut, bump, or bruise. Auburn-brown tendrils of hair form a halo around her face against the white hospital pillow. In the midst of this medical mayhem, Katie looks peaceful. Beautiful, even.

But as I look at her, my hand covers my mouth to stop words that are blazingly clear to my spirit from tumbling out: *She's not in there. She's gone.*

In just one glance, I know. What I sensed over the phone is affirmed. The Katie spirit that filled—overflowed—this tiny frame is glaringly absent.

A flash of panic fires through my brain, and miniscule, infrared sparks of light swirl before my eyes, obstructing my vision. I grasp the bed rail.

But logic and a mother's hope override the horrid reality trying to declare itself as fact to my soul. *She'll be okay. We can fix this.*

"Hey, Bug," Scott whispers, a catch in his throat. He strokes her hair, but then father turns doctor, and he looks to the monitors.

I lift her hand, warm but heavy. Two things about Katie's appearance reveal the depth of her injury, even to my medically untrained eye: The tip of her tongue will not quite stay inside her mouth. A breathing tube is holding her teeth slightly ajar—and her tongue lolls forward, past her teeth and onto her lower lip. It looks dry and uncomfortable. I gently push her tongue back behind her teeth, but it just gravitates forward again, coming to rest again on her lower lip. It's unnatural.

And her eyes won't stay closed. She is unconscious, but her eyelids rest only about halfway down. I gently run a finger down each lid, forcing them shut. But they slowly rise, returning again to about half-mast. The vacant gaze of her eyes is a shocking contrast to the bursting-with-life girl who dashed out of my kitchen less than two hours ago.

The ER doc, a kindly looking man with white hair, enters. Seeing us, he takes a moment to busy himself with the chart in his hands. The fluorescent lights overhead reflect in the tiny beads of sweat gathering above his upper lip.

"I'm Dr. Rogers, the attending physician," he says without looking up. "I am so sorry about your daughter's accident." We nod impatiently.

"Katherine's in a coma. She had no pulse at the scene," he says. "It took the paramedics twenty minutes to get her extricated from the car, and they revived her in the ambulance. She has a fractured skull. Her neck is broken, but it doesn't appear to be displaced. The real problem is the bleeding in her brain. She just got back from CT, where we scanned her head and neck." The doctor then begins to explain Katie's condition using simplistic layman's terms.

In any medical situation with our family, Scott is always discreet about his own past medical career. He prefers to let the doctor be the doctor when it comes to his wife or kids. But today, layman's terms will not suffice. The stakes are too high for discreet. He wants the full medical picture, physician to physician. "I'm a retired emergency medicine physician," he says. "I was an attending physician in a trauma center for twelve years. Can I see her scans?"

"Oh! Certainly," Dr. Rogers says. He leads the way to a small, dimly lit room where CT images can be viewed on a large computer screen. He pulls up Katie's CT, and Scott's face goes pale.

"Oh, Bug," he groans, rocking on his toes.

"Katherine has a significant bleed," Dr. Rogers says quietly. "Her ventricles are completely filled with blood. Her c-spine images show a fracture at C1 and a basilar skull fracture."

"Interpret," I whisper to Scott.

"It's bad," he says, pointing to the expansive spread of white on the film. "All this is blood. This is one of the worst CTs I've ever seen." I know he's seen thousands of CTs in his life. I want to throw up.

"Her pupils are unresponsive," Dr. Rogers adds gently.

Scott and I return to Katie in the trauma room. Nurses whisk around, speaking in urgent, hushed tones. Scott reads through her chart, one eye on the monitors. I stroke Katie's hand, her face, and I shove aside my earlier sense that she is gone.

"Katie," I whisper in her ear. "Come on, girl. You're a scrapper. Fight! Fight. Fight." *She can get through this. We just need to solve the medical issues. We need to figure out the bleed.*

"Tember and Sam need to get here—and fast," Scott says.

Please, please, God, keep her alive until they get here. "I'll call Brooke." I slide open my phone, but in this brick hospital building, I have no reception. I head back outside to get a signal.

◆

As I step onto the ambulance bay, the early summer warmth envelops me, melting away the air-conditioning-induced goose bumps on my arms. As I try with trembling hands to dial Brooke's number, a slow-motion hush washes over me and stops me in my tracks. I raise my eyes.

Ancient oaks line the hospital street. Above, a thin white cloud hovers against a cerulean-blue sky. The almost-summer scent of freshly mowed lawn hangs moist in the air, and fairylike tufts of down from nearby cottonwoods drift by. A deep sense of peace floods through me, and my trembling hands drop to my side. This moment feels holy. Tears begin to run down my cheeks as I lift my face to God.

I am good, I sense Him say. *This tragedy doesn't change My character. It doesn't change who I am. I am good.*

How ludicrous His words sound. Really? He's good? How could a mother with any sort of emotional capacity affirm this sappy "God is good" message, given our situation?

But something in His words rings true. I want them to be true. This tender encounter with God is undeniable, as real to me as the pavement beneath my feet in this ambulance bay. He is wrapping His strong arms around me in this world where pain has the brutal and current—but not final—say. *I am good . . .*

Will I find His words to be true, no matter how this mess turns out?

⟲⟳

With steadier fingers, I dial Brooke's cell number, and she picks up.

"Brooke, it doesn't look good. Please, please get the kids here as soon as you can. Are you guys still at the house?"

"Deanna's running her son home. I'm just leaving the house with Sam and Tember."

"How are they doing?"

"Yes, they are both right here with me." She's not free to speak. I don't ask to talk with them—I would only affirm their worst fears. And I don't want to assure them Katie is still alive when she may be dead by the time they arrive. Let them live in fretful ignorance a few moments more.

With a miracle seeming to be Katie's only hope, we need people praying. A thought occurs to me: It is now after 5:00 on a Saturday night, and thousands of people are pouring into our church for the 5:30 service. They could pray!

"Wait—Brooke? Is Davy still with you?" I ask. The kids' friend Davy was at the house earlier when the phone call came. Davy's father would be at church, and he could get word to our pastor, Bill Hybels, who could ask people to pray.

"No, Davy already went home."

"Call him. Have him call Jimmy and tell Bill—and Willow—to pray!"

"We're on it," Brooke says. "And we'll be there as soon as we can."

I make one more phone call before going back inside: I call my parents in Seattle. My mom answers. Through tears, I try to explain what has happened to Katie. She can barely make out my words. But she hears two phrases clear as day—phrases no doctor has yet spoken to me, and words I will later have no recollection of saying: "no hope for quality of life" and "brain-dead." This is what I tell my mother.

5

I step back into the trauma room, where it's clear that Katie is not doing well. Nurses and techs buzz around her, speaking only what is necessary, intently focused on their individual tasks. Scott and I stand out of the way, watching. The ER doc, however, just stands there, flipping through Katie's chart. Nurses ask him for orders, but he simply rubs his forehead, silent. One nurse casts a knowing glance at another. It hits me—and with panic—that perhaps this doctor doesn't see many traumas as severe as Katie's.

At about 5:20 p.m., a monitor alarm sounds. Katie's pulse on the screen shows a flattened squiggle.

"What's happening?" I ask.

"V-fib," Scott says. "The worst. Katie's heart isn't pumping blood."

An ER tech springs into action. She jumps up onto Katie's gurney, her knees straddling my girl's petite body. She begins forceful chest compressions to restart Katie's heart. With each aggressive, two-armed compression, Katie's chest sinks, her rib cage expands to each side, and her tan, naked belly bulges out. I envision her organs being shoved around inside like bumper cars.

"She's going to break Katie's ribs!" I whisper to Scott.

"Maybe," he says. "But she's doing good CPR."

The compressions continue, but the faint squiggle on the monitor is unchanged. The ER doc at last begins giving orders. A nurse fills a syringe with what I assume is epinephrine, a heart stimulant, and injects it into one of Katie's IV lines. Nothing.

"Shock her, 150 joules," the doctor says.

The ER tech hops down from the gurney and preps the paddles with lubricant.

"Clear!" she shouts, pressing the cold paddles to Katie's warm skin.

A jolt of electricity surges through my daughter, causing her entire body to jump. Our eyes look to the monitor. No change. The tech shocks her twice more. Nothing. The nurse injects another bolus of epinephrine into Katie's IV line. Nothing. Again and again, they repeat this pattern as we watch, helpless.

Long minutes tick by, and Katie's beautiful little body endures more CPR, more jolts of electricity, more physical abuse than I think anyone could possibly survive. Scott stands next to the doctor, riveted to the monitors, attuned to each order being given. I shrink in silence, flat against the back wall, my fists drawn to my mouth. *Don't freak out. Don't pass out. Don't distract. Stay out of the way.* I should not be here, seeing this, and I'm afraid they will ask me to leave. But no one seems to notice me, and I cannot move. I don't want to move. I cannot leave my girl.

As the life support efforts fail to bring back Katie's pulse, I watch Dr. Rogers. Whenever he issues an order, he glances toward Scott. Scott either nods his head or offers a quiet correction, which the doctor then repeats to his staff.

When a young person codes (loses her pulse), an ER team will fight long and hard to get that pulse back. A healthy young body wants to live, fights to live, and the attending physician will be very slow to give up on resuscitation efforts—to "call the code." Our presence—and the fact that Scott is a fellow physician—adds pressure to this doctor, no doubt.

The minutes drag on as this team continues their lifesaving violence against my daughter. The tech doing CPR begins to look spent, her hair plastered against her forehead, dark rings of sweat appearing under each arm. Yet she continues. I fight the urge to shout, "Stop! *Stop it!* Just leave her alone!" I want to push the tech aside and scoop Katie into my arms. I want to stroke her hair, to rip out all those horrid monitor wires and tubes, to close her eyes, and to push the tip of her tongue gently back into her mouth. Instead I must, must, must allow the medical team to continue. It is her only hope.

"More epinephrine?" a nurse asks the doctor. The doc looks at the clock.

"No. She's maxed." The nurses exchange glances. The tech keeps pounding on Katie's chest. The monitor's alarm blares, undeterred. We need a miracle.

I look at my watch. It is now 5:42. They have been working to restore Katie's heartbeat for more than twenty minutes, but nothing is working.

Dr. Rogers turns to us. I fear he wants to call the code. As if reading his mind, the tech stops her compressions. All movement in the room ceases. The piercing blare of the alarm drowns out the gentle whoosh of Katie's ventilator. I stare at the monitor—and at my daughter's lifeless body. It is over.

Then suddenly, to our utter surprise, the alarm ceases and the sound of a heartbeat breaks the stillness. All heads turn back to the monitor, which shows the return of a normal rhythm! Katie's heart is beating! The sound of a strong heartbeat sends the staff into full gear once again. Within moments, Katie is stabilized, and the immediate crisis averted.

Friends who gather at the hospital later that night will describe to us how Davy's dad got the word of Katie's accident to our pastor during the worship songs that open the 5:30 service. Bill took the stage moments later and stopped the music.

"This afternoon, Katie Vaudrey—the daughter of one of our staff members, Scott Vaudrey—was in a terrible car accident," he said. "She is in a coma. Let's pray right now for the Vaudreys and the healing of their daughter." Our church family then poured out their prayers for Katie. The clock at the moment of Bill's prayer read 5:42 p.m.— the same moment Katie's heart inexplicably jumped back to life.

Bill's sermon that night—a message about living our lives fully surrendered to God—was titled "Have You Died Yet?"

Now that Katie is stable, Scott tries to assess the full picture of her medical condition.

"Can I see her chest X-ray?" he asks Dr. Rogers.

"Uh, I didn't order one," he replies.

A shadow crosses Scott's face. I watch as hints of disbelief and restrained anger cloud his eyes. Dr. Rogers looks away, his cheeks reddening.

"It'd probably be good to check for a pneumothorax or a widened mediastinum," Scott says quietly. "Let's order the chest film."

Dr. Rogers nods. "Good idea," he says and finds a nurse to call for the portable X-ray machine.

Scott and I wait in the hallway while they shoot and develop Katie's film. "They took her to CT without first getting a chest film," Scott says, incredulous.

"Is that bad?" I ask.

"Standard of care in blunt trauma would be to get a chest film as soon as possible after you pull a patient off the ambulance," Scott explains. "An X-ray will show if there's a collapsed lung or torn aorta. You get the film before sending patients to CT because, if they have a tear, there is a risk they could bleed out—and should go straight to surgery first. Plus the film might show other reasons for a patient's decompensation. A pneumothorax could explain her heart arrhythmia, and a chest tube could resolve that. Katie has been here for almost two hours, and still no film."

The X-rays come back and Scott studies them in a light box on the wall. He looks relieved. "Normal."

The nurse takes Scott and me to a room down the hall, where the hospital has been sending friends who have arrived as news of Katie's accident spreads. Scott updates them with as much information as we know. I go outside to wait in the ambulance bay for Brooke and the kids to arrive.

At last, I see them coming up the sidewalk. Sam and Tember are red eyed and ashen faced—and I am no better. I wrap them in my arms and take them inside, where Scott meets us in the lobby and hugs the kids. The nurse shows Brooke to the crisis room. We head to the trauma room and to Katie.

When your children are little, you reflexively shield their eyes from a graphic scene on TV and distract their attention when you drive past a dead cat on the side of the road. I realize Sam and Tember's first sight of their sister will be burned into their memories for a lifetime. How I wish I could spare them. How grateful I am that Katie is not all bloody or banged up. It helps a little. But the vacant gaze in her eyes is shocking to behold. And the wires and tubes don't help. Thankfully my kids are "medical kids." They've been in the ER dozens of times to visit their dad at work, so at least the general setting is not foreign to them. But this is a scene like no other. Scott stops us and preps them before we go in.

"Katie is in bad shape," he says. "She has a broken neck and a skull fracture." Large tears begin to pool in the kids' eyes. He pauses to let this reality sink in before continuing.

"The skull fracture has caused some bleeding in her brain, and that's her biggest problem right now. She's unconscious. She's in a coma." The kids listen intently.

"Can she hear us?" Tember asks, her voice a tiny wisp of air.

Scott looks tenderly at his youngest daughter. "No one fully knows how the brain works for people in a coma," he says. "But we will take you in to see her, and you should go ahead and talk to her as if she can hear you."

We enter the trauma room, and Scott pushes back the curtain. Sam and Tember rush toward their sister. Sam, tall and lanky, reaches over the wires and drapes his arms around Katie in a cumbersome hug. Silent sobs wrack his lean body. Tember hangs near the end of the bed, her eyes large at the sight of all the wires. Reflexively, she picks up Katie's foot and strokes it.

"Her foot is warm," she tells me. I feel it, and she is right. I think of all the times Katie playfully shoved one of her bare feet—always cold and clammy—under Tember's shirt to torture her and make her laugh. The difference now is striking. Tears roll down Tember's cheeks and drip from her chin onto the white sheet covering her sister. She whispers to Katie, "I love you! Don't die! Don't die."

A new physician enters the room. He exudes a quiet confidence, which gives me hope. Dr. Rogers trails behind.

"Dr. and Mrs. Vaudrey, I'm Katherine's neurosurgeon, Dr. Yun. I am so sorry about your daughter's accident," he says, shaking our hands firmly. "The bleed in Katherine's brain is substantial, as you know. The break at C1 and the cranial fracture would cause some intracranial bleeding—though the pattern on the CT looks more like an aneurysm. Regardless, our first priority is to try to relieve the increased intracranial pressure that the bleed is causing. We need to measure that pressure, and to do so we need to drill a hole into her skull and insert an intracranial pressure monitor."

Dr. Rogers holds out a clipboard and a pen. "We need your permission for the procedure," he says. "The incision will be made just above her right temple, and it will mean shaving some of Katherine's hair."

Her hair? No mention of drilling a hole into my daughter's skull—just a warning about her hair. "I assure you, we're not concerned about her hair," I say. Scott and I sign the consent forms, giving our permission for them to insert the pressure monitor—and, oh, shave off a bit of her hair.

The nurse motions us from the room so they can begin the procedure. Tember and I move toward the door. Sam, however, doesn't budge. He remains bent over his sister, arms extended, hands cupping her shoulders, his own shoulders shaking with quiet sobs. We all wait a moment for him to compose himself and let go. But he shows no sign of moving. Scott rests a hand on his shoulder.

"Come on, buddy. Let's go to the waiting room so they can get started." Nothing.

"Hey, Sam," he quietly persists. "It's time to go." But Sam is lost in his own world of heartbreak, oblivious to Scott's words. In this moment, he seems incapable of moving.

"Sam, we need to go so the doctors can begin their work," he says. "Come on, son." Scott touches Sam's arm, but he flinches like a wounded animal and draws himself closer to his sister. Scott puts his arms around Sam's shoulders and tenderly but firmly pulls him away. Sam's arms strain toward Katie's motionless body. He tries to stand upright, but his knees give way, and Scott catches him. With a fatherly arm around Sam's shoulders— half supporting, half carrying his son—Scott leads us from the room.

6

AUGUST 2006

Katie would begin her senior year of high school—and Sam his freshman year—in less than a week. Sam was fourteen and all limbs, like a Great Dane puppy. I love this age of boy—where voices squeak, random facial hairs sprout from chins, and jeans are outgrown before they're broken in. He had grown six inches in the past school year, and nothing in his closet fit.

It's a tradition in our house to make a big deal out of back-to-school shopping. In a family of seven, this is one time when each child can be guaranteed a one-on-one shopping date and dinner out with a parent. Scott and I savor this chance to dote on each individual child. But one night at dinner, Katie announced she'd be the one taking Sam back-to-school shopping this year, and I could see nothing but win in this plan. Let's face it: What freshman boy wouldn't rather be outfitted by his stylish senior sister than by his mom or dad?

The appointed afternoon arrived, and as Sam waited in the kitchen for Katie to find her purse, his face tried to read "no big deal"—but I could tell by how fast he was talking that he was excited about spending these hours with his sister. It didn't hurt that he was pretty much guaranteed to be dressed in way cooler clothes when he walked through the doors of Fremd High School on his first day as a freshman. Katie found her purse, and I handed her my debit card. Off they drove in her Taurus.

Four hours, one fresh haircut, and a dinner at Panera Bread later, the Taurus pulled back into the driveway. Sam and Katie burst into the kitchen full of stories and laughter, with bags of Sam's new clothes in hand.

"Sam was a good sport, Mom," Katie announced. "He's gonna be the coolest thing on campus." She made him model at least one outfit for us.

The damage to my debit card was respectable but not overboard. Sam had never cared much about clothes before, so a little splurge this year felt right. And the investment between sister and brother? Priceless.

Fremd is a large high school—close to three thousand students—and Sam started the new year with confidence. Throughout fall semester, whenever Katie spotted him in the crowded hallway, she would holler out to him, "Sam! Hey, Sam! Sam Vaudrey! Everybody, that's my brother Sam! He's the coolest! I love you, Sam!" She embarrassed him, to be sure, but she knew down deep he was feeling loved, was proud of her attentions—and was probably gaining cool points from his freshman friends who all admired his sister, the hot senior.

But one day Sam decided to flip the script. He spotted Katie down the hall.

"Katie! Hey, Katie! Everybody, Katie Vaudrey is my sister! She's so cool!" he shouted. "I love you, Katie!"

Katie blinked, caught off guard. "I love you more, Sam!" she shouted back.

"No, I love *you* more," he countered. And back and forth they went until Katie finally cried uncle. This time she was the one with reddened cheeks. He caught up to her, picked her up with those lanky, strong arms, and swung her around in a huge bear hug. She'd been bested at her own game.

For the rest of the year, the "love you more" game was on. Both looked for prime embarrassment opportunities to proclaim their brotherly or sisterly love. Their playfulness, affection, and mutual respect—both at school and at home—reflected the closeness they shared as sibs and as friends.

7

6:00 P.M., SATURDAY, MAY 31

By the time the four of us leave Katie's side in the trauma room and follow the nurse out, the crisis room is crowded with friends who have heard the news. Sam's friends from church surround him. Katie's girlfriends embrace Tember. Scott and I are shocked at how many people have gathered here for us, all with reddened eyes and praying lips. How grateful I am. For all the bad press Christians get (and, sadly, sometimes deserve), this scene is a beautiful picture of the church at its finest.

We still have not called our two oldest kids, Matt and Bethany, in California to tell them what has happened to Katie. We keep waiting for things to take a turn for the better—or at least for a lull in the crisis—so we can offer them some hope when we break the news. But lulls are not the order of the day. And nothing is heading up and to the right. Before I can initiate a call, my cell phone rings. Matt's number pops up on my caller ID.

"It's Matt!" I say to Scott. "What should I tell him?"

"Just tell him what we know. And get them here, quick," he says.

I pick up. "Hi, Matt."

"Mom. I just got a text about Katie. What's going on?"

I tell him about the accident and break the news to him about Katie's condition, one piece at a time. "She's in bad shape, son. Her neck is broken, but they tell us it's not displaced."

He is quiet on the other end, trying to soak in what I am telling him.

"Honey, she's in a coma." More silence. He repeats what I've told him to his wife, Andrea, who must be standing nearby. I hear her gasp.

Matt is the sort of person who rises to the occasion in a crisis. Though he's a tenderhearted man and only twenty-three, he's the perfect person to get everyone to Chicago as quickly as possible.

"Matt, I need you and Andrea to find Bethany," I say. "I don't want her to hear this through a text. I'm sorry you found out that way. We were just waiting to call you until we knew a little more."

"It's okay, Mama. And yes, we'll find Bethany. I think she's at work." Bethany is a barista at the Starbucks near campus. "Andrea and I will drive over there right now."

"Can you let Adam know too?" Bethany's boyfriend will be a tremendous comfort to her.

"No problem."

"And can I ask you to take care of getting plane tickets? Get everyone on the next flight out. You need to get here right away." Again, silence.

Andrea, my son's bride of ten months, pipes up in the background. "I got it, Mom. I'll get right on it." Matt married an amazing woman. I breathe easier knowing she's there to support Matt and Bethany and help him get the tickets booked. I give Matt our credit card number.

"I love you, son."

"I love you, Mama."

❧

As a mother, my focus is divided. I do my best to keep one eye on my critically injured daughter and the other on Sam and Tember, who are agonizing in their own world of trauma. Scott is afraid to leave Katie's bedside in the trauma room. He stands alongside Dr. Rogers, his eyes on the monitors. Sometimes when Dr. Rogers gives an order, I notice Scott lean over and say something privately to the doctor, and then Dr. Rogers changes the order or alters a dosage. This happens multiple times, until I hear Dr. Rogers instruct his staff to simply follow Scott's orders.

I can't believe this is happening. It seems as if, for all intents and purposes, my husband is now functioning as the attending physician, running the trauma of his own daughter.

I will never forget these images of Scott, who has been out of ER medicine for almost six years—and whose own heart is being torn apart with grief—keeping a laserlike intellectual focus on Katie's case, recalling all the correct medical tests, procedures, and even dosages. When we are alone with Katie for a moment, Scott turns to me. "It was for this day God sent me to medical school." My thoughts exactly. No matter how this turns out, both Scott and I will have the reassurance of knowing everything that could save our girl is being done.

Twice more that afternoon, Katie codes. Twice, Scott runs the code, giving the orders to nurses and techs who administer CPR and use electrical paddles to shock our daughter's heart back to a sustainable rhythm. How much more can her little body take?

Nurse Administrator Nancy approaches me in the crisis room. "Mrs. Vaudrey, there is a police officer here who wants to speak with you." I follow her into the hallway, where an officer waits.

"Mrs. Vaudrey, I'm Detective Wilson, the investigating officer of this accident," he says, "and I wanted to bring you Katherine's personal effects from her vehicle." He hands me a clear plastic bag and Katie's large brown leather purse—the one with lots of buckles and zippers that I just slipped over her shoulder this afternoon. She frequently carries oversized purses like this, which dwarf her small frame.

"I need to keep hold of her cell phone and wallet to finish my report," he says. "We are still checking her call records to determine who spoke with her last, that sort of thing."

It hits me: Katie could have been finishing her conversation with me when she crashed. Horror washes through me.

"Do you think Katie was talking on her cell—and that's what caused the crash?"

"No," he says. "We found her phone inside her purse. We don't know what caused her to swerve. But whenever there is an accident like this, we need to complete an investigation. You can pick up the rest of Katherine's things at the police station later this week." He turns to leave, then stops. "I hope your daughter will be okay."

As he walks away, I open Katie's purse. Her powdered blush and eye shadow compacts are shattered and loose inside. Her wallet, of course, is missing—as is her cell phone. I push aside a hairbrush and a few loose odds and ends—that's it.

I open the plastic bag the officer handed me. It's the sort of drawstring bag a hospital gives you for storing your clothes. Katie's clothes, however, are not in this bag. *They were probably cut from her body upon arrival.* I look down the hall at the trash can just outside the trauma room. Perhaps Katie's cute Bandito Barney's outfit is stuffed inside. I can't look.

This bag holds only a few of Katie's belongings—her earrings, rings, and a brass-and-silver bangle bracelet. I pull the bracelet out of the bag and slip it on my wrist.

One more thing lies in the bottom of the bag—*her blue plaid men's necktie.* I pull it out. The knot is still tied, but the neck loop has been cut—a clean slice. *They had to cut the tie off Katie's broken neck.* I shudder and shove the tie back into the bottom of her purse, cram the plastic drawstring bag on top, pull the purse straps over my shoulder, and return to the crisis room.

8

7:00 P.M., SATURDAY, MAY 31

Dr. Yun and his team successfully insert the intracranial pressure monitor into Katie's skull. Once the burr hole procedure is over, the nurse invites us back into the trauma room, where the neurosurgeon waits. Katie's head is now swathed in a thick turban of cotton. A faint brownish-yellow tinge of iodine taints her forehead where they sterilized her skin before surgery. She looks so small beneath the bulky bandages—more critically injured, more vulnerable.

"Katherine's pressure is dangerously high, five times what it should be," Dr. Yun says. "And in addition to the pressure caused by the blood, the brain tissue itself is now swelling."

A swollen brain cannot be drained of fluid any more than a swollen ankle can. And the skull gives the swollen tissue nowhere to go. But it doesn't occur to me that we are losing this race.

Dr. Rogers approaches. "I'd like to order an angiogram to make sure there has not been a significant injury to the large blood vessels in Katherine's chest," he says. "Maybe that's what is causing her arrhythmias." In this type of angiogram, dye is injected into a patient's aorta, and then a CT reveals where the dye goes, showing the blood flow.

"But those vessels are not the root issue," Scott counters. "Her heart is likely reacting to the pressure in her brain. That's fine if you want to squirt her aorta, but while she's catheterized, let's do a cerebral angiogram as well—so we may get a sense of the source of her bleed."

"Oh. Uh, yes, that would make sense," Dr. Rogers says, adjusting the orders on his clipboard as he walks away.

Scott clenches his jaw.

We leave the trauma room so the procedures can begin.

Dozens of friends, young and old, have heard about Katie and come to the hospital. They now overflow the crisis room and spill into the hallway. I spot Katie's high school friends from church and her best friend Kati Harkin (yes, Katie's best friend is also named Kati—sans the *e*). Friends of Sam and Tember are there, and friends of Scott and mine too.

Two people are noticeably absent: Katie's close friend Whitney, who is away at college, and Katie's sweet boyfriend, Dan, who is on a remote fishing trip with buddies—out of state and out of cell phone range. He doesn't yet know about the accident. He will get back to civilization on Wednesday, but we have no way to contact him before then.

The crowd clogs the hallway, making it tricky for the hospital staff to get by. A nurse moves us to the hospital chapel upstairs, where people can spread out, sit, pray, and talk. A cafeteria worker brings a cart piled high with boxed meals. So thoughtful. I'm too nauseated to eat, but I am grateful the staff thought of this, and I feel like a bad hostess because it's past dinnertime and I never thought to order food.

"Dive in, you guys," I say. "It's way past dinner. You must be hungry." But no one moves.

Matt calls with an update.

"We went to Starbucks and found Bethany," he says. "We took her outside and broke the news to her. Mom, it was awful. She burst into tears and began pacing the sidewalk. We told her boss what was going on and then drove Bethany to her apartment so she can pack. We called Adam, and he's on his way over to be with her. We're home packing. Andrea is online looking for flights. Should we buy Adam a ticket too?"

"Can he get off work? Is he willing to come?"

"Yes."

"Then yes. Buy him a ticket. It will help Bethany to have him here."

"Will do. Next available flight is a red-eye."

"Nothing else? Did you try other airports?"

"Andrea's tried everywhere. Ontario, Long Beach, John Wayne, Burbank—everything is sold out. Should we book the red-eye, or would you rather we take the first flight out in the morning?"

"No. Take the red-eye. I'll pick you up in the morning."

"Got it."

"Thank you so much for handling this, Matt. Tell Andrea thank you. I love you—"

"How's my sister?"

"No change." Silence. I hear him swallow.

"How's Dad?"

"He's now running Katie's trauma. It's a mess, Matt. But you would be so proud of Dad."

"Our dad's a stud."

"Indeed."

"I love you, Mama."

"I love you."

The crowd in the chapel is huddled in clusters, weeping, praying, talking. Our senior pastor, Bill, has asked Chris Hurta, one of our church's most compassionate, skilled pastors, to come to the hospital and see this thing through with us. Chris's gentle, solid presence is just what we need. After praying for Katie in the trauma room, he stations himself in the hospital chapel, comforting friends so that Scott and I can remain focused on our own kids.

A little after seven, Chris gathers everyone together in the chapel to pray. Scott is with Katie, so I join our friends and sit down in one of the chapel chairs. I feel a tug at my arm. Tember, my almost-high-school daughter, climbs into my lap and nestles her head against my neck. I wrap my arms around her. I scan the room for Sam and spot him sitting against the wall with Davy, praying. For the next two hours, we lift our requests for Katie, one at a time, aloud to God.

Since the first phone call, it's been a nonstop adrenaline rush. I now pause and try to collect my thoughts. *Is this happening? Is this real? Surely she will be okay.*

A horrid thought lodges in my mind: *Is this my fault? Is this some sort of karmic payback for the wrongs I've done in life?* I have never believed in karma—it is contrary to my understanding of God's goodness—but in my desperation, I grasp for answers. I meet eyes with my friend Pat, who is sitting across from me. She knows all the worst things about me, my biggest failures.

"Is this me?" I mouth.

"*No,*" she says, grit in her voice. "You didn't cause this. Don't even go there." Her firm, aggressive response, so contrary to her normally gentle nature, slaps me back. I shove aside this futile line of thinking and close my eyes again.

As others pray, my mind slows and begins to focus on my daughter's situation: Katie has a broken neck at C1, the worst possible vertebra you can break—the "Christopher Reeve fracture." Displaced or not, I'm guessing this will mean some degree of paralysis. Recalling Christopher Reeve's quality of life after his horse-riding accident—wheelchair bound with a ventilator breathing for him—I try to imagine Katie's exuberant spirit confined to a paralyzed, helpless body, a metal wheelchair, and a vent.

But these are just physical issues. We can overcome them. What about her mental capacity—her mind? Can she pull out of this coma? Will there be lasting intellectual damage?

I understand more than most the life of someone with a cognitive impairment. My only brother, Greg, who is two years younger than me, has cerebral palsy and an intellectual disability. He lives in a nursing home where he receives twenty-four-hour care. Greg experienced a brain injury at birth, likely from a lack of oxygen. He has never known what it's like to have a nonimpaired mental capacity. But Katie . . . Katie would know. She'd know the difference.

The urgency I now feel is for my daughter's mind. Though she is most recognized for her ability with a paintbrush, Katie's intellect is equally remarkable. I think of her academic success, her love of learning and growing, her meaningful, truthful, challenging conversations.

Images come to mind—television clips I have seen of devoted parents making daily treks to a nursing home where their paralyzed, comatose daughter lies atrophied in a hospital bed. She is unresponsive as they tenderly wash her, feed her, talk to her. I often wondered where such parents find that kind of selfless devotion.

But now I get it. It is not the withered, vacant frame on that hospital bed they are tending to. *It is the daughter they remember*—the girl who, before the accident or illness, filled their home with laughter, wrapped her loving arms around their necks, and danced pirouettes as she headed for work, the girl whose grin lifted their spirits, whose potential was limitless, who gave her love to them freely and with great abandon. This is the girl they now bathe and dress and read aloud to, whose hair they comb, whose contractured hand they stroke.

Sign me up! I pray silently. *If this is Katie's only shot at life, then let me be that parent! Give me the privilege of loving one of my children with that kind of devotion, Lord. Just spare Katie's life!*

But how could I wish such an existence upon my daughter? The image of a withered, comatose Katie sickens me. She who embraces life with such gusto, who finds spiritual expression in capturing beauty in all its imperfect forms through her art, who loves Jesus deeply and is secure about her eternity with Him—spending the rest of her life curled up and unresponsive in bed? Never to paint, never to laugh, never to give a hug, or write, or sing? How can I pray for God to ensnare her in such an earthly existence? Why not release her to eternity?

Yet the mother heart in me is too selfish to pray for her release. I cannot let her go.

Instead I pray, plead, beg God, "Spare her life!"

As tears and snot run down my face and I rock my youngest daughter in my arms, I pray aloud: "Father, spare Katie's life, but please, please, please, above all else"—with clarity and urgency, I beg—"please, Father, make her mind whole."

9

MARCH 1994

"Mommy, how do I become a Christian?" Katie, five, asked out of the blue one morning as I was driving her to preschool. Katie had shown an interest in God from a tender age. As a toddler and preschooler, she loved church, loved singing songs about Jesus, and loved "reading" her *Beginner's Bible* with its colorful cartoon illustrations depicting the stories of Noah, Moses, David, and—her favorites—the stories of Jesus.

How do I explain complex theological concepts in words a five-year-old can grasp? Even trickier, how do I do so in a way that won't manipulate this five-year-old's baseline desire to please her mom? But the spark in Katie's eye and intensity of her gaze told me this was more than a casual question to her. She wanted answers.

I pulled into the church parking lot, turned off the minivan, and took a deep breath. Turning to look in her eyes, I said, "Becoming a

Christian means asking Jesus to forgive you for any wrong things you have done."

She furrowed her brow, thinking.

"Have you ever done anything wrong?" I asked, not heavily but hopefully, with an undergirding of safety.

Katie looked at me with serious brown eyes and a slight tilt of the head, as if preparing me to be shocked.

"Oh, yes, Mama," she said gravely, nodding her head and looking down. "Sometimes I disobey. And sometimes . . . I am mean to Bethany and Matt."

I reached for her hand.

"I've done wrong things, too, Katie," I told her. "We all have. None of us is perfect. We have all done wrong things that deserve consequences. But Jesus is perfect. He's never done anything wrong, so when He died on the cross, He paid the price to remove the consequences for you and me—for our wrongdoings. And He gladly forgives us for those wrong things when we ask. Becoming a Christian means saying yes to Jesus—not only as your Forgiver but also as the Leader of your life."

"But how do I *do* that?" she asked—hoping, I suppose, for step-by-step instructions.

"Well, you can pray to Him and tell Him whatever it is you want to say, honey," I said. "If you want Him to forgive you for disobeying and for being mean sometimes—and for any wrong thing you've done—just ask Him to forgive you. And if you want to follow Him as your leader and live your life as He taught us to live, just tell Him so. Ask for His forgiveness. Ask Him to lead you. And He will."

"That's what I want to do," she said, resolution in her young voice.

We bowed our heads, but I peeked. She folded her hands and squeezed her eyes shut with such earnestness, her dark lashes crinkled. And she prayed.

"Jesus, please forgive me for all the wrong things I've done," she said. "Sometimes I am mean to my sister and brother, and sometimes I disobey. I'm sorry."

Then she asked Jesus to lead her for the rest of her life.

And He did.

10

Scott steps into the crowded chapel and motions to me from the doorway. Tember climbs off my lap so I can get to him.

"Dr. Yun wants to talk to us," he says. "He has the results of Katie's dye study."

Perhaps, finally, we will hear some positive or, at least, productive news. I gather Sam and Tember, and we follow Scott to a bank of chairs against the far lobby wall. Dr. Yun, carrying a clipboard, stands nearby. Sam sits down and Tember perches on the arm of his chair, her legs draping over his lap; Scott and I stand next to the doctor. Our friends gather near the chapel door and grow quiet. They are too far away to hear our conversation, but all eyes are on us.

"Dr. and Mrs. Vaudrey, we have completed the dye study on Katherine. She took the procedure well and is stable," Dr. Yun says. "We ran dye through her carotid artery and down into her heart; then we scanned her. The study reflects only minor damage—just some bruising that could heal nicely in a few days."

He clears his throat. "However, we also ran the dye upstream into Katherine's brain in an attempt to determine the location of her bleed. The scan reveals that because of her extremely high intracranial pressure, none of the dye was able to flow into Katherine's brain."

He glances down at his watch. "It is now after nine o'clock, and Katherine's accident was around three. Because of the size of her bleed and the resulting pressure inside her skull, it is evident that no blood flow has been able to enter her brain since that time. This means her brain has been without oxygen for more than six hours." He pauses before continuing.

"Dr. and Mrs. Vaudrey, I am very sorry, but your daughter has experienced a brain death."

Dr. Yun's words reverberate inside me like an earthquake. *What? No! We are still in this fight! The race to save her isn't over!* Despite the fact that twice today I sensed that Katie was gone—once when the nurse called our house and again when I first saw Katie in the trauma room—I honestly still believe we can bring her back, that somehow she will pull through.

A hushed fog envelops me, and Dr. Yun's words drift quietly into the background. A brilliant scene—a vision?—flashes before my eyes in high-def detail:

From a skyward vantage point, I see Katie's gold Ford Taurus cruising toward work along Illinois Route 68, the scenic stretch of country road canopied by towering oaks between our house and Bandito Barney's. Through the rear window of her Taurus, I can see Katie slumped over the wheel, unconscious as a car approaches in the oncoming lane. Just before the two cars pass, Katie's lifeless body rolls sharply to the left, turning the steering wheel—and her car—into the path of the approaching vehicle.

But right before impact, a brilliant-white, lightning-fast ethereal being—Jesus?—swoops down and scoops her up into His arms. The two cars collide in a violent impact, but Katie is already safely soaring through the trees, a look of utter delight on her face, her hands lifted high, as if she's on the roller coaster ride of her life. Cradled in His arms, she sails toward the heavens, through the trees, until their images blend into the wispy white clouds, beyond the blue sky, and out of sight.

All of this flashes before my mind's eye in a microsecond, and it makes no sense whatsoever. Why would Katie be unconscious *before* the impact when it was the crash that broke her neck, cracked her skull, and caused the massive bleed in her brain?

Nonetheless, this is the illogical scene that plays before my eyes like a Technicolor movie.

I shove the vision aside and snap from my fog. My thoughts turn quickly to Tember, my youngest, sitting across from me on Sam's lap. She is only fourteen. Does she understand that "your daughter has experienced a brain death" translates to "your sister is dead"?

In that instant, before my eyes can even turn to meet hers, a long, guttural wail fills my ears and sends chills down my spine—an involuntary cry of agony from Tember's pierced soul. *She understands.*

Our youngest daughter puts her hands to her face and lurches forward. Sam catches her in his arms and holds her tight as he, too, erupts in tears. He helps her to her feet, and Scott and I wrap our arms around them both, huddling together, clinging to one another as the reality of the doctor's words crashes down upon our shoulders, wave upon incomprehensible wave.

Our friends stand motionless, watching.

Dr. Yun waits. In gentle professionalism, he gives us several moments for the initial waves of shock to subside. At last, in carefully stated words, he speaks again: "I can't begin to imagine how hard this must be, and I am deeply sorry for your loss. However, I must ask you a difficult question. Your daughter signed the organ donor line on her driver's license, and she is an excellent candidate for donation. Would this be something you would consider for her?"

Give away Katie's organs? But I have barely swallowed the reality that she is gone! The sharp juxtaposition of my gutted emotions against Dr. Yun's pragmatic question feels surreal—like an out-of-body experience. But his gentle question forces me to reengage the rational side of my brain. Strangely, as if tapping into someone else's levelheaded mind, I find I can think.

What are our options, really? For six hours, her brain has been devoid of oxygen. It's no longer telling her to breathe. And it keeps forgetting to tell her heart to beat. Three times already, Katie has coded, her heart shocked back to a sustainable rhythm with electric paddles. Even the most basic of human brain functions is not happening for our girl. It is clear that Katie will never awaken from her coma and that her brain is so severely impaired, even her physical survival is not a long-term possibility.

I recall my prayer in the chapel just moments ago. Even though I want to be one of those parents who makes treks to a nursing home where my comatose child lies, I am not being offered this privilege. Katie is trying to die. Her mind is already gone, and her body wants to follow.

We're a medical family. We have all signed the organ donor lines on our driver's licenses. We are all strong believers in organ donation—in theory. After all, what's the point of burying or cremating a body with perfectly good organs that could give someone else life? But now this philosophical issue has become personal. It is staring Scott and me in the face, tapping its watch and demanding a prompt decision.

We have no better option for our daughter. The decision is easy. We will do as she wished.

"Absolutely we would allow it," Scott responds. "Absolutely. We know how important it is, and Katie would want it. We will donate her organs."

"She was all about life," I add, the past tense "was" sticking in my throat. "She would want to help others live if she cannot live herself."

Sam and Tember nod their agreement. We are of one mind.

"I am so grateful," Dr. Yun says. "It's no small thing to give the gift of life to others in the midst of your own loss."

"The decision is effortless," Scott says. He is right.

"Very well. I will have the transplant coordinator come meet with you and explain how the process works," Dr. Yun says. "And there are some papers to sign. Meanwhile, we will move Katherine up to the surgical ICU and begin preparing her for transplant surgery. Once she is settled in, you can go see her."

Scott nods. Dr. Yun leaves and motions for a woman standing nearby to approach. She is the organ transplant coordinator.

"Thank you so much for agreeing to let Katherine be a donor," she says. This is such a reflexive and right decision that her expression of gratitude feels out of place. Plus Katie is nineteen and signed the donor line on her license. I'm guessing asking our permission is just a polite kindness and not an actual necessity.

"After Katherine is settled in a surgical ICU room upstairs," she continues, "we will draw her blood so we can do a crossmatch and determine her compatibility with possible recipients. Organ donation is a two-part procedure: Once matches are found, someone from the donor registry will begin contacting those individuals who are a good match with Katherine so they can prepare for surgery on their ends. The entire process of matching donors and recipients takes about twenty-four hours, so Katherine's surgery will likely be late tomorrow night."

It's a barrage of information. Scott signs the consent form for the crossmatching of Katie's blood.

Everything is happening too quickly, but there is no slowing down. We have just learned that Katie is brain-dead—and now we are being swept along this rushing river toward Katie donating her organs and her heart beating its last.

We have about twenty-four hours to say goodbye to our girl.

11

"WE NEED TO LET EVERYONE KNOW," I say, nodding toward our friends, who are still watching in silence. Scott walks over to them. From his med school training and ER experience, he knows that once people hear, "Your loved one is dead," they will hear nothing else you say, so it's essential to get all the pertinent information out first.

Our friends gather around as he approaches. No one speaks. Scott's back is facing us and I can't hear his words, but I know instantly the moment he reaches the part of our horrid story that says, ". . . and so Katie is brain-dead."

A reflexive, tribal-like wail of grief rolls from the mouths of our friends and echoes off the marble walls of the lobby. "Nooo!" two of Katie's girlfriends cry out.

I tighten my arms around Sam and Tember. Everyone is in tears. They begin to embrace one another. Undoubtedly, many of the adults are crying for our loss, but the teenagers have lost one of their own. Katie and her friends have loved one another deeply and well. They have lived their lives together throughout junior high, high school, and into college. Looking at their beautiful, tearstained faces, I am sickened by their loss.

Scott explains briefly that we are following Katie's wish to be an organ donor. Then he rejoins Sam, Tember, and me. "We need to tell the older kids."

"I want them to hear this news from me, face-to-face, when they land," I say. "I don't want them to find out their sister is brain-dead over the phone. And I can't bear the thought of them sitting on that plane all night, carrying this grief alone."

"This kind of news travels quickly," Sam says. "Someone is bound to text them." *He's right.* I turn quickly toward the crowd in hopes of halting any well-intended messages. Scott catches my arm.

"We should release them to go home now, too," he says. "I feel bad—they've been here for so many hours. They must be exhausted."

Katie's friends don't look anywhere near ready to leave. My guess is they'll want to see Katie one last time to say goodbye. But in their current emotional state, I fear they might become overwhelmed—and I have no reserve to comfort them. I am bone-dry.

I swallow. "Let's offer them a chance to say their goodbyes."

The weeping grows quiet as I approach. Katie's girlfriends stand huddled together near the front of the crowd—Ester, Darla, Melissa, Caitlin, Marie, Kati Harkin. And then I spot Casey, the remarkable young woman who has mentored Katie and her friends for these past four years. She stands behind the girls, arms around them like the wings of a mother hen. I exhale. *It will be all right. Casey is here.*

"Hey, everyone." I say. "Thank you so much, guys, for being with our family through this mess. We are heartbroken. And we are deeply grateful for you. Katie is being tucked in upstairs in the ICU so they can get her ready for her organ donation surgery tomorrow night. Tomorrow will be just for our family"—I am making this up as I go—"but once Katie is settled in, we invite you to say your goodbyes to her tonight. Or if you'd rather remember Katie as she was the last time you saw her, we understand that too. Whatever works best for you—that's what we want."

"One more thing," I continue. "Matt, Andrea, Bethany, and her boyfriend, Adam, are catching a red-eye from LA. They don't yet know that Katie has been pronounced brain-dead. I want them to hear this news from me in person, not by accident via a text from a friend. Can you guys please, please help that not happen? Don't text about this until after they land at five tomorrow morning, okay?" They nod solemnly.

I scan my eyes over these people. They've been here for hours. They are weary, disheveled, with pale faces and reddened eyes. I'm flooded with gratitude for each one—and for God, who wired into human beings the innate desire to be known deeply, to love one another well, and to live in community together. *This is what it looks like when people live as He intends. In the midst of unspeakable pain—such selflessness, such generosity of spirit, such utter beauty.*

My friend Gail approaches and wraps me in her arms. My shoulders relax and I let her hold me. For a brief moment, I give myself permission to receive—to not "be on" for my heartbroken younger children but simply to be a mama who has just lost her daughter.

"I prayed God would make her mind whole," I tell Gail. I think about the vision—and the look of utter joy on Katie's face as she soared toward eternity in Jesus' arms. "He answered that prayer."

❧

During the next hour, Katie is transferred to an ICU room. Scott's role as his daughter's ER physician is finally over. He stands talking with our friends, numb with shock but grateful for their presence. Sam, Tember, and Katie's friends stand in clusters, holding one another, talking. Several kids from this morning's drama party are here, along with Deanna and her family—and the leaders from our church's youth groups. We are not alone in this, and we are not parenting our children alone. We never have been. Community is in full swing.

My mind turns to Matt and Bethany. "The kids likely will call me as soon as they get to the gate at LAX," I say to Scott. "I will find truthful words to tell them without spelling out the final verdict. Then I'll try to meet them at the gate at O'Hare tomorrow and tell them the news in person, hopefully before they read about it in a text."

A little after ten o'clock, my phone rings—Matt. *Give me the right words.* I pick up.

"Mama. We're at the gate," Matt says. "The plane leaves in an hour. Andrea and Adam are here with me. Bethany is walking around somewhere. I think she's in search of a Starbucks. How's Katie?" he asks.

I swallow. "She's stable, but she's in a coma, and it's looking very grave." Three truthful statements.

Silence. He sniffles.

"I love you, Matt."

"Love you, Mama."

"I will be there when you land."

❦

Ten minutes later, my cell phone rings again. Bethany this time. It's the first time I've talked with her since all of this began.

"Hi, Mom," she says. Her nose sounds stuffy. Like Matt, she has been crying.

"Hi, beautiful."

An elongated pause hovers in the air. No words seem to fit.

"Bethany, how are you doing?"

"I'm all right," she says, exhaling. "Thanks for flying Adam out too, Mom. That helps a lot. We are all hanging together and doing all right. Andrea's been great about taking care of details. Mom, how's Katie?"

I swallow again and repeat my three truthful statements. Before she can ask any questions, I change the subject. "Did you get packed all right?"

"Eventually," she says. "Matt and Andrea dropped me off at my apartment so they could go home and pack. But my roommates were gone, so I was all alone. I was so rattled, I couldn't think. But I read somewhere that people in comas can sometimes be reached by stimulating their senses, so I put together a basket for my sister—scented oils, a mix tape she made me of her favorite songs, stuff I'll bring her at the hospital." *Ugh.*

"Then I tried to pack, but I couldn't concentrate. Randomly, this girl who was my freshman RA stopped by and found me standing there, crying, with only pens and underwear in my suitcase. I couldn't think of anything else to pack but pens and underwear!" We laugh.

The RA stayed with Bethany until Adam arrived. Adam packed her suitcase, tucking in a black dress and shoes, unnoticed—just in case.

"I'll pick you guys up at the airport in the morning and take you straight to the hospital," I tell Bethany. "Try to sleep on the plane, if you can."

"Yeah, right!" she says. We both laugh. My energetic daughter has not slept on a plane or in a car since she was about two years old. Too much life happening around her—and too much going on in her mind.

"I'll try," she promises.

"See you in a few hours, Bethany. I love you."

"I love you, too, Mom. Tell Dad I love him. And the little kids." In our family, the "little kids" are Sam and Tember. She doesn't mention Katie. Does she know? Perhaps at some unconscious level, we all know.

12

THE CROWD IN THE CHAPEL BEGINS TO THIN. Gail's husband, Bill, offers to take me to the airport in the morning to get the kids. He'll pick me up at four o'clock while Scott stays here with the younger kids and Katie.

Soon it's just Katie's friends and a few of my girlfriends—Leanne, Gail, and Susan. Leanne's husband, Jimmy—the one who slipped our pastor a note during the church service—spent the past several hours here unnoticed, pacing the halls downstairs, deep in prayer for us. Just last night, their daughter Ester and Katie were catching up over coffee, recapping their freshman experiences and plotting a beautiful summer together. Now Katie is gone. I don't know what time Jimmy finally left the hospital, but it was late. And I know his prayers will continue on our behalf. These are just a few snapshots of people we will never forget.

Once Katie is settled into her ICU room, Scott, Sam, Tember, and I go in. Though our girl looks the same as she did downstairs—wires, monitors, the breathing tube, her tongue resting on her lower lip, her eyes at half-mast, the cotton turban, the neck collar—she seems more gravely ill here, and more absent. But her physical beauty is unchanged. Her graceful arms and hands lie at her side. She looks like a vacant angel.

The organ donation lady enters. "Everything is moving ahead nicely for Katherine's donation," she says. "Her surgery will be sometime around midnight tomorrow. Dr. Vaudrey, can I have some time with you to go over the paperwork and get some signatures?"

An ICU nurse adds, "We've set aside two adjoining rooms where your family can spend the night. I'll take you there." I haven't even thought about sleeping plans. The kids are exhausted in every way. I hug each one, and they kiss Katie goodnight. I will stay here while Katie's friends say their goodbyes.

"Come wake us up as soon as the big kids get here in the morning," Tember says. "Don't let them go see Katie without us! Promise!"

"I promise," I tell her.

They follow the organ donation lady, Scott, and the nurse to those rooms, and I return to Katie's friends and my girlfriends in the waiting room.

"Katie is all tucked in," I say. "You guys can begin your goodbyes now, if you'd like."

For the next three hours, Gail, Leanne, Susan, and I keep vigil in the ICU lobby as Katie's friends make their goodbye treks. The group of junior high girls Katie mentored when she was in high school are here, along with Sarah and Hannah—the high school seniors to whom Katie entrusted her girls when she left for college. Katie's girlfriends sit on the carpet, talking, crying, and telling stories, along with Casey, who has her shepherding eye on the whole group. How Katie adored this young woman who poured herself into these girls, modeling adulthood, marriage, and motherhood so beautifully. *This is a memory of Casey I will never forget.*

In groups of two or three, the girls disappear into Katie's room to say farewell to their friend. For many, this is their first brush with death. *What are they saying to Katie as she lies there hovering between this world and the next? What prayers is heaven receiving from their young hearts? Father, comfort them. May these moments mark the trajectory of their lives in a way that leads to healing and depth and life.*

They exit her room, eyes red, but to a person, everyone leaves with an aura of peace.

Casey and Melissa are the last to say goodbye to my daughter. They stay in Katie's room quite awhile. Afterward Casey hugs me and says, "Melissa and I were both struck by the sense of . . . holiness we sensed in that room. There's no other way to describe it. We could feel God's presence. We knew we were not in there alone."

❧

When the last of Katie's friends and mine have said their goodbyes and headed for home, I find myself alone in the lobby. The hallway lights are dimmed for nighttime, and a solitary nurse sits at her station, filling out charts. I walk to my daughter's room—the last room on the left—and push back the blue curtain doorway.

There she lies. All is quiet, save for the beeping of monitors and the rhythmic whoosh of the breathing machine. I lift her right hand and place it in mine, just as I often did nineteen years ago, when she was a sleeping newborn. *Is this real? Or is it a parent's worst nightmare?* It is both. Less than twelve hours ago, this very girl raced through the kitchen and bounded out the door to head to work, full of life and joy—a sparkling future before her. Now she hovers between death and *death*, her only movement the rhythmic rising and falling of her chest as a machine forces air in and out of her lungs. How could this be? How can this be?

We have become one of "those" families—whose living room wall will someday boast up-to-date pictures of their grown children and grandchildren, but with a photo of one child frozen in time. I remember seeing such a picture years ago at a friend's parents' house: Their handsome son—my friend's brother, dead for fifteen years—wore a 1970s letterman's jacket, a mullet haircut, wide collars on his silk shirt, and a puka-shell necklace. Surrounding his stale senior portrait were recent photos of his younger siblings—now years older than he would ever become—with their spouses beside them and kids on their laps. This will be our family someday, with Katie's senior portrait increasingly outdated among the current pictures of Matt, Bethany, Sam, and Tember. No college graduation portrait for her. No wedding photo, no husband, no children on her lap. The unthinkable has happened. My child has died.

I lift Katie's hand and kiss it. *Oh, the artistic skill that has oozed its way through these delicate fingers onto canvas or paper with paintbrush or charcoal or pen.* I stroke her cheek. Her skin is smooth, warm. I notice that the breathing tube is pinching her lower lip, and I step to the other side of the bed to adjust it. As I do so, I spot something tucked into Katie's left hand—a key chain made of plastic lettered beads that read "Lil Sis"—and I recognize it immediately as the counterpart to the "Big Sis" key chain Tember gave Katie for Christmas a couple of years ago. Tember must have slipped it into her big sister's hand when she said good night. After Scott and I left the house this afternoon, she must have found her half of the key chain set and brought it to Katie. I love the purposeful boldness of this youngest child of mine.

I push Katie's tongue back into her mouth yet again, wet my thumb, and rub the iodine stains from her forehead using the universal spit-wash method protested by children everywhere—the one moms use anyway to rub peanut butter smudges or ice cream drips from their kids' faces. My daughter does not protest.

Katie's lips look uncomfortably dry. I pull a lip gloss from my pocket—the C.O. Bigelow mint-flavored gloss she talked me into buying for myself over Christmas vacation—and coat her parched lips. Her unblinking eyes are now moist with some type of ointment, likely intended to keep her corneas lubricated for transplant. The ointment makes her eyes look more comfortable. She is no longer able to experience discomfort, I realize, but I feel better knowing my daughter's eyes and lips are moist.

A sacred aura fills the room. Despite the chaos and sheer horror of this day, I feel none of that now. The tranquility and peace here defy logic. *I am not alone. Perhaps this is the presence and holiness Casey described.*

Katie rests peacefully in her bed, machines breathing rhythmically for her. There is nothing for me to do. I know that I need sleep and that the night-shift nurse will keep her ear tuned to Katie's monitors, but it's hard to leave my daughter's side. *Her body is just a shell at this point,* I tell myself. *Katie is already home.*

Tomorrow is my last day with this daughter of mine, and then I'll have no more days after that. I want to spend the next twenty-four hours carefully. I don't want to look back and think, *If only . . .* I am terrified of regrets. But what difference can I make, really? What can I do for her as these hours tick by? What else but sit here?

Life is so filled with doing. Tomorrow will be about being. I simply will be with my daughter. I will sit by her side. I will hold her hand. I will spend every minute just being near her.

"Goodnight, Katiebug." I kiss her hand, her forehead, each eyelid, her lips. I turn, and with automated steps, walk out of the room.

payne's grey

[peynz grey] / a very dark grey with a strong blue undertone

The almost pitch-black leaves us groping along the walls,

but a drop of white added to the mix has created just enough light

for us to navigate one more step, and then another.

When things fall apart,
the broken places
allow all sorts of things to enter,
and one of them
is the presence of God.

SHAUNA NIEQUIST, *BITTERSWEET*

13

AUTUMN 1994

Katie, age five, sat perched on a barstool at the kitchen counter, legs swinging. A childlike but accurate drawing of a coffee cup, complete with cartoon lines of steam rising from its rim, graced the white paper in front of her. A loosely stacked harvest of completed drawings was piled at her side.

"Done!" she said, holding up the paper for my approval.

"Nice, Katie! Can I have a sip?" I reached for the paper and took a pretend taste.

"Mom, it's not a *real* coffee . . ."

"But it looks real," I said, winking.

Giggling, she retrieved her drawing and asked, "What should I draw next?"

It was a typical school morning at our house, and the big kids had just left for the bus. Our rural school district offered full-day kindergarten every other day, and today was a home day for Katie. Little brother Sam, two, sat in his high chair, patiently nudging scrambled eggs onto his spoon with a jam-sticky finger. Baby Tember was still asleep.

Katie loved this oasis of "just us" time. Some mornings it was "What should we read next?" or "What should we play next?" But today it was "What should I draw next?" She almost always chose some form of art—watercolors, Sculpey clay, colored pencils—to occupy our time together, which was a pleasure for the artist in me as well. I often drew story illustrations for the children's program at our church—and Katie was a quick study of my drawings. Her cartooning style was beginning to mirror my own. But this morning, Katie was working freehand with crayons and a stack of printer paper.

"Draw these," I said, placing a bunch of bananas before her and moving a cereal box out of the way. I took my coffee cup and the last of the breakfast dishes to the sink. Bananas were not Katie's favorite subject. But nor were coffee cups, cereal boxes, teapots, or loaves of bread. For her, the subject matter wasn't the point; it was the challenge of matching eye to hand to paper that captured her interest.

I turned off the kitchen faucet and set down my sponge to watch as she began her sketch. She flipped her coffee cup drawing over, revealing a fresh canvas ripe with possibilities. She stared at the bananas for a moment. I could almost hear her wheels spinning as she planned her attack. She pulled a yellow crayon from the box, then reconsidered and swapped it for a brown.

Katie's face was a curious mixture of intensity and levity whenever she drew. Her piercing brown eyes, her furrowed brow, and the tip of her tongue—which she unconsciously flicked back and forth against her lip in rhythm with each stroke of her crayon—all these reflected a focused delight. I watched as the stubby crayon in her five-year-old hand transferred the bananas to paper with striking precision.

She set down the brown and reached for the yellow. Soon the outline of each banana was filled in, with a few brown bruises added for accuracy. She held her drawing up, comparing it to the real thing and grinning at me. I nodded my approval and gave her another wink. She wriggled in her seat and added this drawing to the growing stack of papers beside her. She looked up again, eyes sparkling.

"Okay, Mama, what should I draw next?"

JUNE 2002

When the kids were ages eight to seventeen, we moved from Washington State to a neighborhood in the northwest suburbs of Chicago, where

Scott entered seminary and began an internship at Willow Creek Community Church. Though he loved being an ER doc—and he was good at it—he also loved the work he did as a volunteer at our church in Spokane, helping people explore faith at deeper levels and investing in our church's volunteer leaders. He had felt an increasing pull toward full-time ministry, and we finally took the plunge.

"This family could use a little adventure!" Bethany declared at the family meeting when we announced that, yes, we would be moving. The kids were champs about the move to a new state, new schools, and a new church—though we felt sad leaving the school and church friends we loved. Scott and I were especially proud of Matt, our oldest, who kept a positive attitude despite facing his senior year of high school without knowing a soul.

At the end of that first year in Illinois, Katie graduated from middle school and was excited about becoming a freshman at Jacobs High School in the fall. She attended church camp with Bethany and Matt that summer and came back motivated to live her life with more purpose.

"I made a vow," she told me one morning after camp.

"Really?" I asked. "What vow?"

"No boys during my freshman year. No dating."

I smiled.

"I'm serious, Mom. I want to focus solely on my friends, on reflecting God's love to them. *Twenty-three kids*, Mom. I feel like God will help me make a difference in the lives of twenty-three kids."

Why twenty-three? I have no idea. But I loved that her goal had specificity.

Later that month, she wrote these words in a journal: "I want to love more purely than I ever have before. Blessed is each situation in our lives! For it is the perfect preparation for a future only He can see." A little melodramatic, perhaps, but it reflected her heart for people.

～◎～

Katie wasn't a sidelines kind of kid, and she admired people who took action. One night at dinner, she announced, "If I have a daughter someday, I want to name her Jael."

"Why Jael?" Matt asked.

"She was a strong woman in the Bible who defended her people by killing off one of their enemies.[1] She drove a tent stake through the bad guy's head! Jael didn't just wait around for the men to come to her rescue. She took matters into her own hands. That's how I want my daughters to be."

"It's a great name," Bethany said. "If you don't use it, I will!"

14

Katie's interest in art gained momentum throughout junior high, and she was champing at the bit to continue developing her craft in high school. Her art teacher at Jacobs High School, Ms. Ellis, brought the perfect blend of high standards, foundational skills, and heavy dollops of encouragement. Katie thrived.

When she brought home her first finished project—an eighteen-by-twenty-four-inch drawing of a beautiful young woman done in ebony pencil—Scott and I were speechless. The drawing looked like a photograph.

"Here's the image I used as a reference," she said, handing us a perfume advertisement torn from a magazine. The likeness between the perfume model and the woman smiling up at us from Katie's drawing was almost indiscernible.

"Holy moly, Katie!" Scott said. "We knew you had talent, but this . . . we had no idea."

She grinned. She was finding her sweet spot.

"Her art is fearless," Ms. Ellis told me when I bumped into her at school one day. "She tries every medium I throw at her. Her work is large and bold and beautiful. She is accurate—and fast. We call her 'The Machine.'"

Like a runner knocking large blocks of time off her personal best with each race, Katie was gaining ground with each piece of art she

---

[1]Katie was referring to the woman whose story is told in Judges 4:17–5:31.

completed. Her drawings of people especially amazed me. She could capture moist eyes, wrinkles in skin, strands of hair—even delicate lace in gloves—with photographic realism. When she was sixteen, she entered one such drawing, *Masquerade*, in the art fair for her school district, and it took first place. "*Masquerade* is representative of how even grown-ups play hide-and-seek," she said. "Everyone hides behind something. People even hide behind beauty—but there is still a child inside all of us." The district framed and hung the piece in the lobby of its headquarters.

By the end of her sophomore year, Katie had taken all the art classes offered at Jacobs. When we moved to a new neighborhood closer to work and church, Katie began as a junior at nationally recognized Fremd High School, whose robust art program offered a wealth of opportunity for her to stretch her wings. Katie was ravenous, taking every art class she could squeeze into her schedule and tackling every art medium Fremd offered. Delicate watercolors, multitextured oils, bold acrylics, sculptures, pottery, and metalwork—she threw herself into each new medium. She entered shows and brought home prizes.

She said yes to every opportunity to push herself as an artist—including tackling two performance-art pieces: During Fremd's music performance week, she painted a thirty-six-by-thirty-six-inch abstract oil on canvas in the school's hallway as her friend Mindy played a stunning cello solo. And she said yes to painting a watercolor floral during the prelude to the wedding of our friends Eric and Sue. The week before the wedding, I dropped Katie a helpful hint: "Maybe you should time yourself by doing a few practice runs, honey. You only have twenty minutes on stage, start to finish . . ."

"Mom," she said. "*Practicing* would ruin the artistry of the moment! I'll be fine." Clearly I was unenlightened as an artist. She taped a giant piece of watercolor paper to some plywood, gave it a light tea wash, roughed in a few pencil lines, and called it good.

On the day of the wedding, she took the stage, her eyes afire with focus. Energized by the tight time frame and the high stakes, she set her

brushes flying and finished the thirty-by-forty-eight-inch painting—
a soft floral in peaches and greens—just as the ceremony began.

Katie loved creating beauty in all its varied forms—and she herself was
growing into a lovely young woman. But it didn't bother her if someone saw her when she didn't look her best. Even at the peak of teen
self-consciousness, she would readily take out her upper retainer—and
the fake front tooth it held as a placeholder for an adult tooth she was
missing (dental implant to come later). She would flash a goofy, gap-
toothed grin and talk with a thick hillbilly accent, just to get a laugh.
If she accidentally got hit in the face playing volleyball or basketball,
she'd discreetly slip out her retainer and cry out in "pain," pretending
the offender had knocked out her tooth. She regularly met friends for
coffee wearing sweats and no makeup, went a couple of days between
showers on the weekend, or dared a girlfriend to feel the bristly stubble
on the one hairy leg she forgot to shave.

But when it came time to look her best, Katie tackled her appearance with commitment, wielding the same deft skill with her makeup
brushes that she demonstrated with her paintbrushes in art class. If we
were going out as a family and she wasn't done putting on her makeup,
she'd holler from the bathroom, "Wait! I'm not cute yet!" But ready or
not, in sweats or a dress, the girl was cute.

From the earliest days of driver's ed, it was apparent that Katie's free-spirit
personality and the skills required to be an attentive driver were a mis-
match. Katie's driving led to stories that live on in Vaudrey family lore.

One summer afternoon, Scott and Matt picked Katie up from driver's
ed, and Scott agreed to let her drive them home. He moved to the passenger's seat, rolling down his window for fresh air while she buckled
up behind the wheel and tossed her driver's ed notebook onto the dash.

"Matt! Wait till you see what a great driver I am," she said, grinning
at him in the rearview mirror. Matt double-checked his seatbelt and
gripped the seat in front of him in mock terror.

All went well as they merged onto the four-lane road for home. But when Katie sped into an eight-lane intersection and took a sharp left, everyone lurched to the right, and her driver's ed notebook flew out Scott's open window, spinning its way across the asphalt.

"Aaagh!" she screamed. "My notebook!"

"Never mind the notebook—just slow down!" Scott said. Katie hit the brakes and pulled into a nearby gas station, shaking. Matt, her dutiful older brother, hopped out and, dodging traffic, retrieved her notebook—which had been run over by passing cars and now bore a distinct tire tread across its front cover.

"Thanks, Matt!" Katie said. "Phew! That was a close one, heh-heh-heh! Sorry, everyone!"

"Bug, you've got to slow down around corners!" Scott admonished.

"I know, Dad," she said. "I will. But you gotta admit, it's pretty ironic that it was my *driver's ed* notebook that got run over. I can't wait to show my teacher!"

Once she got her license, Katie put down half the money for a gold '97 Ford Taurus. Scott and I paid the other half. But driving remained a challenge. In the first year alone, she ran into the side of our garage with her Taurus, backed into a giant brick building with my minivan, and finally rear-ended a flatbed construction truck—which scared her and improved her attention behind the wheel.

When she bought the car, we reminded Katie that she would also be assuming the cost of keeping it fueled and in good repair. This presented its own set of challenges. Running out of gas was not an uncommon occurrence, and spending money for noncritical repairs seemed a waste in Katie's carefree economy. But her definition of "noncritical" didn't exactly match ours—and once, when Sam was a new driver, it nearly caused considerable harm.

The latch on Katie's driver's-side door stopped working, but she kept driving the car unrepaired by using the manual lock to hold the door shut. She failed to mention the broken latch to anyone because she knew we'd make her fix it. Sam borrowed her car one day, unaware. He rounded a corner and the door flew open, almost pulling the Taurus into the path of a Hummer. He swerved to avoid the

Hummer and narrowly missed hitting a light pole before bringing the car under control.

"Katie!" he yelled when he got home. "How could you not tell me about your car door? You about got me killed!"

"Oops!" she said, trying to laugh it off. "Sorry!"

But Sam was angry. And so were we.

"How long has your car door been broken?" Scott asked.

"Only a couple of months," she said.

"A couple of months? Katie, you can't just ignore repairs," he said. "You could have caused Sam a serious accident."

"But the repair guy wanted me to pay $300 to fix the stupid latch!" Katie protested.

We all stared at her, incredulous.

"Fine, I'll get it fixed," she said, as the harm she had almost caused her brother sank in. "Sorry, Sam."

Sam forgave her. And she took the car to get fixed, begrudgingly shelling out the $300—but looked for opportunities over the coming months to remind us of the "hardship" of spending that kind of money on "a mere door lock."

～҉～

The transfer to Fremd was more than just an artistic boon for Katie—it was a social boon as well. She dove into her new friendships at school and at church and began dating a young man named Dan, whom we liked very much. During those years, she developed some of the deepest friendships of her life.

That fall in her 3-D art class, Katie worked hard on crafting a small pewter sculpture of a penguin as a Christmas gift for Dan, in honor of their mutual fondness for these playful, comedic creatures. But a week before Christmas break, she came home from school in a fury.

"Someone stole my penguin!" she said. "It's almost done—I just need to polish it—and now it's gone!"

"Could you have misplaced it?" I asked.

"No! I stored it in a cup in my art station yesterday, and this morning the cup was empty."

"Ugh, I'm so sorry, Katie. Can you make another penguin?"

"You don't understand, Mom! Each step takes *so* long. I would have to resculpt it from clay, fire it, make a mold, and then pour the pewter and polish it. All I had left to do was the polishing. Plus I don't want to make another one—I want to find *that* one! I am so angry!"

"Sweetness, I'm really sorry."

"I'm getting my penguin back," she said, teeth clenched. "I'm making a 'Wanted' poster!" She disappeared into her bedroom and emerged an hour later, poster in hand. She'd drawn a picture of her penguin—very sweet—but the words were not so sweet:

Wanted: Penguin Kidnapper. Whoever stole my pewter penguin statue from Studio Art 3D—GIVE IT BACK! No questions asked. If it's not returned, I will find you out! You have been warned.

"That's a little aggressive, honey," I said, "Perhaps a sassy, lighthearted poster would be more effective at coaxing the person to return your penguin."

"This is a coldhearted art thief I'm dealing with, Mom," she said, grinning—but with fire in her eyes. "You can't go soft with a penguin-napper!" She held the poster high. "I'm making copies."

The next morning, she hung her "Wanted" posters around school. Three days later, she came bouncing into the kitchen after school. "My posters worked!" she announced. "The penguin-napper returned my penguin!"

Whoever had taken her penguin statue had indeed returned it, unharmed, by placing it next to the faucet of the art room sink, where someone would be sure to find it—which they did—and return it to its rightful owner. Katie polished the tiny, whimsical figurine and brought it home to wrap.

"Win-win!" she said. "I got my penguin back, and I have a great story to tell Dan!"

Life is a series of stories, and she added this one to her pile.

15

I step into the room the hospital has set aside as a place for us to sleep. Scott and the organ donation lady are just finishing up the paperwork that details which organs we want to donate. Katie would say to give them all, so whatever Scott has decided is fine with me. The lady hands me a clipboard, and I add my signature to the necessary lines. She thanks us and is gone.

I peek into the room next door where Sam and Tember lie in twin hospital beds, still dressed in their street clothes but fast asleep. A mound of spent Kleenex towers on the nightstand between them.

Scott slips off his Birkenstocks, strips to his boxers, and climbs into one of the beds in our room. I change into the scrubs and slip-free hospital socks folded neatly on the other bed and set my cell phone alarm for 3:45 a.m. so I can meet Gail's husband, Bill, downstairs. He'll take me to O'Hare to pick up the California kids. I slip between the crisp hospital sheets and lay my head on the cool, white pillow.

It feels weird for Scott and me to be lying in separate beds and to simply say, "Good night" to my husband of twenty-four years as if this were just another bedtime. But what else is there to say? What words can describe this life-altering day?

I lie still for a moment. "Good night, Scott."

He sniffles and clears his throat. "Good night."

At the end of a normal day, my husband often struggles to turn off his brain and find slumber; I cannot imagine he will be able to sleep tonight. But within moments, to my amazement I hear deep, rhythmic breathing coming from his side of the room.

Thank you.

I jolt awake and look at my watch—3:30 a.m. *Where am I?* I sit up and the mattress beneath me crinkles. *A hospital bed. Katie.* All that has transpired comes crashing into my mind. The nightmare has followed me into a new day.

Scott's steady breathing fills the silence, and I turn off my phone alarm before it wakes him. I slip out of bed, pull on yesterday's clothes, and sneak out of the room. Before heading to the airport, I must see my girl.

The hallway lights are still dimmed, and all is quiet. The nurse at the ICU station nods as I walk by but avoids making eye contact with me—my first taste of the awkward ways people respond when your kid has died.

I push back the curtain to Katie's room, half hoping to find her sitting up in bed, smiling. But there she lies, just as I left her forty-five minutes before. The gentle rise and fall of her chest and the steady drip-drip-drip of the saline plinking into her IV line provide the only motion in the room. *Never in her life has Katie lain so still in bed.* Since childhood we have teased her about her arms-flailing, legs-thrashing habits while sleeping. Anyone who ever shared a bed with her—in hotel rooms, on camping trips, or during sister sleepovers—paid the price with bruises the next morning. Her stillness now is unnatural. All the Katie-ness has fled.

I lift her hand and stroke it. I notice the deep-purple fingernail polish she wears—Lincoln Park After Dark from OPI. It took me three trips to Ulta last Christmas before I could find the signature color she had requested for her stocking. The polish on her middle fingernail is chipped.

Katie is still wearing the Philadelphia collar—a stiff neck brace intended to protect her spinal cord from injury—from when they stabilized her at the accident scene. It looks terribly uncomfortable. My head knows she can't feel a thing, but heart overrides logic, and I call for the nurse.

"I'm just wondering," I say. "Does the Philadelphia collar still serve a purpose? She's already brain-dead. I'm pretty sure we're not worried about the risk of paralysis at this point. Could we please take that thing off? I want her to look more like herself when our older kids arrive later this morning to see her."

"Good point," the nurse says. "I need to get the doctor's permission to remove it, but I think he will agree with you. I'll call him."

I kiss Katie goodbye, lay her hand by her side, and hurry downstairs where Bill, my airport chauffer, awaits at the curb.

~~~

At O'Hare, I explain our situation to a ticketing agent, whose eyes widen. "I don't have a ticket, but can I please get a pass through security to meet my kids at the gate?" I ask. "I don't want them to learn about their sister from a text message on their phones when they get off the plane." The agent calls a supervisor, who authorizes a pass that gets me through security. The Arrivals board indicates the kids' flight has already landed—twenty-five minutes early.

My mind races. *How do I break the news to the kids that their sister is gone?* I get one shot at doing this right—and whatever I say will be forever etched in their minds. I think through different approaches, but every approach ends with "and your sister is brain-dead." No "right words" can soften this blow.

I rush to ascend the escalator that leads to their concourse, but a stream of people from the LAX flight is already descending. *Dang. No meeting the kids at the gate. No reaching them before they open their phones.* I stand there watching, helpless and sick to my stomach.

It's a two-story escalator so tall that the top of it disappears into the floor above. At first, only people's feet are visible from where I stand. I watch pairs of shoes descending into view, my eyes straining to spot any that might belong to one of my kids. Soon I recognize a pair of white Nikes attached to two slim legs. *I know those legs.* Bethany, my beautiful, graceful oldest daughter, descends into view. Matt, Andrea, and Adam are close behind. Bethany spots me and we lock eyes. Ashen-faced, she holds her opened cell phone in her left hand. She lifts her phone toward me.

"Is it true?" she mouths, a look of horror in her eyes.

No need for perfect words. *She knows.* I nod. As she steps off the escalator, her delicate frame begins to wrack with sobs. I catch her in my arms. The rest of the kids step off and we move to the side, clinging together, weeping.

"What happened?" they ask. "You said she was stable. Why did she die?"

"Her heart is still beating," I explain, "but last night the doctors declared her brain-dead. The things I told you over the phone were true—she is stable, she is in a coma, and it's very grave. But I wanted you to hear this final news from me, face-to-face."

"Some girl I barely even know just texted me, 'So sorry for your loss,'" Bethany says, glaring at her phone. "I didn't want to believe it, but somehow in my gut, I knew. I just knew my sister was gone."

As we walk toward baggage claim, I wonder for the first time—but not the last—whether I did the right thing by not telling them the full truth the night before. Matt and Bethany are so different from each other. What might have been best for him would not have been best for her, and vice versa. I had to make a decision on what would be best for both of them together, and I had decided to just get them to Chicago in one piece and then tell them in person.

Another thought hits me: Maybe I chose to tell them in person for my sake, not theirs. Maybe I could not bear to tell them last night. I had already witnessed Tember and Sam receiving this news. The horrific wail that erupted from our youngest daughter's throat will haunt me forever. I don't know that I could have handled two more such reactions—and over the phone at that, where I could not have caught them in my arms and comforted them as I had just done at the bottom of the escalator at O'Hare. Maybe I put off telling them last night because it was best for me. My face reddens at this thought. Mothers are supposed to do what's right for their kids, after all. We're supposed to make sacrifices for them. Had I been selfish?

Right or wrong, I'd done the best I could at the time—and I won't get a do-over. God will need to fill the gaps.

❧

During the drive back to the hospital, the kids pepper me with questions. I explain all the medical stuff that has happened and tell them that Katie is being prepped for organ donation surgery—they affirm the decision—and that Dad and the "little kids" are still at the hospital, where we all spent the night.

"How is Dad?" "How is Sam?" "How is Tember?" They want a status report on each family member. A million questions flood their minds, and I do my best to answer each one.

Bill drops us off at the hospital entrance.

"Thanks so much," I say. "I am forever grateful."

"Is there anything else you need?" he asks. "Anything else I can do?"

"Toothpaste," Bethany says. "I forgot toothpaste."

"What flavor?" Bill asks.

"Cinnamon."

"I'm on it."

On the ICU floor, we find Scott in Katie's hallway. He has already been to see his middle daughter. Now he embraces our oldest kids in his arms, and in his eyes I see a mixture of deep compassion and wretched helplessness. I know he would do anything to be able to keep the kids from the reality they are about to face. Irrational as it may be, I know he feels like a failed protector.

I remember Tember's request: "Don't let them go see Katie without us!" We head to the room where Sam and Tember still lie sleeping. Bethany sits down on Tember's bed, Matt on Sam's, and they gently rub their younger siblings awake. Tember opens her sleepy eyes and, seeing Bethany's face, throws her arms around her sister's neck, holding her tight. Tears force their way from between tightly closed eyelids. Matt wraps his kid brother in strong arms, and Sam buries his face in Matt's chest. We give them some time.

"We're so sorry, you guys," Bethany says to the two of them. "Sorry you had to do this without us yesterday."

"We're all together now," Matt adds. "Let's go see our sister."

Sam and Tember get out of bed, giving hugs to Andrea and Adam. Still wearing their drama party clothes from yesterday, they simply need to put on their shoes, and then Scott leads the way.

I walk ahead and step behind the curtain doorway to Katie's room.

The nurse has removed the neck brace, and Katie looks more comfortable, more herself. I try to view her through her siblings' fresh eyes.

They step into the room. Someone lets out a tiny gasp. The flood of pain in their eyes makes me feel ill. Bethany immediately hovers over Katie with a maternal air, picking up her sister's hand and stroking it, as I have. She blinks her long lashes and two tears escape, rolling down her cheeks and dripping from her chin.

Matt is eerily silent on the other side of the bed, his hand resting on Katie's arm, his lower lip quivering. Andrea grips and strokes his other arm, her tears falling to the ground, one after the other in rapid succession.

Matt later writes a blog post about his reaction to seeing Katie for the first time:

As I round the corner and the nurse moves out of my line of vision, it becomes real. There is no more busying myself with travel details, no more fooling myself, no more believing the best and hoping for a miracle. Katie lies motionless on the bed, a half-dozen tubes coming out of her. Her brown hair curls from beneath a gigantic bandage on her head. Her eyelashes and the rest of her makeup are untouched, ready for her first day of work at a new job. Her perfect white teeth peek out from behind the ventilator tube in her throat. But it is her arms that catch my eye. All five of us kids have the exact same shape of forearm, and there are hers, with bandages holding IVs in her skin. Her nails are painted a vibrant purple. *This surely is Katie.* This is my sister.

I find myself holding her hand, which is warmer than I can ever recall it, like a cake fifteen minutes out of the oven, cool enough to eat but warm enough to melt the frosting. The warmth makes her real to me. I tell myself, "She's not dead. Look, she's breathing"—my brain's attempt to protect me. But deceit is a lost cause.

Katie won't be coming back to APU in the fall. She won't be painting the mural for our apartment as we'd planned. And she won't be in the wedding pictures for the rest of my siblings like she was for mine.

My sister is gone.

And so at last we are gathered as a family—as complete as we ever will be again. We'll face this crisis shoulder to shoulder, together.

We spend an hour or so around Katie's bed, sharing stories, wiping tears, and engaging in quiet conversation. Bethany smooths Katie's blankets and fusses with her dreary grey hospital socks.

"So do they know what caused the accident?" she asks.

"No," I say. "The cops told us she swerved to the right onto the gravel shoulder, then came back onto the blacktop before suddenly making a sharp left turn into oncoming traffic. They don't know why she turned to the left." I recall my vision of Katie slumped over the wheel before impact, but I don't mention it because it was just an illogical vision, not an eyewitness account. It's weird. If I told them, would they think I had cracked?

Let's face it: How do I know whether this image was from God or from my own overwrought imagination or wishful thinking? I don't know what to do with the vision. It's more than a little odd. I keep my mouth shut.

"Was she on her phone?" Sam asks.

"No, the cops found her phone inside her purse," Scott says. "She must have just been dinking around with her stupid CD player."

I bristle at his words, feeling defensive for Katie but unable to deny the likelihood that he is correct. Why else would she have swerved? She was such a distractible driver. Over the years we all warned Katie about keeping her eyes on the road. Somehow her death feels all the more senseless because it was likely caused by something so preventable.

We are exhausted. Scott, Sam, Tember, and I have not been home since four o'clock yesterday afternoon. Our poor dogs have been alone in the house since we all raced out the door. The older kids were on a plane all night and need to sleep. Everyone needs food, showers, and clean clothes; Scott, my introvert husband, needs to get some time alone. They need to go home. *What do I need?*

I want to be with the other kids; I want to be the helper mom who blows up air mattresses and puts fresh sheets on beds and doles out clean towels for showers and fixes a big country breakfast; and I certainly could use sleep and a shower as much as anyone. But more than all that, I want to be with Katie. The thought of leaving her is inconceivable. I simply cannot do it.

I pull Scott aside. "I can't leave her. Even if she is brain-dead, I can't leave her body here all alone. I love that little body of hers. I've looked after it her whole life. I carried it inside me, and I feel connected to it in a way I can't explain. I know it makes no logical sense, but I will regret it if I walk out of here. Until this is all over, I absolutely cannot leave."

"I get it," Scott replies. "You are her mommy. It doesn't need to be any more logical than that. And I absolutely cannot stay. I'm about to lose it. I need to get home and be alone and bawl. I've gotta get out of here."

"Yep, and I get that," I say. "You go. Take the kids. Spend the day with them, feed them, help them process. And get some time alone. And I'll spend the day here with Katie. We'll tag-team this mess."

"Perfect. I'll come back and visit after lunch. Then I'll bring the kids back again tonight, and we can say our final goodbyes."

"Bring one of Katie's hats when you come back—maybe a knit one from my mom—to help cover up her bandages." I want her to look as Katie-like as possible for every nurse and doctor who comes through the door. And maybe also for me.

So Scott and I split our duties as parents. Off the other kids go, under Scott's capable care. And I turn around to keep watch over our middle child.

In the corner of her room, I find a chair—the cheap, plastic stacking kind. I pull it close to Katie's bed and settle in. I reach to tuck her blanket under her feet and notice that her grey hospital socks have been replaced by cute, white footie socks—with purple trim. *Who changed her socks? One of her sisters? A nurse?* I smile and tuck the covers around her feet.

Just Katie, me, and God. These Sunday hours will be a sanctuary amid the shock—a sacred vigil for me. And for Scott, back at the house, these hours, too, will be sacred, tender, and absolutely necessary, shoring him up for the grueling days ahead.

From the very beginning, our grief looks starkly different—and equally right for us both.

16

FALL 2007, AZUSA PACIFIC UNIVERSITY

Katie had graduated from high school in June and would start as a freshman at Azusa Pacific in September. Bethany would be a junior. Matt had just graduated from APU in May and married Andrea in July—the most joyful occasion for our family to date. We all adored Andrea, and everyone was thrilled to welcome this remarkable new daughter into our family.

In August, Katie packed her bags for college, and the two of us flew to California. Her best friend, Kati Harkin, was also attending APU, but they planned to be on different floors in Trinity Hall—"so we can double the number of friends we make!" they told me. After dropping off my daughter's luggage in her empty dorm room, the two of us hit the stores for dorm supplies.

For some kids, a new laundry basket, pillow, or shower caddy were just necessary purchases for college. But Katie always attached memories and meaning to things people gave her, large or small. As we shopped, even the mundane purchases were received as gifts, and she was over-the-moon happy about each one. Our budget didn't have much room for extras, so she spent forty dollars of her own money on a comfy butterfly-style chair and fifteen dollars on a hot pot, both of which she deemed essential for her plan to create a home-away-from-home atmosphere for new friends in her tiny dorm room.

By the time I flew home on Sunday, Katie seemed to be settling nicely into her new freshman world. It's never easy to leave a child at college and return to a more empty house, and the absence of Katie's joyful nature left a gap at home that we all sorely felt. But it helped that her exuberance spilled out into the e-mails she began to send.

A few days after arriving home, we received this:

September 3

Hello, family!

College experience, Day Four. My dorm room is pretty much set up, and it's dang cute. Trinity Hall is beautiful and new, and it's been 107 degrees consistently here (yes! 107 degrees!). Trinity's lawn is so nice, and Kati and I have been playing Frisbee, and we played on a huge Slip 'N Slide and ate free ice cream.

My floor is called "4th North." Yes, it rhymes. I feel like I have APU's finest girls on my floor. And my room has started to be the hub of all the action. I love it! Yesterday, girls kept stopping in, and eventually I had four girls on my bed, two on my roommate's bed, both desk chairs and both comfy chairs filled, and girls scattered on the floor. People love it in here, and I looove that they love it. It's wonderful.

My roommate is sweet and very shy, but she loves that our room gets a lot of traffic. She's so easygoing, but I'm learning to read her better: The only electrical outlet in our room is by the mirror on her side of the dresser, so my curling iron cord is always hanging over her dresser drawers. I noticed, and I was like, "Ahh, sorry, that's so inconvenient!" And she just said, "No, it's totally fine! I just keep my curling iron in my drawer . . . ," which is her sweet way of saying, "Get your curling iron out of my space, you sweaty hog!" (It's all in the interpretation.)

More soon! I MISS YOU GUYS AND I LOVE YOU! I have two homes—one in Illinois with my family, and my APU home. It's so wonderful to have two places you love so much.

Katie

❧

Katie's initial college plans had been to major in psychology and get a master's in art therapy. She decided to hold off on taking any art courses during her first semester and discipline herself to focus on academics. I was curious how it would work out for her to stop creating art, cold turkey.

She called in late October. "Mom! It's time to register for spring classes, and I'm going crazy being out of the art studio. I never should have tried to make it a whole semester without taking any art."

"I wondered how that might turn out for you," I said.

"I hate it," she said. "I'm changing my major. I want to be a studio art major, and I want to paint for a living. I don't want to be a painting teacher, or even a therapist who uses art. I want to be an actual painter. Next semester, I want to take as many art classes as I can fit in my schedule."

"What about your gen eds?" I asked.

"I could take one or two gen eds next semester, I suppose. But I want to dive into my art. I can't explain it, Mom, but I just *need* to be painting."

"Go for it, Katie," I heard myself saying, against logic. "Take the art classes. It's sort of like eating your dessert before finishing your veggies— and it might mean taking freshman biology as a junior—but if it's worth it to you, I trust you to manage your schedule."

"Thanks, Mom! And I don't care if I'm the only junior among a bunch of freshmen. Right now, I just gotta paint."

In a later e-mail, she wrote, "I have an agenda with a canvas."

And she did. When the spring semester began, Katie managed to squeeze three full-credit art classes plus studio time into her schedule, giving her eighteen hours each week to create art. Because of her strong portfolio from high school, the art department chair offered her one of the coveted studio spaces normally reserved for juniors and seniors. Katie was thrilled to have her own little nook for creating—and she called home with a request: "Mom! Can you mail me my art toolbox? I am setting up shop in my studio space, and I want all my best brushes and equipment!"

"Sure thing, honey," I told her. "I'll get it in the mail tomorrow."

The toolbox was actually a fishing tackle box filled with top-quality oil and watercolor brushes, paints, and tools that my artistic mother had passed down to Katie a year prior. Grammy had always been meticulous about caring for her brushes. But cleanup wasn't nearly as much fun for Katie as painting. Let's just say those brushes got a rude awakening when they landed in Illinois. I lectured Katie about the importance of taking care of her tools—to little effect—but nonetheless she got a lot of miles out of those brushes throughout her senior year.

I shipped the toolbox to California with a note that hinted about cleaning. I received this e-mail when it arrived:

Hey, Mom!

I'm so excited about my new art stuff. I took your advice
and scrubbed everything out (heh, it was a lot messier than
I thought . . .) and now it is clean as a whistle. I can't wait!

Love you,

Katie

The girl could be taught.

Katie began exploring photography in her new graphic design class. I got this e-mail shortly after the start of her second semester:

Mom! My next project is going to be a tribute to Bethany—
beautiful and tasteful—and she's going to like it. I already did a
photo shoot of her for the project. I'll tell you about it as it goes
along. She doesn't know yet, though, so don't tell.

I am two weeks ahead in my regular classes. I like to get
my "real schoolwork" done quickly so I can just focus on my
painting during the week. My days are maniacally long, but I
like them. The sun is shining now. I am very grateful for that.

I called Matt and Andrea yesterday and invited myself over for dinner. We had steak and cheesecake and mashed potatoes. Then we had tea and watched *Aladdin*. They love hosting, and I love seeing them. It was wonderful. Bethany and I have been having lots of fun too.

Oh! Kati just texted me. She just learned how to shut off the water in the dorm bathrooms, so I've got to go pranking.

I miss and love you guys.

AND DAD, YOU HAVE TO COME VISIT! I'LL WILT OTHERWISE!

Katie

Grammy and Pop-Pop (my parents) mailed fifty dollars of monthly "fun money" to each of their grandkids during their college years. This freed them up to enjoy an occasional trip to the movies, Starbucks, or In-N-Out Burger. But when a child sponsorship organization, Compassion International, hosted a chapel service at APU, Bethany and Katie were gripped by the difference sponsorship could make for a child living in poverty. They each sponsored a Compassion child of their own, dedicating thirty-eight dollars of their monthly fun money to their respective kids. We liked their idea of fun.

Katie's Compassion child was a five-year-old girl from Indonesia whose first and middle names are Kristen Anjelin. Katie called her Anjelin, which sounded way more exotic than Kristen. In one of her art classes, Katie painted a large watercolor of Anjelin from the photo that came in her sponsorship packet. She wrote this description of her work:

> When I was young, my family sponsored a child named Trifonia. Years into her sponsorship, her country, Rwanda, became plagued with war and mass genocide, and Trifonia simply disappeared. We got a shiny new replacement child in the mail, and I never heard about Trifonia again. Impoverished children

are invisible. Warlords and traffickers treat them like they're replaceable, but they're not. This is a portrait of my Compassion child, Anjelin, from Indonesia, who just turned five, who is real, alive, and irreplaceable.

Scott had not yet seen Katie's new life at college, and to keep our daughter from wilting, we flew out in early February to visit the kids and celebrate Katie's nineteenth birthday. Before leaving home, I baked and packed a chocolate cheesecake—her birthday dessert of choice. We stayed in a hotel with a pool, and Katie's older sibs and her friends met us there to celebrate. After swimming and pizza and presents, I lit candles on her chocolate cheesecake, and we all gathered around to sing "Happy Birthday." Scott filmed our elated girl as she blew out the candles commemorating her nineteenth year.

Dorm life, with its close proximity to new friends, clearly suited Katie. We toured her dorm, saw her room, met her friends, and got a glimpse into her life as a college student. Although she got homesick sometimes—she especially missed Sam, Tember, and Dan—the life she was building in California was Katie at her best: with friends who challenged her, classes that broadened her worldview, and an art community she loved.

Later that day over coffee with Kati Harkin, our two Katies recounted one of their recent dorm adventures. "Kati came to my room one day," our daughter began, "and she told me, 'Um, I have three dollars. And you know, I noticed the other week that goldfish were only ten cents each at Albertsons . . .' I told her, 'I'm in!'"

The girls' faces were lit with mischief. "So we rallied a few other girls," Kati Harkin continued, "including one who has a car—and an hour later Katie and I found ourselves with thirty goldfish to distribute. We chose 4th South—our faux rivals—to prank."

"And we tried as quietly and unassumingly as possible to walk down to their bathroom, hiding thirty goldfish in plastic bags under our sweatshirts!" Katie said. "We were very stealth."

"Very," Kati Harkin added. "It's a big community bathroom with lots of showers and sinks and toilets. And we filled each sink to the brim and placed a fish in it, then added a fish to each toilet. But a few of the goldfish died during the commute—so we put those little buddies in each shower's soap dish."

"And then we scurried out of there as fast as we could—but very nonchalantly!" Katie said.

"Very," Kati Harkin agreed. Then turning to her friend, she added, "Until you lost your focus and felt the need to say hi to someone—right as we were closing the door to 4th South!"

Katie shrugged and grinned. "You know focus is not my strong suit."

"You are many great things, Katie, but inconspicuous? No way." To us, she continued: "As soon as the first woman on that hall found her bladder full, Troy, the resident director, came knocking on Katie's door, and we were busted."

"We got written up," our daughter confessed. "But the good news is, Troy and his wife really like us! And he's our newest favorite person to prank. Totally worth it."

Our daughter was thriving, inside and out. She and Kati Harkin were closer than ever, and their plan to double the number of friends they made by living on different floors was panning out nicely.

The next day, she paraded us over to the art department to show us her studio space. Clearly the art classes she was taking were breathing life into her soul. She let us peek at a few pieces she was working on. One in particular caught my eye—a seven-by-twenty-one-inch still life drawing of some of her paintbrushes. The title: *My Voice*. Yep. Her voice indeed.

I got a call from an excited Katie one Saturday afternoon in March.

"Mom! I just saved 4th North!"

"What?" I asked. "What are you talking about?"

She explained.

It was laundry day for Katie and some girlfriends on 4th North. Waiting for her clothes to dry, Katie was relaxing in a chair by a door that led to a balcony. Suddenly, the door popped open and two young men tossed a smoke bomb into the laundry room. Then they took off running. Katie—recognizing that it was just a smoke bomb but nonetheless indignant that anyone should "attack" 4th North—gave chase across the balcony and down the stairs. The first guy raced across the street and ducked into a building. Katie—barefoot but fast—chased the second guy clear across campus before finally losing sight of him. She walked back to 4th North, dejected.

"When I got back to my dorm," she told me, "the APU Campus Safety officers and a real Azusa city police officer were there! Since I was the only one who had actually seen the guys who threw the smoke bomb, the police asked me to give an official statement as an eyewitness. I ended up talking to the Campus Safety officers for a long time—and they offered me a job!"

"That's terrific," I said. "But, honey, just out of curiosity, what would you have done if you had caught up with those two smoke bombers?"

"I would've brought 'em to justice!" she said with mock toughness. "But seriously, Mom, I just had to give chase. It was instinct. I had to *do* something."

I thought of penguin-nappers and yellow jackets and Jael. Chasing smoke bombers across campus, barefoot, fit Katie to a tee.

A couple of weeks later, she called home, elated.

"Mom! I just finished my first shift as a Campus Safety dispatcher!" she said. "I have a whole manual of real police codes to memorize! I already know what a 211 is—and a 415. And I get to wear a real uniform."

"That's terrific, Katie," I said. "Congratulations!"

"But there's a downside, Mama. The smallest shirt size for my uniform is a men's medium. The short sleeves come down past my elbows, and the bottom of the shirt hangs to my knees!"

"Could you get it tailored to a women's small?"

"Already checked! It would cost thirty-five dollars—and I'm not paying thirty-five dollars for a work shirt."

"So the princess has met her match?" I asked.

"Hardly! I just roll up my sleeves and wear the shirt with leggings and a belt, like a dress. It's pretty dang cute!"

Undoubtedly.

She loved her new job as a Campus Safety dispatcher, as this e-mail attested:

April 14

Hi, Mommy and Daddy!

Life is good and busy! This dispatching job is humbling because there's a stigma about Campus Safety, and it's not easy work. It's good for me. And the paycheck will be really nice. Woo-hoo!

The students here mock and belittle the Campus Safety officers, who are really just good, different guys. I'm understanding in greater depth the Dwight Schrutes of the world. I'm finding myself saying, "Campus Safety" with more pride in my voice, and I'm defending their honor whenever people complain about Campus Safety—which is frequently.

I'm excited about my roommates for next year! There are five of us—Marissa, me, Amber, Red, and Courtney—and we are all easygoing. They are kind and sweet. We got an apartment in Crestview—same as Bethany! It has a balcony and two bathrooms, plus our own washer and dryer. We will be living in luxury. Our unit is not near Bethany's, but all the apartments are pretty close!

Miss you and love you,

Katie

As her freshman year drew to a close, Katie became reflective. During finals week, she wrote this prayer in her journal:

I've learned a lot in these months, Jesus . . . I have changed so much in eight months. In four more months, God, I want to return to this place different than I am right now. These eight months did not fail me, and I don't want to waste my days.

Jesus, help me number my days. Remind me to be in constant dialogue with You. I am so much more myself when I am Yours. I want a deeper capacity to love—I want to love in a way that transcends me. I want my family and friends and Dan to feel valued and loved, cherished, in a way that transcends me. Light this fire in me, God.

❧

Katie wrapped up her freshman year with straight As, an abundance of new friendships, and plenty of excitement about returning in the fall to live near Bethany with her new girlfriends. Bethany planned to stay in California through the summer to work, so Katie sweet-talked her big sister into storing all her stuff in Bethany's apartment for the summer.

Katie packed up her stuff, said goodbye to her friends, and on Thursday, May 1, rode with Bethany to the airport.

17

6:30 A.M., SUNDAY, JUNE 1

The attachment I feel to Katie's body surprises me. I want to be near it, to touch her skin, to feel her warmth.

When each of my babies was a newborn, how I savored the privilege of caring for their tiny, fragile bodies. I loved bathing them, patting them dry with a soft towel, caressing their delicate skin with Johnson's Baby Lotion, and dressing them in fresh clothes. I loved wrapping them in soft blankets and kissing their noses and foreheads, the palms of their tiny hands, their toes, and the pudgy folds of their necks.

Long before they were old enough to be cognitively aware of what these loving caresses communicated, I always believed that at some level beyond cognition, they knew. They knew they were being loved.

Now here lies one of my babies, all grown up. Her beautiful little body, so capable for so many years, is once again helpless and in need of a mama. Does she know the meaning of these kisses I am showering on her hands, her nose, her forehead? She is not cognitively aware. But perhaps at some level that transcends words, she knows. She knows she is being loved.

It's six thirty in the morning. The second hand on the industrial clock above Katie's door marks the time in steady, unforgiving ticks. I have about eighteen hours remaining to offer my love in these tender and tangible ways to my daughter. The privilege of being able to touch her, stroke her hair, push her tongue back in her mouth, close her eyes, cover her feet with a blanket—each of these is a short-term privilege. I won't be able to nurture her fragile body tomorrow, or the next day, or ever again.

I cannot believe I am sitting here in a hospital room, next to Katie on life support. This pain in my chest goes deeper than anything I've ever experienced—yet there is such a strange familiarity to it. *When have I felt like this before?*

Three other times in my life I have felt this type of earth-shattering emotional pain—though not at this depth: my junior year of college, when Scott and I found ourselves expecting our first baby and I dropped out of college (glad to marry Scott and glad to become a mama—but mortified at being an "unwed mother" and heartbroken to drop out of school); in 2004, when Scott and I went through significant marital struggles—mostly at my hand; and in 2006, when Sam was diagnosed with retinitis pigmentosa, a progressive eye disease that leads to blindness.

During each of these seasons—when the pain seemed unbearable and I wondered how we would possibly make it through—I sensed God's presence in such tangible ways. Through the kindness of others, through timing that seemed beyond coincidental, through a resilience and strength that far surpassed my own, and through a peace that certainly didn't match the circumstances, God was faithful. He provided the guidance and strength we needed. He carried us.

In those seasons, I learned there is a commonality to emotional trauma—that pain is pain, no matter its source. And true healing from deep trauma requires facing the pain head-on. No shortcuts, no avoiding, no easy back trails. Just raw, honest grieving, which means walking out of the pit one step at a time. It's hard work. From your vantage point at the bottom of such a pit, you think the pain is more than you can stand, but it's not. And there is life along the way.

Looking back, each of these painful seasons was powerfully transformative. I encountered God in ways I'd never experienced Him before.

I grew. I became a better version of myself. And as I walked out of each of these pits one step at a time, I found ever-increasing glimpses of healing and beauty along the way. I had lived. We had lived. And we had learned lessons about life and love and God during those seasons that have marked us forever.

As I look down at my daughter in this hospital bed, I recognize it's these past experiences that make the pain in my chest feel so familiar. But will the lessons I've learned from those experiences hold true for *this* depth of pain? Can our family survive a blow of this magnitude? Can I?

The pit we are now in feels bottomless. I cannot begin to comprehend better days ahead without my daughter. But I have always found God to be faithful. And I know what it takes to climb out of pits, no matter their depth. I can take a step. One step. One step at a time.

In the stillness, exhaustion sets in. I snuggle my forehead against Katie's side and drape my arm across her legs. A moment later, her legs move! I bolt upright. A surge of hope washes through me. I try to calm myself with logic: *You know she can't move. She has no motor function left in her brain. She is brain-dead.*

But hope trumps logic: *Perhaps all the tests were wrong! Perhaps the miracle I have been begging for has occurred. She moved! I felt it with my own hand!*

"Katie!" I say in a loud whisper. "Katie, move your leg. Can you move your leg?" I grab her foot and gently shake. No movement but the rhythmic rise and fall of her chest from the vent.

Louder now. "Lift your leg, Katie. Can you wiggle your toes?" No response. I feel silly talking to her—I hope no one else is listening—but I can't hold back.

I squeeze her toes. "Katie! Wiggle your toes!" I run my thumbnail up the inside arch of her foot, trying to trigger a positive Babinski sign—an automatic reflex that would show something is synapsing in the nerves between her foot and her brain.

Nothing.

"C'mon, Katie. Move your legs!" I say with command. I shake her legs with increasing rigor, and then I pinch her big toe—hard. Still nothing. Finally I throw back her blankets, and—

And then it all makes sense.

Each of her legs is wrapped in some sort of automated blood-pressure cuff. The nurse must have applied them during the night. *For preventing blood clots in her legs.* An air pump sounds, and the cuffs inflate, stirring the blankets. And then slowly they exhale—along with my brief, irrational surge of hope.

I lay the blankets back down on her legs, tuck in the edges, and resume my station in the plastic stacking chair. *Of course she didn't move. What was I thinking? Did anyone hear me?* I feel stupid—but only for a moment.

If a mama can't chase the tiniest glimmer of hope in a situation like this, then who can?

A little before seven thirty, Dr. Yun and a nurse appear. "Mrs. Vaudrey, we must conduct a final test on Katherine to certify for the State of Illinois that she is brain-dead," he says. "By law, in order for a death certificate to be issued in the case of brain death, two such tests—conducted at least twelve hours apart—must result in clinical findings of zero brain activity. We completed the first test last night, and I am here now to conduct the second test."

"Okay," I say. "Can I stay with her?"

He looks at me for a moment. "If you like. The test is called ice water caloric stimulation, in which ice water is squirted into each of the patient's ears. If there is any brain stem activity at all, the ice water will trigger rapid side-to-side eye movement in the patient. If no brain activity is found, the eyes remain stationary. We will conduct the test in both ears."

Seriously? I am surprised by how untechnological the test sounds.

The nurse wheels a metal cart into the room. It holds a pitcher of water packed with ice cubes, a pink bowl, and a giant, needleless syringe. She fills the syringe with ice water from the pitcher and then hands it to the doctor. She pulls back Katie's hair and pushes the pink bowl under her right ear. With his thumb and index finger, the doctor opens Katie's right eye wide, exposing her entire iris. Her brown eyes have flecks of green, gold, hazel, even a slight splash of blue around the edges—all the colors of autumn—and the look startles me. I avert my gaze and swallow hard, but then I look back. *Please, Lord, last chance!* I pray. *Any movement at all! Even a flicker . . .*

The doctor gently inserts the tip of the syringe into Katie's right ear and squirts the ice water deep into her ear canal. The nurse catches the backsplash in the pink bowl.

Katie's eye stares straight ahead, motionless. Nothing.

The doctor fills the syringe twice more and empties it into her ear canal. No movement. Not even a flicker. He quietly shakes his head to the nurse, who scribbles something on her clipboard. They move to Katie's left ear, where the same procedure is repeated with the same results.

Dr. Yun turns to me. "I'm so sorry, Mrs. Vaudrey, but Katherine shows no sign of brain stem function whatsoever. Her brain death is confirmed."

I nod, my throat too tight to speak. I rest my hand on Katie's warm foot.

He looks at his watch. "Time of death, 7:45 a.m."

The nurse scribbles the time in her chart and hands it to him. He signs it, nods to me, turns, and leaves. She follows him out the door, pushing her metal cart. The ice cubes clink inside the water pitcher, and I think of lemonade and summertime. The tinkling sound dances down the hallway, fading, fading, until I can hear it no more.

18

THURSDAY, MAY 1, 2008

We were all giddy with excitement.

Katie's flight home from college was due to land at O'Hare at 10 p.m., and by 9:30, Sam, Tember, Scott, and I were at baggage claim, pacing, with butterflies in our stomachs.

I saw Katie coming down the stairs long before she was close enough to recognize by face—the bouncy walk, the flowing skirt and layered tops, the dark hair pulled into a messy bun and loose curls brushing against her face—I knew it was her. Katie was home!

I trotted through baggage claim and scooped her into my arms. The rest of the family was at my heels, and we were soon an entangled mass of hugs and chatter. Then Katie stepped back and took us all in, one by one.

"Sam, you've grown another two inches since Christmas, I swear!"

"Hey, sis!" he said, wrapping his arms around her and swinging her around, just like he used to do at Fremd.

"And Tem, you're more beautiful than ever!"

Tember grinned an orthodontics-filled smile as her big sister held her tight and stroked her silky hair.

"I have missed you so much," Tember said, her lashes wet.

"Bug," Scott said.

"Daddy!" she squealed, standing on tiptoe and holding him tight. Scott closed his eyes, and the corner of his mouth twitched. As she withdrew her arms from around his neck, she stroked both his cheeks with the back of her fingers. "I love you, Daddy!"

"I love you too, Bug. So good to have you home."

At last it was my turn. I hugged her again.

"Katie, I've really missed you! I am so glad you are home."

"Mama! Me too! How's your wrist?" She picked up my left hand and kissed the surgery scar on the wrist I'd broken last fall.

"It's all right. Surgery number four next week, though," I said. "Outpatient."

"I'll take you!" she said—and turning to her dad—"I'll take her, Papa. I'll take good care of her!" Then to us all, she added, "I have so many stories to tell! And we have a whole summer to catch up!"

As we headed to the baggage carousel, the butterflies in my stomach began to settle. Three of my chicks would be home in the nest. It wasn't the full five-count, but it was a solid majority.

FRIDAY, MAY 2

Katie slept in the next morning, her internal clock still set on Pacific Daylight Time. By the time she awoke and made her way downstairs, Scott and the kids had already left for work and school. I poured her a cup of coffee, and we sat at the kitchen table.

"I want to be really purposeful about my summer, Mama," she said. "At the last APU chapel for the year, Jon Wallace [APU's president] challenged us to make our summers count. He told us, 'You have one hundred days until school starts up again in the fall. Don't just loll away your summer. Make the most of each day. Don't come back the same.' I want to spend my one hundred days well."

Later that morning, I found her sitting on her bathroom counter, dry-erase marker in hand. Along the top of the bathroom mirror, she had written, "Katie: You have 100 days. Don't go back the same." The next morning, I noticed she had lowered the number to 99. Each day thereafter, she dropped the number by one, counting down the days until school started—and reminding herself to make each day count.

MONDAY, MAY 5

The weekend went quickly, and Monday was a school day for Sam and Tember, who had another five weeks to go before their summer break began. When Monday morning rolled around, Katie was standing at the kitchen counter, blurry eyed but cheerily mixing pancake batter. It was six o'clock.

"What are you doing up, Katie?" I asked when I came into the kitchen. "You're on vacation! Go sleep in!"

"I want to make Sam and Tember a hot breakfast," she replied.

"I can do that for you, honey. I'm up by five anyway." The truth was it was cereal or bagels for the younger kids on most mornings. Now I was feeling pressure!

"That's okay, Mom," she said. "I want to cook it myself. I want it to come from me."

Make each day count.

So the kids awoke that morning to the smell of chocolate chip pancakes in the kitchen. Katie served breakfast, saw the kids off to school, and then climbed back into bed. And she continued to cook for them each school morning—pancakes or eggs, something special to start their day.

FRIDAY, MAY 9

Friday morning, Katie drove me to a day surgery center for the arthroscopic surgery on my wrist. The procedure went well, and afterward Katie helped me into the car with my still-numb wrist in a fresh cast, my head groggy from the anesthetic, and a bottle of pain meds in my pocket.

"Let's get Thai for lunch!" I suggested. Katie was game: It was my nickel, after all, and our favorite cuisine.

We chatted over chicken curry, glass noodles, and peanut sauce.

"After this, let's go see a movie!" Katie suggested. "Have you seen *Baby Mama* yet? It's a comedy with Tina Fey and Amy Poehler!"

We spent the rest of the afternoon munching on popcorn and Junior Mints, sharing a large Mr. Pibb, and laughing at the antics of our two favorite comedians.

The anesthesia on my wrist was beginning to wear off, and when the movie ended and we stood to walk to the car, my wrist began to throb. Katie was all sympathy—giving me plenty of "Ooooh, Mama" and "I'm so sorry you're hurting!" She drove me home, made me a bed on the living room sofa, and brought me juice so I could pop a pain pill. Then she snuggled in next to me to watch some *30 Rock*.

This role reversal of being "mothered" by my daughter felt awkward but wonderful. It touched me on some deep level that caught me by surprise. I soaked it in, feeling deeply loved by my girl.

❧

Katie landed a waitressing job at Bandito Barney's that would begin on May 31. With time on her hands before her start date—and with my wrist in a cast—she offered to make herself useful around the house. I sent her to Home Depot to pick out bedding flowers for my oak barrels and planters. She returned with two flats of hot-pink petunias.

"These'll liven the place up nicely," Katie said. Grabbing a pair of canvas garden gloves—and changing into her striped bikini—she headed out into the springtime sun to fill my planters with the cheery petunias. She was right—their hot-pink petals added a summery zing to the place.

SUNDAY, MAY 11

My parents had flown in from Seattle for Mother's Day weekend. My head was still cloudy with painkiller fog, but two things stood out: the incredible peppercorn steaks Scott and the kids prepared, and a

Mother's Day card from Katie. "Your joy is one of the main ingredients to this home's climate," she had written. "Don't underestimate your contribution!"

Her words captured some of my deepest hopes as a mom. In a family full of quick wits and strong personalities, I viewed myself as more of a "good audience" than a culture former. But joy was baseline for me, and it's something I had been intentional about fostering in our home over the years. Could what she wrote be true? I felt a quiet mixture of hope and pride as I read and reread her words.

WEDNESDAY, MAY 21

On Bethany's birthday, Katie called her big sister so they could "be together" as Bethany unwrapped Katie's gift—a book she'd created in her graphic design class from the photo shoot with her sister. She had chosen her favorite shot—a beautiful profile of Bethany—and had reproduced it in black and white on each page. To each reproduction, Katie had added a different color or texture or image that represented a memory from their shared sisterhood or a character trait of Bethany that Katie admired.

I had the privilege of overhearing Katie's half of their conversation as she explained each page of her gift: "See the photo with the princess crown that I Photoshopped onto your head? I want you to know I'm sorry for always acting like the princess in our family—and for how that left you feeling like you had to be the tomboy." Page by page, Katie described the characteristics she most admired about Bethany—her strength, her warmth, her kindness, her leadership, her humor—and apologized for the "sister scars" she'd caused Bethany over the years. Bethany had expressed similar sentiments to Katie almost three years prior—the night before Bethany had left for college. But Katie, age fifteen at the time, had not reciprocated. Now, at long last, Katie was making things right. She was owning her contributions to whatever bumps they had experienced together as kids and teens.

For the next two hours, they shared the kind of laughter-and-tears conversation I imagine only sisters could share—stories of childhood adventures, apologies for past wrongs, commitments to stand in each other's weddings, and promises for plenty of coffee dates, dinners together, and girls' nights out at APU in the fall.

Having watched these two grow from infancy to young women—loving each other so well but also inflicting inevitable stings along the way—my heart soared as I heard Katie's long-overdue words of reconciliation toward Bethany. When at last they hung up, Katie said to me, "I can't wait to live near Bethany in Crestview next year! She is so good to me, Mama. You know, lots of times growing up, when it looked like she was the cause of our little conflicts, often it was me just trying to make it look that way—trying to make her look mean and me look innocent. I had a lot of stuff I needed to apologize for."

I recalled her preschool confession in the minivan: "Sometimes I am mean to Bethany and Matt." More than kids realize, parents see what's really happening between the siblings, so her confessions were not news to me, but I appreciated her words nonetheless.

"It feels so good to have a clean slate with my sister," she continued. "She's my hero!"

In the days that followed, there was a renewed freshness to their sisterhood. The length and frequency of their phone conversations increased, they texted each other constantly, and there was palpable lightness and joy between them, even across the miles.

MONDAY, MAY 26

On Memorial Day, May 26, our friends Leanne and Jimmy and their kids came over for a barbeque. After dinner, the kids cleared the table and then headed downstairs to our rec room. The four grown-ups moved outside to the Bug Room. After doing the dishes, Katie brought us coffee and slices of the apple pie she had baked earlier that day. Its crust was filigreed with delicate swirls. All the world was a canvas.

"So what has God been teaching you in school this year?" Jimmy asked Katie.

"Good question!" she said, pulling up a chair. "My biggest learning is that everyone is so different. People come from all kinds of worldviews and were raised with different values, and I realized it's not necessarily wrong that they were raised differently from how I was—it's just, well, different. I can be pretty judgmental sometimes in viewing my way as right. And I am excited about living more open-mindedly, learning from how other people think and the choices they make."

Pure Katie. She sometimes took a while to spot where she was off base—she could be stubborn, judgmental, and a little prideful. But once she got it—once she saw where she needed to make a course correction— she went after it wholeheartedly.

Her bathroom mirror read, "77 days."

WEDNESDAY, MAY 28

Katie's boyfriend, Dan, came over early Wednesday morning to say goodbye before he headed out for a weeklong fishing trip with buddies from junior high school.

"I'll be out of cell phone range the whole time, but you can always leave messages on my phone," he told his girl.

And so she did.

~⦿~

Katie's waitressing job included an all-day training on Wednesday, and she came home that night enthused.

"Mom! They hired fifty new employees for summer," she said, "and the owner and managers are the nicest people. The crowd there on the weekends can get a little rough, evidently, but the staff is awesome. The best part is that everyone there is so different from me! I don't think any of the people I met today consider themselves to be Christ followers. I can't wait to get to know them better."

Like a kid in a candy store, Katie was excited to make friends, learn from people who were different from her, and perhaps invite her new friends to consider the Jesus she loved and followed.

FRIDAY, MAY 30

The kids and I spent Friday morning getting the house ready for the next day's drama team year-end celebration. By noon, we were about done with the prep work, and Katie was growing restless.

"Mama, I need to paint," she said as I pulled a pan of brownies from the oven. Painting was something spiritual for her, and when her impulse for creative expression struck, it was almost a primal urge.

"Go for it," I told her. "We can finish up here."

She ran upstairs. Minutes later, she breezed past me in her bikini, wooden easel in one hand and a fistful of brushes in the other. "I'm multitasking!" she said. "Tanning while painting!"

Her ponytail swayed as she bounced by, her skin glistening with oil—and not SPF 30 tanning oil, mind you. Pure baby oil. She might as well have lathered up with Crisco. I could smell the familiar Johnson & Johnson fragrance of her infancy as she walked by. She set up her easel on the sun-soaked back deck.

"Mom! We're out of watercolor paper!" she moaned, trotting back inside and heading to the basement where the art supplies were stored. Soon she was back, carrying a twenty-by-thirty-inch sketch pad designed for pencil or pen and ink, not watercolors.

"No worries," she said, setting the pad down and filling a cup with water at the kitchen sink. "I'm just doing a rough draft anyway." Then she headed back outdoors, where she planted the oversize tablet on her easel and whipped out her paints. "No peeking!" she hollered over her shoulder, adjusting her easel so I couldn't see. I went inside to do dishes, closing the slider behind me.

I loved to watch Katie work, but she rarely let people see a piece until it was complete. I usually gave her space, but today I couldn't help stealing an occasional peek at her through the kitchen window above the sink.

There she stood tanning in the sun, paintbrush in hand, her bronzing skin increasingly dotted with flecks of paint from her flying brush. Her face wore the familiar mixture of concentration and delight.

I turned off the water and set down my sponge. Even without seeing what she was painting, I never ceased to be amazed by her natural skill and speed. She studied the hawthorn tree just off the deck—evidently the subject of this project—and began transposing what she saw onto the paper.

Forty-five minutes later, she called me outside, the tablet held close to her chest.

"Mom! I'm going to paint a piece for you and Dad, and you are really going to like it!" she said. "Here's the rough draft."

She turned the tablet toward me.

It was lovely. Delicate strokes of green, brown, and blue captured the hawthorn tree with stunning accuracy. Translucent shadows of red traipsed along its branches and down its trunk, which was anchored in the bed of strawberries I'd planted beneath the tree last summer—some in bloom, some with ripening red fruit peeking from behind shiny green leaves. The copper wind chime I'd made Scott for our twentieth anniversary hung from a lower branch on the right. And to the left stood Scott's copper citronella-oil lantern—one of his beloved possessions of summer and a stalwart soldier in his never-ending strategy of mosquito warfare.

The painting, though quick and rough, showed balance and delicate beauty. I could only imagine how lovely the finished product would be.

"Nice, Katie!"

"I'm calling it *The Bleeding Tree*."

"*The Bleeding Tree*? Sounds . . . significant."

"Oh, it is!" she said, flashing a mysterious grin. "You're going to love it. I can't wait to tell you what it means!"

"Me too!"

Katie had never painted something exclusively for Scott and me before. Judging from the hints in its title, the streaks of red on the tree trunk, and the two copper items—one from each of us—I suspected she was painting something that reflected the growth and healing God had brought to our marriage on the heels of a hard season a few years back. Now our marriage was sweeter than ever, and our kids had witnessed its transformation. Perhaps this painting mirrored her worldview that God doesn't waste pain but seeks to use it to bring greater beauty and growth to our lives.

But this was only a guess. I would have to wait until she finished the final draft to hear what the artist intended.

That afternoon, Katie moved on to other things, leaving her easel and tablet outside. Cleaning up is never as much fun as painting, after all.

Tember would be graduating from middle school on Tuesday, but her eighth-grade dance was tonight, so Katie busied herself with creating a "beauty salon" in the girls' bathroom for when Tember got home from school.

"That girl has watched me get ready for so many dances," Katie told me. "It's time for me to watch her!" She set out a pair of her own earrings and a necklace that matched Tember's dress. She pinned a matching bow on one of her own purses and set it out for Tember to borrow.

When Tember got home from school, the salon was ready. Katie painted her little sister's nails, styled her hair, and helped her get dressed. I couldn't help but listen as their sisterly giggles and stories filled the air.

"When it's my senior prom," Tember confided, "you will be away at college, and Bethany will have graduated. No one will be around to help me get ready."

"Tember, I promise you," Katie said, "wherever I am, I will fly home for your senior prom and help you get ready. I will be here. I wouldn't miss it for the world!"

Tember's girlfriends arrived to carpool to the dance, and Scott took photos of the eighth graders in their cute dresses.

"I want a picture with just me and Tember," Katie said. She stepped next to her kid sister, and they wrapped their arms around each other. *Click.*

◦◦◦

Later that night, Jimmy and Leanne's daughter Ester arrived home from college, and she and Katie met for coffee to catch up. I waited up for Katie to get home because she was always full of chatter and stories after a girlfriend date, and it was worth the wait.

"Mama! Ester and I had the best conversation," she said, bursting through the kitchen door. "We talked about how odd it is to go away for college and then come home where everybody is still the same—but *you're* not the same. We both learned so much at school this year, and we both changed so much. We are super glad we went far away for school. It gives you a different perspective than if you had stayed local. We are going to make a habit of getting together this summer to process everything we've learned. And I got to meet her new boyfriend! Mom, it was such a great night! How was Tember's dance?"

"Wonderful! She had lots of fun. She's already in bed. Katie, thank you so much for helping her get ready tonight. It meant the world to her."

"To me, too! I'm crazy about that girl."

And with that, she bounded up the stairs and headed to bed.

Her easel and tablet stood forgotten on the back deck. A light rain began to fall.

❧

8:00 A.M., SATURDAY, MAY 31

Early Saturday morning, everyone scurried around with last-minute touches to get the house ready for the drama party at nine. Katie put away her easel and tossed the rain-spotted rough draft of *The Bleeding Tree* into the trash.

2:50 P.M., SATURDAY, MAY 31

Katie races down the stairs and into the kitchen, where I am cutting brownies into squares.

"Mom! Where are my keys?" she asks, pulling on her black flats as she scans the room. "It's ten to three! I'm gonna be late!"

19

9:00 A.M., SUNDAY, JUNE 1

The organ donation lady stops by Katie's room to see me. "Surgery has been scheduled for 12:30 a.m.," she says.

Surgery? I hadn't thought of Katie's donation as a surgery, but of course it is.

Scott calls. I update him about the results of the caloric stimulation test in Katie's ears—he is not surprised, but he groans just the same.

"Katie's surgery will be at 12:30 a.m.," I say.

"All right. We'll come by around ten o'clock. The kids are doing pretty well. They ate and showered, and now they've crashed. A bunch of them are snuggled together, watching reruns of *The Office* in the living room."

"Probably just what they need—a chance to veg after this emotional overload. Are you in the Bug Room?"

"Yep."

"I'm glad. Love you."

"Love you too."

～⌘～

At lunchtime, the nurse brings me a tray. I bite into a strawberry, but it tastes like sawdust.

I return to my plastic chair to hold Katie's hand. When my arms grow weary, I rest my hands in my lap and find myself picking at hangnails—a nasty, nervous childhood habit. Looking down, my hands now remind me of the hands of a woman I saw once in Scott's ER. She sat in her waiting room chair, rocking, hints of mental illness behind her eyes, her lips mouthing silent conversations. Her cuticles were raw and bloody.

My cuticles are raw now too. But in spite of myself, I pull at one more bit of dried skin until it cuts into flesh and bleeds. I apply pressure with my thumb.

Unbelievable how the world can change. It hasn't even been twenty-four hours. This time yesterday, Katie had been so full of life, heading off to work. And the day before—Friday—she had been overtaken by an urge to paint us a picture . . .

The Bleeding Tree! That rough draft has become Katie's final finished work—and it lies crumpled in the trash. I grab my phone and call Sam's cell phone. Utterly reliable, he is just the right person for this small but vital task.

He picks up at the first ring. "Hey, Mama." He sounds so grown.

"Sam! Go to the garage trash can and find that painting Katie did on Friday. She threw it away. It was just a rough draft—but can you find it?"

"I'm on it," he says.

He gets the urgency. We hang up. Who knows how much party garbage he will need to sift through to find that painting?

He calls back a short time later. "Got it."

"Is it ruined?"

"No. It's bent and a little wet—but salvageable."

I exhale. "Fantastic. Nice work, Sam. Thank you! Put it on my desk for now, okay? Maybe Mr. Pinley can help restore it." Katie's high school art teacher at Fremd was an important player in her creative development and over the years became a family friend after Katie entered his department as a student.

"Will do."

I am so grateful for my boy. Rescuing this painting is a small win, but I'll take it.

～◎～

A nurse I recognize from the ER yesterday stops by. "Did you hear about the witness to Katherine's accident?" she asks.

"What? No! There was a witness?"

"Yes," she says. "The officer who handled the accident last night was here again this morning for another case. He told us a witness called the police department. Evidently Katherine passed by this guy's car before crashing into the second car. The witness saw her swerve onto the shoulder of the road, then pull back onto the pavement. When he passed her, she was slumped over her steering wheel, unconscious. He then glanced up at his rearview mirror and saw her car turn into the path of the other vehicle. He said she was definitely passed out, unconscious, before the impact."

"An aneurysm!" I say. "The neurosurgeon mentioned yesterday that Katie's CT bleed pattern looked more like an aneurysm than a cranial fracture. An aneurysm in her brain must have burst, knocking her out!"

This feels like the best news ever. I hug the nurse. It doesn't change the bottom line. Katie is still gone. But somehow, knowing that nothing could have prevented her death—that it wasn't the result of Katie's careless distractions—brings tremendous comfort.

I can't help but think of my vision. Katie was indeed slumped over the wheel before impact, just as I had seen. An eyewitness saw it as well—with his own eyes. Maybe Katie's unconscious body had rolled to the left, turning the wheel into the oncoming lane, just like in the vision. And perhaps Jesus—or some heavenly being—really had scooped her into His arms before impact, carrying her into the next reality.

I call Scott to tell him about the witness, and he is also relieved. "And it explains her CT," he says. "Too much blood for a skull fracture. It didn't add up."

The news spreads throughout our family and beyond. How bizarre that we are celebrating *how* our nineteen-year-old daughter and sister and friend has died.

20

SCOTT RETURNS ALONE to the hospital in the early afternoon, bringing a loose, grey knit cap my mom made Katie for Christmas. I pull it over her bandaged head, and she looks a little better. I rummage through my wallet and pull out last year's family Christmas picture and a photo of all three daughters from Matt and Andrea's wedding, placing one picture on either side of Katie's head on the pillow. "*This* is Katie," I tell every nurse and doctor who enters, showing them her photos. "This is what she *really* looks like."

The organ donation lady has been in and out all day, monitoring Katie's oxygen levels, urine output, heart rhythm—all the things that will clear the way for the best possible outcome for her organ recipients. When she sees Scott, she approaches us to go over each donation one last time.

When healthy donors agree in advance to share that which is no longer of use to them—not just organs, but even bones and skin—it is remarkable how many of their body parts can help patients in need. Scott has said yes to most everything on the list. Katie's heart, however, is not ideal for donation because of the slight bruising it sustained yesterday from all those electrical shocks.

"A nine-year-old boy in Wisconsin is awaiting a heart transplant," the coordinator tells us, "and his family is considering Katherine's heart for him." They would prefer a heart in perfect condition, of course. But they are fighting the clock. What if they turn down Katie's bruised heart and their son dies before a perfect heart becomes available? Such a torturous decision.

"The surgical techs will come get Katherine for surgery at twelve thirty," she says as she leaves.

Scott stands to leave. "I'll be back with the kids around ten." He kisses my forehead, then Katie's. His eyes linger on his daughter, and he exits the room.

The afternoon and evening are quiet again, just Katie and me and God. A sense of surreal peace hovers in the air. I am prayerful, numb, yet in touch with a depth of pain I didn't know was possible. I am laid open, eviscerated, raw.

The organ donation lady pops her head into the room, interrupting my solitary vigil. "I just wanted you to know," she says, "the family in Wisconsin decided to wait for a better match for their son. We can still use the valves in Katie's heart, but not the heart itself."

Dang. I wanted them to pick Katie's heart. I feel a weird sense of rejection that her heart was passed over. *That family has no idea the sheer volume of life and love that pulsed through this heart.* Yet if it were my son, would I risk saying yes to a bruised heart?

As the organ donation lady exits, I feel God's presence wrap around me in an almost physical sense, like a weighty, warm blanket. He is tender, yet powerful in His nearness—steadying me, calming my trembling soul, keeping me from slipping under.

Father, protect that little boy until someone else's tragedy can save him.

SUNDAY EVENING, JUNE I

My friend Sandy McConkey is flying into O'Hare from Washington State this evening. She and her husband, Bobby, are our closest friends from our years there, and their three sons, Aaron, Brian, and Collin, are like cousins to our kids. Yesterday, when Sandy heard the frantic voice message I left on her machine, she booked the next available flight out of Spokane. Bobby, Brian, and Collin will arrive tomorrow—Brian is forfeiting speaking at his own high school graduation to be here—and Aaron will arrive Wednesday after finishing his college finals. I can't imagine our family navigating what lies ahead without these people by our side.

When I spot Sandy in the hospital corridor, relief washes over me. We hug and I bury my face in her neck. She is like a sister to me and a second mom to each of our kids—and I cringe at what it will be like for her to see Katie in this condition. Nonetheless, I lead her to my daughter's room, and we step inside.

"Oh, September," she says, water pooling in her clear blue eyes. We stand together, holding each other and just looking at our girl. Sandy breaks the silence.

"She still looks beautiful."

～◎～

Scott and the kids arrive promptly at ten o'clock. They look refreshed but numb—until they spot Sandy. Hugs and a fresh round of tears erupt. Sandy is family, and it feels complete to have her here.

We crowd into Katie's room, sharing oddly normal conversation. Out in the hallway, my girlfriends Leanne, Susan, and Gail have arrived; but they hang back, ready to step in should we need anything, giving us space as a family.

～◎～

Since yesterday afternoon, Katie's IV line has been pumping saline through her body—standard procedure to flush her organs for donation. She's received several liters of saline—and she's beginning to show the effects of all that fluid. Her lips are puffy. The outlines of the delicate bones and veins in her hands are no longer visible under the skin. Her neck is swollen—from the fractured vertebra, I presume. Her heart-monitor alarm keeps going off as her heart struggles to keep beating.

"She's not looking so good," Scott says to me privately.

"I know. Feels like we are torturing our poor girl."

Katie's body is trying to die.

⌇⌇⌇

Around eleven o'clock, Scott gathers us together: "Hey, kids. It's time. Each of you take ten or fifteen minutes—or however much time you need—to say your own goodbyes to your sister. Sandy, you too. Then Mom and I will do the same. And then let's gather around her and pray over her together. We'll say goodbye as a family."

One by one, each of the kids takes a turn behind the blue curtain that separates Katie's room from the hallway. Long, somber moments, prayerful moments, quiet tears, fitful wrestlings, numbness, exhaustion. And each goodbye ends with a nod toward eternity—and hope.

Sandy says her goodbyes next, and then it is Scott's turn. He is in her room for quite a while before he steps from behind the curtain, his face white. He wipes his eyes with the heels of each hand.

"Well, I didn't expect *that*," he says.

"What?" I ask. "What happened?"

"I leaned over her and nuzzled my forehead against hers. All I could think to do was to thank God for such a generous gift as a daughter like my beautiful Katiebug. I cried and held her face to mine. I told Katie how much I love her and how proud I am of the life she lived. And when I was through—and I pulled my head back and looked into her face—she had tears streaming down her cheeks! *She heard me! She heard me*, I thought. *And she's crying! She's alive!* But then I realized the tears on her face were mine. Forehead-to-forehead, my tears had dropped and pooled into her eyes, and two perfect tears were now running down her cheeks. Katie was crying *my* tears."

"Oh, honey," I say, hugging him close. "I am so sorry." Everyone in the hall is now weeping too.

"I'll never forget that image," he says.

⌇⌇⌇

My turn has come, and I step behind the curtain. There she lies. Remnants of two tears moisten her cheeks. I have had eighteen hours to say goodbye to my daughter, but as the noose of time tightens, I become panicky. I cup her face in my hands and pray.

God, turn back the clock, I beg. *You're the God of time. No one will be the wiser. Just turn back the clock and then give Katie a tiny symptom of the aneurysm that lurks in her brain. Give her a bad headache or blurred vision—anything! Then we can rush her to the hospital and save her life.* My plan seems ingenious! Why didn't I think of it before?

Then this thought occurs to me: *Perhaps God already has turned back the clock. Maybe in the first version of this nightmare, Tember mooched a ride from Katie so she could visit friends in our old neighborhood near Bandito Barney's, as she often did when one of us was heading that way. The Mercedes that struck Katie's Taurus impaled its full force into the passenger's door of her car. No one in the passenger's seat could have survived.* I shudder. Had the drama party been on a different day—had Tember been free to visit a friend—I could be grieving the loss of two daughters right now. *Thank You, God, that September was not in her sister's car.*

But I am too greedy to take back my request for Katie. *Turn back the clock.*

I kiss Katie's cheeks, her forehead, each hand. I notice the "Lil Sis" key chain is gone, and the small chip in her nail polish has been freshly painted over—undoubtedly the handiwork of Tember and the bottle of Lincoln Park After Dark she was carrying moments ago when she stepped from behind the curtain. Sister loyalty. Tember is helping Katie go out in style.

Too soon, my fifteen minutes are up. No more minutes, no more words.

"I love you. Goodbye, Katiebug. And thank you."

❧

Scott gathers us around Katie's bed. "God never promised us a lifetime of Katie on this earth," he says. "But He promised us something better: an eternity with her—and with Him. While losing Katie will never make sense to us from an earthly vantage point, how blessed we are that someday we will see her again. We grieve deeply, but we grieve with hope."

The unsettling, blunt truthfulness of Scott's words strikes home. He is right. We were never promised a lifetime with Katie or any one of our children whom we love so much. Each day is a gift. And someday we will see this child again.

We each lay a hand on our girl, and Scott prays: "Thank You, God, for the gift of Katie. Thanks for how deeply she loved each of us. Thank You that she came to know You at a young age and is now experiencing eternity in Your presence. Thanks for how well she lived out the one and only life You gave her—all nineteen years of it. Help us accept this new reality with honesty and grit and grace."

He pauses. He swallows. "Together we commit our daughter and sister and friend into Your care. Amen."

I look around this room. How blessed we have been. How blessed we are, even now.

It is past midnight. Sandy gathers up the kids, and they head for home where she can mother them and tuck them in while Scott and I see this thing out to the end. My girlfriends stay, praying for us in the hall. Twenty minutes to go.

～❧◇～

Right on time and much too soon, two surgical techs arrive. One grabs Katie's IV pole and monitor cart, the other begins pushing her gurney toward the blue curtain door. Before I know it, she is in the hallway and being wheeled toward the big stainless steel doors with circle-shaped windows at the end of the hall—the entrance to the surgical suite.

A monitor wire is dragging behind her. I chase it down the hall and set it onto her lap. The surgical techs don't slow down. I trot next to the gurney because Katie's right foot with its purple-trimmed sock is now exposed, and I try to tuck her blanket around it to keep her warm. They keep pushing, pushing. I don't mean to be chasing them, but my legs keep following. This is my last chance to see Katie's body alive, and my eyes don't want to lose sight of her. *You are stealing her away! Slow down! You're taking her away too fast!*

They reach the steel doors but don't break stride. They shove the gurney through, and the doors swing shut, swallowing up my daughter. I reach for the doors—and collapse. Scott catches me and holds me, gently but firmly pulling me back.

My eyes strain to stay fixed beyond the circle windows of those stainless steel doors, and this is what I see: my little girl laid out on that hospital gurney, with all those wires and the IV pole, being pushed by two strangers down the hall, turning left around the corner. And then, like an empty sailboat being sucked out to the open sea, she is gone.

21

MY GIRLFRIENDS, SCOTT, AND I STAND weeping in silence for several moments. Finally Scott speaks. "Do you want to go home?" he asks me, his arm still tight around my shoulder.

"No," I say. "Not until it's over. I'm sorry. But not until her heart beats its last."

"No problem, honey. We'll stay as long as you want."

The pain-weary look on my husband's face shows the sacrifice he is making by staying even one minute longer. He wants to get out of this hospital *now*. But I simply cannot leave, not while our daughter is down the hall, alone in a strange OR, giving the final gifts of her life. Scott doesn't hesitate to go with my desires rather than his own.

We all decide to wait in the hospital rooms where our family slept last night. When we step into Sam and Tember's room, a familiar face greets us.

"Beth!" I say. "What are you doing here?" Beth is a friend who attended seminary with Scott and is on staff with him at church.

"Hey, guys," she replies in her gentle Carolina accent. She stands and we hug.

"We were just down the hall," I say. "You could have come and joined us."

"I know," she replies. "But I just wanted to be nearby, praying for y'all."

"When did you get here?"

"About seven," she says.

Five hours. This woman has been here alone for more than five hours, just praying, not wanting to disturb us. *The sheer beauty of people.*

Scott steps into the room next door to begin crafting an e-mail update to our friends and family. We have been unable to keep up with the phone calls and e-mails we've been receiving, so he sends a group e-mail. Impersonal, perhaps, but it's the best we can do.

I climb onto Tember's bed. Except for about forty-five minutes of sleep last night, I have been awake now for forty-two hours. I elevate the head of the bed so I can recline but still talk with my friends while Katie is in surgery.

❧

Scott gently shakes me awake. "It's over, honey. The surgery is over." He bends and kisses my head.

I open blurry eyes in a panic and look to the clock—2:37 a.m. *Dang! I fell asleep!*

"You conked out midsentence," Leanne tells me, smiling.

The organ donation lady stands in the doorway.

"What happened?" I ask her. "Did everything go all right?" Bizarre question, when the "all right" I'm looking for means my daughter's heart has successfully beat its last.

"The surgery went perfectly," she says, "and everything on the transplant list was able to be harvested." *Ugh. Harvested . . .*

"What time did her heart stop beating?" I want to know.

She looks down at her clipboard. "Katherine's heart stopped at 2:18 a.m.," she says.

I turn to Scott. "Let's go home."

❧

When we step through the kitchen door, the house is dark and silent. We ascend the stairs and climb into bed. We lie there in silence, staring at the ceiling. Scott reaches over and takes my hand. We are together, yet alone. Scott's loss is his alone to carry—I don't know what it is like for a father to lose his little girl. And my loss, too, is mine alone—he can't know what it is like for a mama to lose her daughter.

I think of the psalmist's words in Psalm 139:

You have searched me, LORD,
    and you know me.
You know when I sit and when I rise;
    you perceive my thoughts from afar.

You discern my going out and my lying down;
>   you are familiar with all my ways.
Before a word is on my tongue
>   you, LORD, know it completely.
You hem me in behind and before,
>   and you lay your hand upon me.

PSALM 139:1-5

There is Someone who fully understands. *I am not alone. He knows.*
I can't comprehend how I will face tomorrow or all the Katie-less tomorrows yet to come. But for tonight, I close my eyes, and into His arms I fall.

Here is the group e-mail Scott sends to our friends:

Dear Friends and Family,

Katherine Rachelle Vaudrey died this morning. Her heart beat its last as it was removed by the organ transplant team.

I have always suspected there could be no worse loss than that of losing a child. Thus far, the pain of losing Katie is every bit as awful as I would have anticipated.

The rest of our kids—Matt; his wife, Andrea; Bethany; Sam; and Tember—were with September and me this evening as we all said goodbye to Katie before they wheeled her away to the OR. The unity and pride of my family leaves me with a level of gratitude that nearly matches my level of grief.

Katie brought life to every room she entered. Tonight, she brought life to the bodies of several dying people: As I type this note, a woman at Northwestern Community Hospital is being prepped to receive Katie's liver. It will save her life.

A 37-year-old man will receive Katie's pancreas and one of her kidneys. This will likely save his life. A third patient will receive her other kidney. It will likely save her life.

And finally, as I type this note, a 26-year-old woman at Loyola Medical Center is having her hopelessly diseased lungs removed. Yesterday, she was told she had less than 24 hours to live unless they could find an organ donor match. When she wakes up in a few hours, she will be breathing with Katie's fresh, healthy lungs. They will save her life.

September, the kids, and I are in a good place. We are overwhelmed with sadness and loss. But as we think through alternative ways this scenario could have played out, we are feeling a renewed appreciation for God's love, provision, and sovereignty.

At this stage, we are anticipating a reception and a memorial service this coming Friday and Saturday at Willow Creek Community Church. We will send you details once they are known. We would be honored if you would join us.

We so appreciate you!

Scott and September

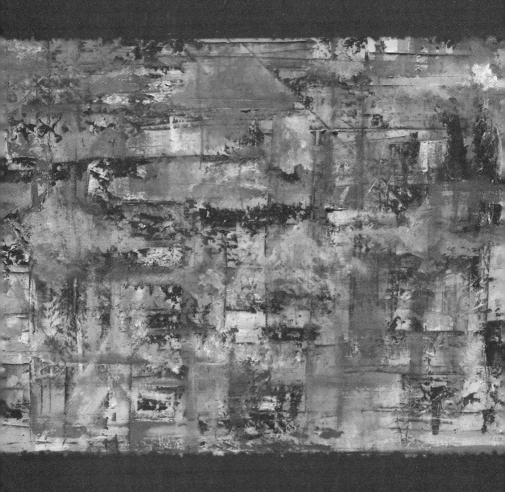

indigo

['in-di-goh] / a hue ranging from
deep violet blue to dark grayish blue

The tumultuous, swirling sea capsizes our world,

gorging itself on life as we knew it

and threatening to suck us under.

Fighting, kicking, and gasping for air,

we keep our heads just above the deep-blue abyss

We have this hope as an anchor for
the soul, firm and secure.

HEBREWS 6:19

Oh no, You never let go
Through the calm and through the storm. . . .
Lord, You never let go of me.

FROM "YOU NEVER LET GO," BY MATT REDMAN

22

My pillow is wet when I startle awake at four thirty. As the muddiness of an hour's sleep clears from my head, I remember: My daughter is dead.

I must get up. I must move. Silently, I slip out of bed and tiptoe downstairs. The house is silent and dark. A pile of unfamiliar shoes by the front door reminds me that while I was away, the house filled with people who are mourning the death of my daughter.

The death of my daughter. These words shock me. There I stand, in my same kitchen—with my same coffeepot on the counter; my same brownie pan, washed and drying upside down by the sink; my same oak kitchen table with its scar on one end, a reminder of when Sam superglued his pet rock there at age three; my same candlesticks from Grandma on the table, tapers partly burned from the last dinner our family shared.

Everything looks the same. But nothing is the same. The entire world has been scrambled. *I have a* dead *daughter. My daughter is* dead. *Katie is* dead. I whisper the *d* word aloud several times, hoping familiarity will rob it of its sting.

I pace, unable to sit, unable to think what to do. My chest aches. I want to bawl. I cried plenty of tears in the hospital but always with an awareness of the people around me—and a sense of responsibility for how my tears might affect my watchful children. Now, at last, I can cry alone. I can weep openly, wholeheartedly, for my loss as a mom.

I step outside onto the back deck and breathe in the sultry June air. The hawthorn tree Katie painted just three days ago stands unchanged in its bed of strawberries at the edge of the deck, casting an early morning shadow onto the lawn. I cross the deck, pass under the tree, and walk barefoot through the damp grass to the far edge of our backyard, where a thin line of woods separates our property from a pasture of undeveloped land. There, alone at last, I weep—silently at first, then in heaving, throat-aching sobs. Foreign, anguished sounds—wails rolling unencumbered from my chest.

I search for God. The veil between us is paper-thin. I feel smaller, more human, more vulnerable than I have ever felt before—fully in touch with the agony this world holds and fully in touch with God's rugged, tender presence. The air is electric. *Is Katie here too? Is she hovering unseen, nearby?* I turn, scanning the yard, the woods, the sky—half expecting to spot her peeking at me from behind a tree, an impish grin on her face.

I long to lay my body down on the ground, prostrate before God, and just surrender. Give in. I long to stretch out my arms and feel the soil beneath me—the solidness of the earth and the smell of spring sod—to demonstrate with my body how utterly helpless I feel. I long to grab God by the ankles and shake Him and demand He give me my old life back—and if He will not grant me this, I want to cry uncle, to shove this mess into His lap and demand that He fix it in some only-God way that far outstrips my human imagination.

All this I long to do, but I hold back. Instead, I stand there on the lawn rocking on my toes, hugging myself, paralyzed. Why do I resist?

The grass is wet, I reason. *I'm wearing just pajama pants and a T-shirt.* If I lie down, I will stand back up, braless, with a wet T-shirt covered in bits of grass. How embarrassing. And what if someone sees me lying facedown on the wet lawn? What if Jeremiah—the grad school intern who lives in our spare bedroom just off the deck—wakes up and spots me from his window? It would be weird. People would worry. They would think I have lost it.

These are good reasons to hold back, I rationalize. *No surrendering. Not now.*

Memories of Katie flash through my mind unbidden. I see her standing at the stove just last week, helping me make a batch of apricot jam. "I so look forward to becoming a wife and mom," she confided. "When I get married, I want to have six kids, and a house with an art studio filled with sunshine, and a little baby crawling around on the floor while I paint."

A crawling baby didn't sound like a workable painting environment to me, but I smiled at her idealistic optimism. She stood there stirring that hot jam with a wooden spoon, her hair pulled into a ponytail, a loose curl plastered to her forehead from the steam. How I loved this daughter of mine. *You are too good to be true.* I wanted to speak those words aloud to her, but as a mother of five equally loved and remarkable kids, I didn't want to risk anyone mistakenly sensing favoritism. So I held back.

Now, suddenly, I raise my hands—palms grasping toward heaven—and I rage at God.

Noooo! No, God! Nooo!

Don't You understand? What about the paintings Katie had yet to paint, the drawings yet undrawn, the homemade apple pies with their fancy, filigreed crusts never to be made again?

God, give me my kitchen table crowded once again with all five kids—stories being told, good food shared, laughter reverberating through the air. Give me Katie's quick, full laugh! Give our family one more conversation, one more dinner, one more game of Speed Scrabble or The Settlers of Catan. Let me watch Katie tell a story again with her contagious exuberance; let me laugh once again at her silly antics. Let me eat her homemade kettle corn—and later I'll gladly wipe up the splatters she always left on the stove. Let me listen once more to the lessons she felt You were teaching her in college—her growing humility, her broadening compassion. Let me feel the embrace of her arms around my neck and the silky heaviness of her head on my lap as we snuggle together on the couch watching 30 Rock.

And oh, God, what about the wife she longed to become, the mother she longed to be? What about the sun-filled art studio and the little baby crawling around? What about the six children she wanted to have—my six grandchildren? Oh God, no, no, no . . .

And what about our other kids? How will they survive a blow like this? How will our family survive? We were seven, God. Make us seven again!

How can I get through the week that lies ahead? How can I face my kids? I am not enough! Don't You know? I am not enough. Give me the strength to face my children when they awake. Give me strength to comfort them in their agony when I am drowning in my own.

Dawn comes, as it always does. Everyone will be waking soon. Utterly spent, I drop my arms and wipe the wetness from my face with my T-shirt. I turn toward the house and walk to face the day.

Everything is still quiet in the house. I let the dogs out of their kennel in the laundry room, and they bound to greet me. Alice and Henry, our toy Australian shepherds, are people magnets. Henry is all wiggles, glad to have me home. I rub his head, then off he races to pee, through the doggie door and into the backyard. He is a happy, shallow boy.

Alice, on the other hand, is clearly distraught. Her radar for human emotion is spot-on. She knows something is not right with her people, and she is beside herself. I bend down to pet her, and she tries to jump into my arms. I scoop up her little eight-pound body and bury my face in her fur. She is trembling.

"It's all right, girl. Mama's home," I say in as normal a voice as I can. She isn't buying it. I set her down. She sneaks a kiss on my ankle and looks up.

"Outside, girl." I open the laundry room door. "It's all right, Alice. Go on outside."

She hesitates, then hangs her head and begrudgingly obeys.

Before me lurks a finish line: my daughter's funeral on Saturday. I feel paralyzed by myriad, unknown tasks to be done between now and then. Where to begin? *What would I normally do on a busy Monday morning?*

I make coffee. Then I sit down at my kitchen desk, turn on my laptop, and robotically click open my e-mail. My in-box is filled with messages from friends. I am shocked at how fast and far the news of Katie has spread. I begin clicking through each note. How soothing it is, just hearing from these people, knowing that they are aware of our pain, that they care, that they love our daughter, that they are praying for us, that they are heartbroken with us. Their words are a cool compress on my blistered soul, and they bolster my spirit. *Can this be a part of God's response to my demand for strength to face this day?*

23

THE HOUSE BEGINS TO STIR. One by one, the kids find their way to the kitchen. It feels awkward to see them for the first time. I hug them and whisper, "I am so sorry" into their ears. What else is there to say?

The kids rummage for cereal, bagels, toast. Sandy scrambles a skillet of eggs. Bethany brews a fresh pot of coffee and fills our cups.

We need to formulate some sort of plan for Katie's memorial. Scott calls a family meeting. "You, too, Sandy," he says. "You're family." Fittingly, we gather in the family room.

Once we are settled, Scott and the kids begin updating me on all that happened on the home front while I was at the hospital.

"You and I have an appointment with the funeral home today at two," Scott says.

"What funeral home?" I ask.

"Some place in Palatine. Someone from church set it up for us. It's where they are taking Katie today. Ahlgrim Funeral Home . . ."

"All-Grim Funeral Home?" Bethany asks. "Seriously? That's like 'Dr. Whitehead's Dermatology Clinic' or 'Dr. Graves, Geriatrics'!"

Everyone laughs. How I love this girl! Her irreverent humor cuts through the heaviness. We are still Vaudreys, and it is still okay to laugh. We will get through this.

Scott brings us back to business. "Okay, so Mom and I think Katie should be cremated," he says, "and we think Katie leaned that way too. Do any of you feel differently?"

No one protests.

"Then cremation it is," he says. "Now to plan the memorial."

Andrea mentions the idea of a wake, but none of us knows exactly what a wake is. "It's sort of a pre-memorial open house, where people can stop by and express condolences to the family," she explains. "We had one when my grandpa died. It's a nice way to connect with everyone."

This sounds appealing—a chance to express our gratitude to all the people who mean so much to us. We decide on a Friday night wake and a Saturday morning memorial service, followed by an informal gathering of friends and family here at the house.

"I don't want Katie's service to be all heavy and depressing," Tember says. "She'd hate that! We need to celebrate her! And I don't like calling the open house thing a 'wake.' It sounds creepy."

When our easygoing youngest child gives a strong voice to something, we all pay attention, and her words ring true.

"Let's call it a life exhibit," Bethany suggests. "The Life Exhibit of Katie Vaudrey." We all agree that this captures the heart of what we want Katie's wake to be. Not a tribute to loss, but a celebration of her life and of the values she lived out: beauty, creativity, joy, love of friends and family. Slowly, plans for the Life Exhibit begin to take shape. It will be an intimate display of her art interspersed with personal mementos and photographs.

"All of Katie's art from this past semester will be here in a couple of days," Andrea says. "I called my dad yesterday, and he agreed to gather everything up and FedEx it to us." Her dad, a former professor at APU, lives near the school.

"Her stuff is spread all over," says Bethany. "At my place, in her friends' apartments, at the art department . . ."

"He's on it," Andrea says. "He's glad to be able to help."

"That's awesome, Andrea," I reply. "Tell him thanks."

When she hears about our plans, my girlfriend Susan, who hung out with us till the end at the hospital, again serves our family by offering to run point on organizing the Life Exhibit with the help of Katie's friends from church. "Think 'New York art exhibit,'" Susan hints. She's an artsy, hippy soul. Whatever she is envisioning, I know Katie would approve.

Plans for the memorial service begin to take shape as well. This is our one shot at saying goodbye to our girl and honoring the One who gifted her to us for nineteen years, and we gratefully accept every bit of assistance being offered. Bowman—a good friend of Matt's and a talented graphic designer—agrees to create a slide show for Katie's memorial. He stations himself in our home office, scrolling through nineteen years' worth of our family's photos and videos, pulling clips and pictures that tell the story of our girl. My girlfriend Leanne runs point on organizing the service itself. "Everyone at church has been hit hard by Katie's death," she tells us, "and the chapel only seats five hundred. We need to prepare for the sheer number of people who will be there. Let's move the service to the Lakeside Auditorium. It holds about two thousand." We don't expect to need that many seats, but we feel better knowing that no one will be turned away.

Our church's college pastor and Katie's mentor, Jon, agrees to lead the service. Brandon, one of our worship leaders and also a friend of Katie's, will lead the music with his band, and our senior pastor, Bill, will give the message.

"What about eulogies?" Scott asks.

"I think you should speak," I say. "I know it's not traditional for immediate family to give a eulogy, but I think you should speak for Katie."

"Absolutely," the kids concur.

"Fine," he says. "Who else?"

"I think Matt should speak, representing the sibs," I say. "He's the oldest." I am full of opinions, having had all of Sunday at the hospital to think about this stuff.

"Then all the kids should speak," Sam says. "We all love Katie, and we all have our own unique relationships with her."

"You guys agree?" Scott asks. "Are you all in? No one should feel pressured."

They all nod. "We're in," Tember says.

"If everyone else in the family gets to say something," I say, "I want to say something too."

It's a done deal. We will all give short eulogies. And we'll invite Kati Harkin and Dan—Katie's two closest friends—to say a few words too.

Eight eulogies. It's a long list, but we're a big family and no one wants to trim anyone out.

The girl will go out in style.

Meeting adjourned.

~❧~

The wake is scheduled for five o'clock Friday afternoon, and the memorial for ten o'clock Saturday morning. The next step is to meet with the funeral director. I have never been inside a funeral home nor met a mortician. On the drive over, I imagine he will be a tall, thin, serious man in a dark suit, sort of a modern-day, dignified Lurch from *The Addams Family*.

At two o'clock, Scott and I arrive at Ahlgrim. The lobby is just as I imagined: silk flowers, polished French provincial furniture, the scent of floral air freshener, and elevator music playing in the background. A display of ornate vases with lids glistens in a glass curio in the hall.

The funeral director—sure enough, he's tall and thin in a navy suit—approaches. With his white hair, piercing blue eyes, and dignified presence, he looks the part. Definitely not Lurch, but perhaps his handsome, friendly cousin.

"Scott and September?" he asks.

"Yes," Scott says.

"I'm Karl," he says, "and I'll be helping you with arrangements for Katherine's service. I'm so sorry for your loss."

Karl shakes our hands and is very good at eye contact. I stifle a nervous urge to giggle, but he quickly wins us over with his gentle demeanor—a mixture of calm professionalism and warmth. I have heard he attends our church. Was he there Saturday night when Bill interrupted the service to ask everyone to pray?

Karl leads us to a large room lined with caskets and invites us to sit opposite him at his immaculate cherry desk. Speaking slowly and clearly, he exudes a quiet assurance that things will be done right, just as we want them.

When someone dies, there are more decisions to be made than I ever imagined. For example, even if your loved one will be cremated, you still must purchase a casket for him or her to be cremated in. Embalming costs extra. People being cremated don't usually get embalmed. "But if you want a viewing before cremation, then embalming is recommended, especially if it will be several days between the time of death and the viewing," Karl informs us. I get the picture. *Embalming, please.* Also, for a viewing, you must make decisions about hair, makeup, clothing, and jewelry.

"The wake is Friday, but we want a private viewing for Katie's boyfriend, Dan, on Thursday, if possible," I tell him. "He has been out of town since this happened—he won't learn of Katie's death until Wednesday—and his mom and I think he'll want an opportunity to say goodbye."

"Wise—and kind," he says. "A viewing can be helpful, especially for young people. So we will plan on embalming. Bring us the clothing you'd like Katherine to wear, and we will dress her before you arrive."

"We donated Katie's organs," Scott says, "and the hospital told us she'll be wearing a plastic suit of some kind."

"We deal with this often," Karl says. "It's not a problem. The suit will be covered by her clothes."

"I want her to look as Katie-like as possible," I tell him, "so I want to do her makeup and hair myself." Scott shoots me a surprised look. "No regrets," I whisper. He nods.

"All right," Karl says. "We'll leave her hair and makeup for you."

We need to pick out a casket. And for cremation, we need to select an urn.

"We have a lovely assortment of urns on display in the front lobby," Karl says. *Ahhh . . . the vases in the curio.* "And we offer an inexpensive pressboard casket for those choosing cremation, but I'd encourage you to look around before you decide."

Scott and I wander the room and examine the caskets on display. Some are simple but elegant, some are ornate, and some are downright gaudy. We walk past caskets with themes like Catholic patron saint, Harley biker, American patriot, and hunter's camouflage. Scott and I exchange a few wide-eyed glances. I guess there is no accounting for a variety of tastes. But all of the caskets are of fine quality. We are shocked at the sticker price that some people (or their families) are willing to pay for a fancy casket. It's like buying a car.

"We don't want to seem cheap," Scott finally tells Karl, "but since Katie is being cremated, we really don't want to spend a ton of money on a casket. It seems wasteful."

"I completely understand," he assures us. "Let's go with the press-board casket."

I feel a little guilty choosing the cheapest option for our daughter.

"She'd be appalled if we spent thousands on a casket for cremation," Scott says, as if reading my thoughts. "She would declare it bad steward-ship of money."

The director nods. "For the viewing, we can make a gurney look like a comfortable, tall twin bed. Then after the viewing, we can place her in the casket for cremation." *Perfect.*

"I'll bring you her pillow and her favorite quilt to lay on the gurney," Scott says. The director suggests a second blanket to cover her legs and waist. I start writing a list.

"Send everything over by Wednesday," Karl tells us. "And choose clothing that covers as much of the body as possible—long sleeves, boots, pants, that sort of thing. In Katie's case, with her organ donation surgery, this will be even more important. Mrs. Vaudrey, be here by eleven o'clock on Thursday. We'll schedule Dan's private viewing for two o'clock. That will give you plenty of time to get Katie ready."

I nod and write down the times.

"Also, someone needs to write an obituary for the *Herald* and the *Trib*," he continues.

"That would be me," I say.

"The print deadline is two thirty tomorrow. I'll e-mail you their obituary guidelines." I give him my e-mail address and write everything down, not trusting my addled brain to remember any of this once we walk out the door.

My cell phone rings. I recognize Fremd High School's number on my caller ID. It must be Curt Pinley, Katie's former art teacher, returning the call I placed earlier. He has already learned of Katie's death and is heartbroken, our son Sam told me earlier this morning. But now I have a monumental favor to ask of him, so I excuse myself to answer his call. Scott continues talking with the director, making decisions we normally would make together. We are tag-teaming this thing once again.

Curt expresses his shock and sorrow when I answer my phone. I can hear the devastation in his voice. I give him a too-brief update on all that has happened. "Our friends are organizing an art exhibit for Katie's wake," I explain. "Her art from college is being shipped from California and will arrive here in a day or two, unframed. Plus most of her high school portfolio is also unframed. We'd like to display as much of her art as possible—which means everything needs to at least be matted. Is there any chance you and your students could mat her entire portfolio by Friday?"

"Absolutely," he says without hesitation.

I then tell him about *The Bleeding Tree*. "Would you be willing to take a look at it and see if it can be restored?" I ask. "No hurry. It was just a rough-draft watercolor she threw together on pen and ink paper, but it was her final work of art."

"Absolutely," he says again. "It would be an honor."

"Thanks, Curt. I'll have Sam bring everything to the school as soon as it arrives." I write down this task on my growing list. "Katie loved you, Curt. Thank you so much for giving her wings as an artist."

"It was my pleasure. That girl was something, for sure. What a talent! We had a sparring sort of relationship, she and I. I gave her a hard time, and she gave me a hard time right back, and we both were good with that." I knew this to be true from the stories Katie told me during high school.

"She and I had different ideas about religion," he continues. "I'm not that into the God thing, but your daughter talked about God like she knew the guy. When she graduated last year, she gave me this book called *Blue Like Jazz*, and she would e-mail me from college and nag me about reading it. The book is religious, sort of. I'm not a huge reader, but I like how this author talks about God. He isn't all hellfire and brimstone. Katie knew that would've turned me the other way. The author, Miller, he's just like . . . a normal guy, talking straight about his struggles. I like that."

I didn't know Katie gave Mr. Pinley a book, but I recognize immediately that she handpicked a title she knew would resonate with him. The book tells of author Donald Miller's journey of figuring out where God fit in his life. I grin at Katie's astute selection for her mentor-friend.

The *Blue Like Jazz* gift was a continuation of a lifelong pattern of Katie's that began around age six. She came bounding in after school one day and asked, "Mama! Can we buy a Bible for Heather? She wants to learn more about God!"

She and her friend had evidently been having conversations about God on the school bus. Heather was the first of many friends to receive a Bible from Katie, who wanted to be sure they could read about God for themselves, firsthand.

Curt continues. "Katie came by to see me a few weeks ago as soon as she got home from college, and right away she began nagging me about that dang book," he says, chuckling. "I only have fifteen pages left, and I'm gonna finish it for Katie."

By the time I hang up and return to the casket room, the funeral director is handing Scott our credit card. *Bizarre. We are earning frequent-flyer miles by purchasing a casket and funeral services on plastic.* We shake Karl's hand and head for home.

We forget to pick out an urn.

24

BACK AT HOME, Sandy's sons Brian and Collin have arrived from Spokane. The house continues to fill up—and become more complete.

Around dinnertime, the doorbell rings, but I am lying down on the sofa in the family room and pretend to be asleep. *Too much.*

Matt answers the door. It's Kaleen and Wally from church, and they have brought over a huge dinner from El Molino, my favorite Mexican restaurant. Matt and Andrea help them unload the trays of food onto the kitchen counter.

From my hiding place on the sofa, I can smell the spectacular meal. I hear Wally and Kaleen chatting with Scott, and I hear the clatter of plates and silverware as the hungry people in my kitchen dive into dinner. *I should get up off this dang sofa and be a good host and welcome our friends and thank them!* I feel ashamed, but I don't move. I am paralyzed. I am an ostrich, face buried in a throw pillow, eyes closed. I lie motionless, hoping no one will notice me.

Soon a cool, gentle kiss lights softly on my cheek. I open my eyes and look up. It's Kaleen. Two tears glisten at the brims of her eyes.

"Don't get up," she says. "We love you. We are so sorry."

"Thank you—" I rise up on one elbow and try to speak.

"Shhh . . . ," she says. "Lie down. Just know we love you and are praying for you. Now, shhh . . ." She strokes my hair like I am a child. I let her. Then she pats my throw pillow. I lie down again and close my eyes. I listen to her quiet footsteps as she walks away. She asks nothing from me except to express sorrow and love. I hear Kaleen and her husband say goodbye as Andrea walks them to the front door, thanking them profusely.

So many wonderful people—we don't deserve this outpouring! But these friends aren't offering their help because we deserve it. They are doing so because that's what Christ followers do. As best they can, they are trying to be the community of Jesus for us. And they're doing a fantastic job. People offer spare bedrooms for our out-of-town guests. They buy us hotel rooms and loan us cars. They drop off groceries—and Kleenex. Lots and lots of Kleenex. Scott's administrative assistant at church has created a meal schedule, and night after night—for six more weeks— these meals will keep coming. It absolutely saves us.

Our appetites all respond differently to grief. Bethany, Scott, and I are on one end of the spectrum: Food is a lost cause for us. We have no appetite whatsoever. Everything makes us queasy. On the other end of the spectrum is Tember, who stands at the kitchen counter in her size-two jeans, polishing off the third "edible arrangement" someone sent.

"I'm just a sad, fat monster," she says with a smile and a shrug, stuffing yet another piece of cantaloupe into her mouth.

All throughout the house, people cluster in quiet conversation, or cry together, or laugh their heads off telling Katie-stories or watching *The Office* on TV. Some are writing, planning, or choosing photos and video clips for the memorial service—or for the photo boards Katie's siblings and friends are making for the Life Exhibit. I find Andrea curled up on the sofa in a world of her own, rereading the second Harry Potter book. I smile at my newest daughter. She has been selfless and relentless in caring for her husband and his family all day. Now she has found—and earned—a way to escape and refuel.

The funeral is in just five days. We put Bethany in charge of choosing music for the service. She and Kati Harkin spend hours upstairs, sitting on Katie's bed, scouring her laptop and iPod to find her favorite songs. It gives me peace knowing that the music will be perfect—and that Bethany and Kati have something productive to do with their grief.

It is past midnight when Scott and I finally climb the stairs.

In bed in the dark, again staring at the ceiling, Scott says, "Well, we made it through a day."

"One day," I say.

He slips his hand over mine. "One day."

~⊙~

The next few days are a blur of activity, but a couple of patterns keep me sane.

My early morning routine—startling awake around four o'clock, then grieving alone outside with God—gives me sturdy footing to face each day. I don't fight the tears. I invite the brutal waves of emotion to simply pummel me without resistance. I cry hard, hoping that by releasing some of the steam from this pressure tank of grief, I lessen the likelihood that I will leak excessively on my kids later in the day. They will see me cry, of course—anything less would be disingenuous. But I don't want them to feel any sense of responsibility toward comforting me when their own hearts are a wreck.

I check my e-mail each morning and read new messages from friends and family who are aching, praying, and grieving with us. I linger over each kind word and write short notes in response. The sheer power of community bolsters me with its strange paradox of pain and love. Both are palpable. I can feel people's prayers. *There is no way I should be thinking as clearly as I am able to think this week, or functioning as well as I seem to be functioning—knock on wood—given all that has happened.* Yet somehow, inside, I am solid, unshaken. This fortitude I discover inside myself isn't from me. I'm not that good. I'm not that strong. I recall a verse of Scripture about "the peace of God, which transcends all understanding."[2] And I get it. This is what that peace from God feels like.

Tuesday morning, I notice Alice acting funny. Then Henry tries to climb on her. *Terrific. The dog is in heat.* We've been planning to breed a litter of registered pups from the two of them—but not now! The awkward timing strikes me as funny: A house full of people in crisis, and our two dogs are now going at it at every turn.

Sure enough, throughout the week every time we turn around—with company, without company, indoors, outdoors—no matter: Henry is making a move on Alice. If math has anything to do with it, Alice will be giving birth to about one thousand puppies.

Later, on Tuesday, Deanna and Brooke show up at the house. "We're here to clean!" Deanna announces when I open the door. The two of them brush past me, and Deanna's spitfire sprite of a daughter, four-year-old Anya, is at their heels.

"I know you'll have a houseful of guests this week, and we are going to scrub your toilets, wash your towels, and change your sheets!" *Friends like this—unbelievable!* I should feel mortified or at least sheepish that I need friends to clean my house, but I feel only relief.

Deanna and Brooke get right to work, and our kids cluster around adorable Anya, who brings a much-needed spark of brightness to the day. Sometimes God gives you a freebie, a little something extra to help you along. He does so today through Anya.

Over the hours that her mom is at the house, Anya hears us repeatedly shooing Henry away from Alice. "Henry! Get off of her! Get down!"

---

[2] Philippians 4:7

we keep saying. Each time, Henry obeys resignedly. But hope springs eternal, and soon he is back, looking for action. "Henry! Get down!"

Anya catches on. When Henry makes yet another move on poor Alice, Anya takes charge. "Henry!" she says, wagging her tiny finger in his face. "No climbing!"

This brings down the house. "No climbing" sticks. It becomes the euphemism of the week—and one we must repeat often to poor Henry. It remains part of our family's vernacular to this day.

Our kids' college friends begin arriving, having driven across the country from California or landed at O'Hare. The house is bursting at the seams, but there is such comfort in being together that no one wants to get a hotel. The basement and kids' rooms are wall-to-wall air mattresses. Somehow there are enough beds, pillows, blankets, sofas, and quilts to go around. We are all together. No one complains.

Sandy and Andrea find their niche in the kitchen, rolling out custom-cooked orders at breakfast and lunch. Each dinner is a home-cooked or catered meal delivered by friends. Being on the receiving end of people's generosity and kindness helps me understand firsthand how important it is to rally around those who have suffered deep loss. These practical gifts are lifesavers for our family.

Adam, Bethany's boyfriend, makes it his personal mission to ensure that Scott, Bethany, and I—the three Vaudreys whose stomachs rebel against food in a crisis—are eating. He lures Scott into eating lunch by fixing a sandwich of his favorite foods: sausage, sourdough, and Velveeta. He keeps pecking away at Bethany with offerings of toast, Malt-O-Meal, and fruit smoothies. He makes me a smoothie at lunch one day.

"This is for you to drink now, Mrs. Vaudrey," he says, adding a straw and aiming it my direction.

"Thank you," I say. He waits, watching. I take a sip. It is the first food to cross my lips since my hospital strawberry two days ago. The tart coolness of the fruit is refreshing. I manage to down a few more sips before the sawdust flavor returns.

My mother and I talk by phone each day. She and my dad will be flying in from Seattle on Wednesday. My five children are their only grandkids, and they are devastated by Katie's death. I feel guilty that I don't have one spare ounce of anything to offer them. Mom doesn't ask for my comfort or make it about her. She understands that my bank is empty and that I need to spend what few emotional dollars I have on my own family.

I have yet to speak with my dad, though he has left messages. My dad is rather stoic but so tender toward his grandchildren. I know our first conversation will be hard for both of us, and I keep putting it off. I relay messages of love to him through my mom, with promises to call soon.

My parents are rocks. A whole cotillion of my aunties and uncles are flying in from all over the country, and my mom and dad handle all their hotel reservations, trips to O'Hare, car rentals, everything. They are truly amazing in a crisis. And Matt, likewise: Scott's parents, brother, and sister are flying in from Spokane, and he handles all the plans for them.

Katie's death is especially devastating for my brother. Despite the two thousand miles that separated Katie and her uncle Greg, she was purposeful about investing in her relationship with him, and he adored her. In fact, Katie was chatting with him via Skype to the computer in his nursing-home room on Saturday morning before she left for work.

Greg has no shelf upon which to put this kind of loss. Mom tried breaking the news to him slowly—in small bites over two days—so he could absorb it all. The first day she simply told him, "Katie's been in a bad car accident, and she is very sick in the hospital." But when she arrived in his room on the second day, he turned his electric wheelchair to face her.

"Katie is dead, isn't she?" he asked.

"Yes, son," my mom said, resting a hand on his arm. "Katie died."

His eyes filled. "When I woke up this morning, I knew she was dead," he said. "She really loved me, you know. She told me all the time. And I told her, 'I love you, too, Katie.'"

My brother will not be able to come to the funeral. His health makes him too fragile to fly. So on Saturday, when the rest of us will be gathering together to grieve my daughter, he will be sitting in his wheelchair, alone in his room in Seattle, eating his breakfast from a cafeteria tray. This image brings more pain than I can absorb. *God, cover this. Please— just cover it.* I push Greg out of my mind.

I finish writing Katie's obituary by Tuesday's 2:30 p.m. deadline. Flowers and cards have been arriving at the house, and we are touched by each one. But soon we are running out of space to hold them all, and the house looks a bit jungle-like. I recall obituaries that read, "In lieu of flowers, please send a charitable donation to . . ." This seems like a good plan for Katie, who sponsored her little girl, Anjelin, through Compassion International. Bethany has decided to continue Anjelin's sponsorship in honor of her sister—but on top of her own sponsored child, the extra thirty-eight dollars per month is beyond her college-student "fun money" budget. I add Compassion as an option to the obit and hit send.

In the coming weeks, the donations people send in Katie's memory are enough to cover Anjelin's sponsorship for the next eight years.

25

Tember's eighth-grade graduation ceremony from Carl Sandburg Junior High has been at the top of our family's radar in recent weeks. Tuesday—graduation day—has now sneaked up on us amid all that has happened, but we cannot miss this opportunity to celebrate Tember.

Each eighth grader's family was allotted a mere four tickets to the commencement, but the school scores us nine extra tickets to accommodate everyone in town—thank you, office ladies at Carl Sandburg!—and on Tuesday afternoon, we shift from planning a memorial for one daughter to celebrating the graduation of another.

In the upstairs bathroom, Bethany helps Tember get ready, just as Katie helped Tember prepare for the dance last Friday. At five o'clock, our youngest girl descends the stairs, wearing not the graduation dress she and I purchased a couple of weeks back but a summery white dress of Katie's. Her long brown hair is piled into a mass of curls. Bethany has snipped sprigs of baby's breath from some of Katie's bereavement bouquets and tucked them into Tember's hair—her subtle way of making sure Katie is present for this milestone event in their sister's life. A pair of Katie's mother-of-pearl earrings dangle from Tember's ears as well. As I watch her walk down the stairs, I blink and swallow hard. But when I notice her feet, I can't help but smile: Above her new graduation shoes, her right ankle is wrapped in an ace bandage from where she whacked her anklebone with a baseball bat in gym class a few days back. With a slight limp, she stands balanced between childhood and womanhood— and she looks stunning.

Thirteen of us—five McConkeys, seven Vaudreys, and Adam— stream out to the front yard for pictures. The afternoon sun casts a golden glow, making everything look as surreal as it feels. Scott snaps pictures of our graduate; then we take some family shots—our first family photos without Katie—and we work hard to put smiles on our faces.

There is one shot I would normally ask for in a setting like this. But now—with Katie gone? *Don't put it off. Don't avoid. Lean into the pain.*

"How about a sister shot?" I ask. "Andrea, Bethany, Tember—let's get a shot of the three of you girls."

Andrea gets what I am trying to do. "Okay, Mom," she says and steps next to Tember. She and Bethany wrap arms around our youngest daughter, and the three remaining Vaudrey sisters smile for the camera. *Click.*

And no matter how Scott aims the camera, Henry and Alice manage to position themselves in the background, in full swing.

We shout in unison, "Henry! No climbing!"

In the crowded Carl Sandburg gymnasium, we find an empty row in the bleachers and fill it. We sit through speeches and songs and then the reading of names. When at last the principal calls "September Michelle Vaudrey," we cheer her on. Our beautiful, brokenhearted fourteen-year-old walks confidently (no limp) across the stage and receives her diploma. The crowd, fully aware of her loss, erupts in applause, expressing their affection—and their sympathy, too.

After the ceremony, we swarm Tember with hugs, flowers, and "Congratulations!" We take more pictures, then head to Chevys Fresh Mex for a celebratory dinner.

Tember opens cards and gifts, including the same present we'd given Bethany and Katie at their eighth-grade graduations: a gold cross inset with tiny diamonds.

As the waiter takes our dessert orders, I glance at my watch—nine o'clock. Just three days ago at this time, Dr. Yun was telling us Katie was brain-dead. Now here we sit, celebrating Tember in spite of all that has happened. We've pulled it together. It isn't easy, but it is so the right choice.

Our desserts arrive, and one by one, we go around the table, sharing words of affirmation about our youngest, the guest of honor. Tember is loved beyond measure by all thirteen of her biggest fans—and by the one fan whose presence is sorely missed. Tember feels the love.

❧

Katie's art arrives from California on Wednesday in two giant, flat FedEx boxes. I bring them into the living room, alone, to open.

I have seen photos of a few of the pieces Katie created at APU, but most of them I have only heard about from her phone calls and e-mails. I lift each piece out of its box and remove its tissue wrapping. More than fifty pieces of new art! Many were mere homework assignments, but a few dozen are significant finished pieces. I am floored by the vast volume of art and the diverse media my daughter conquered during her one semester of art classes at APU.

I look in particular for one painting that Katie described over the phone this spring: an India ink watercolor wash she painted with her sumi-e Japanese brushes. She told me the piece portrays each of our kids as toddlers. Katie was rarely satisfied with a finished piece of her art, but I could tell over the phone that she was very happy with how *The Siblings* had turned out. At last, I come across a long, narrow piece of heavy watercolor paper—about two feet wide and four feet long, wrapped in tissue. *The Siblings*!

I open the delicate wrappings, and my jaw drops. There on the paper my five kids play as toddlers, frozen in time, captured through simple brushstrokes of translucent black and grey India ink. Each child's portrait includes an object painted in opaque red ink, something representative of his or her toddler personality—playful Matt with a red ball, Bethany with her favorite stuffed bunny in red, Katie the fashion plate wobbling in a pair of my red high heels, Sam my snuggler with a red binky in his mouth, and Tember with a red lipstick in one hand and a red toothbrush in the other, reminiscent of the week when she discovered a "sink" just her height in the bathroom: she colored the inside of the toilet bowl with one of my red lipsticks and then brushed her teeth in the toilet water.

Any artist will tell you that watercolor is the most difficult of the paint mediums. Once the brush touches the paper, there is no turning back. Yet on one sheet of paper, Katie captured each of the five kids with playful, simplistic accuracy.

What could she have accomplished in another semester? Another year? A lifetime? What kind of mark might her art have made on the world?

I repack the boxes, and Sam drives them to Curt Pinley at the high school to be matted.

It is wonderful to have everyone together in the house, but it heightens the reality of everyone's loss. One complication of losing a child is that you grieve not only for your own loss but for everyone else's, too. I am devastated by the catastrophic pain that Tember, Sam, Bethany, Matt, and Andrea are going through. And of course I am leveled by Scott's loss. Pain upon pain, layer upon layer.

I am also heartbroken for the loss Katie's closest friends are experiencing—her friends from church; her roommates and friends from college; and her boyfriend, Dan, who is still out of state, fishing. His pain is yet to come. I love these kids, many of whom have spent countless hours at our home hanging out, watching movies, roasting marshmallows over a bonfire in the backyard, or eating Italian beef sandwiches around my kitchen table at lunch break—every Friday during Katie's senior year. In losing my daughter, am I also losing my "Mrs. V" relationship with her closest friends? The tentacles of loss from one person's death reach further than you can imagine.

On Wednesday morning, at the end of their fishing trip, Dan and his buddies canoe as planned through the wilderness waterways back to the remote outstation. His parents and brother are waiting for him at the dock. I don't envy their task.

His mom calls me shortly thereafter. "It was awful," she says. "He is a wreck."

"I'm so glad he has his whole family around him," I tell her. "We're praying for you all."

Half an hour later, this remarkable young man calls me. His first words reflect such a selfless, others-focused character: "Mrs. Vaudrey," he says, his voice cracking, "I'm so sorry for your loss."

☙⚭❧

My parents flew in from Seattle around noon on Wednesday and are at a hotel nearby, waiting for the rest of my aunts and uncles to arrive from New England. Long overdue, I make my first call to my dad. It is his seventieth birthday.

Over the years, my patient father's birthday has been regularly over-shadowed by milestone events in our family: Scott graduated from college on Dad's birthday. Scott graduated from med school on his birthday. Several of our kids graduated from high school on his birthday. The guy just can't get a break in the birthday department. He always takes it in stride. But this year is the worst. On his seventieth birthday, we are planning his middle granddaughter's funeral.

I dial his number.

"Hey, honey," he says, recognizing my phone on his caller ID.

When I hear his gentle voice on the other end of the phone, a goofy idea pops into my overloaded, sleep-deprived brain. I start singing:

Crappy birthday to you,
Crappy birthday to you,

Crappy birthday, dear Daddy!
Crappy birthday to you!

He laughs at my ridiculous song. And then the floodgates of grief that separate us open wide and we cry.

"I love you, Dad."

"I love you, babe."

Few words are exchanged in our brief phone call. Few are needed.

Near bedtime, Scott heads out to the backyard to soak in our hot tub. "Let me grab my suit, Dad," Matt says. "I'll keep you company." I head up to bed.

Matt has kept his emotions well guarded thus far. Perhaps he feels he should be the grown-up of the kids, since he is truly a grown man now—a six-foot-three-inch college graduate, a new husband, and a teacher. He has taken his role as pillar of strength for the family seriously from the very first phone call, and he has been a tremendous help every step of the way.

An hour later, Scott comes upstairs to our bedroom.

"Good hot tub?" I ask.

"Yep." He sniffles.

"Did Matt say much?"

"Our first few minutes were silent," he says. "We just soaked there together in the quiet. It was validating for both of us, I think. No words were necessary." Both men are introverts, so that makes sense.

"But soon, I saw a shift in him," Scott continues. "His wall of bravery got breached by a tidal wave of grief. I caught his silhouette in the moonlight and saw this involuntary quiver on his lower lip." He chokes up. "Honey, he looked just like our same little boy, back when he wore that little blue baseball cap everywhere he went, with his blankie as his Batman cape and his toy dump truck tucked under his arm. He covered his face with his hands and started to cry, and through his sobs he told me, 'There's supposed to be five of us, Dad . . . *five Vaudrey kids.* We're supposed to be five.' It about wrecked me. I just held him and said, 'I know, son. I know.' And we just sat there together in the water and cried."

Scott wipes his eyes. "Such a bizarre juxtaposition of emotions: On the one hand, I was drowning in grief for him. On the other hand, I was bursting with pride. I am so proud of him and the other kids, so grateful for how deeply they love one another, for how close we are as a family. And we can't love each other this deeply without paying the full brunt of grief that comes hand in hand with loss."

26

WHEN I WAKE ON THURSDAY MORNING, an illogical sense of stillness envelops me. Life has thrown its worst at our family, yet still we stand. I sense God is hovering, present, carrying us. I think of how, in the ER on Saturday, Scott caught and carried our son Sam out of the trauma room; God is carrying each of us, just like that. And today I will certainly need His strength: In a few hours, I will head to the funeral home to get Katie's body ready for her viewing with Dan.

I still feel a sense of protectiveness over her body—the same protectiveness I have felt over each of my kids. I am Katie's mama, and so long as her body needs help, my job is not yet done. Her body began inside mine, and I was its first home. Throughout infancy and toddlerhood, I nursed and bathed and snuggled that tiny body. In childhood, I bandaged skinned knees, pulled loose baby teeth, and cut her hair. I bore witness as that little-girl body began its transformation into womanhood. I bought Katie her first lip gloss—Bonne Bell Vanilla Swirl—which she was liberal in applying. I saw that body through pierced ears, overplucked eyebrows, green-tinted contact lenses, and a thankfully short-lived season of dreadlocks. I helped Katie slip myriad prom dresses onto her body until we found just the right one. And I was there for her senior portraits photo shoot, marveling at what a beauty our little girl had become.

This same body that I adored throughout its lifetime gave its final gifts—its lungs and kidneys and liver and pancreas, its corneas, skin, and even bones—to complete strangers, extending and saving their lives.

This is my girl. I am ragingly proud of her. I don't hesitate at the thought of caring for her body once more. One final time.

For a fleeting moment, I wonder, *What will other people think of my volunteering for this funeral home task? Is it weird of me? Morbid? A sign that I am refusing to let her go?* Maybe. I would understand if people think so. But I know Katie would want me to do whatever I can to lessen the shock of this viewing for Dan. And the idea of a stranger doing her hair, applying her makeup, being the last one to check her over before he arrives—that is unthinkable to me. It would be a cop-out I would always regret. Today will be no picnic, but today isn't for me. It is for Katie.

All bravado aside, I don't want to tackle this task alone. But neither Scott nor the kids have a desire to see Katie at a funeral home. Their goodbyes at the hospital feel complete to them.

"We're willing to come help you," Bethany says. But I can tell she and Tember are horrified at the idea of seeing their sister in a morgue.

"Nope, I got this," I assure them. And I am relieved, frankly. If any of them were to come, the mama/wife part of me would reflexively focus on comforting them rather than accomplishing the task at hand.

Sandy is the perfect person to join me on such a mission as this.

The thing about Sandy is she's beautiful and feminine and gentle. Even her voice is sweet and comforting. You might think she'd be overwhelmed by a task like this, but she has an inner strength that makes her more resilient than you might guess at first glance. If Katie were choosing a helper for me today, she absolutely would choose Sandy.

Downstairs in the kitchen, I find her at the stove, again attending to everyone else's breakfasts. I step beside her and tell her what my morning holds. She blinks her blue eyes thoughtfully as she listens.

"Will you come? Will you help me?" I ask.

"Absolutely I will come with you," she says without hesitation. "We will do this together. I am hugely honored that you would ask."

Once again God is providing the strength I need through the help of a friend.

Yesterday, Bethany and Tember selected an outfit for their sister: a black turtleneck, black down vest, flowing grey skirt, and her "pirate boots"—long, suede scrunch boots with soles worn thin and a hole starting in one toe. Vintage Katie. She wore those boots everywhere. Scott drove the bag of clothes to Ahlgrim, and Karl, the funeral director, promised to have Katie dressed and ready by eleven.

Sandy and I load a paper grocery sack with makeup, jewelry, hair spray, Katie's curling iron, and a brush. Kati Harkin adds a cute, newsboy-style cap—"to cover the shaved part of her head," she tells me. *Perfect.* I place a goose-down pillow and Katie's well-worn blue-and-white childhood quilt, which I sewed for her third birthday, into another sack. *She dragged that threadbare blanket everywhere: to summer camp, sleepovers, and college—and then back again.* Today, once more, it will do its job.

Tall, kindly Karl in his navy suit meets us in the front lobby and ushers us toward a set of double doors. "Katherine is here in our chapel," he says. "She is dressed and ready, lying on the gurney at the front of the room. The viewing is at two o'clock. The room is yours for as long as you need it until then." He nods and leaves us alone.

Just like in the hospital, my daughter and I are separated by a set of double doors, but this time I can go to her. I had envisioned Sandy and me walking in together, but now I realize I need to see Katie alone first.

"Can you wait here for just a bit?" I ask Sandy. "I want a minute by myself."

"Absolutely. Take as long as you want," she says, taking the bag of supplies from my arms and sitting down in one of the straight chairs against the wall.

I swallow, push open a door, and step inside.

The room is long and narrow, and I enter from the back. I hesitate to look toward the front of the room, but here we go. My head turns, and I see the gurney. A body lies motionless on top.

Is that Katie? It can't be. It looks nothing like her. My feet rush up the aisle, my arms reach for her, and a reflexive wail escapes my throat, echoing off the walls.

There must be some mistake. This waxen figure before me cannot, cannot be my daughter. This body is wearing Katie's clothes, but it bears no physical resemblance whatsoever to the electric, full-of-life girl who only five days ago raced out the door for work. The face is too white, the neck too thick, the features too swollen.

Then I see the hands. Folded gently and naturally across her abdomen, they are graceful, beautiful, and delicate, the kind of hands that would look natural holding a watercolor paintbrush. They are artist hands. And the nails are painted unmistakably in OPI nail polish—Lincoln Park After Dark.

Katie.

My mouth fills with a metallic taste and saliva. I gag. With trembling fingertips I touch Katie's ashen face. I trace the faint smattering of freckles traipsing across the bridge of her nose—freckles long ago masked by her love of the sun. I haven't seen them in years. I'd forgotten she even had them.

Like a blind person using her fingers to see, I keep touching, touching, touching. I touch her lips. I run a fingertip down each eyelid, as I did countless times in the hospital. Her eyes are shut at last, her long lashes lying in repose.

I stroke her cheek, her forehead, her hair. I touch the incision on her scalp from the burr hole surgery—a thin red line with a few black spider-leg stitches. I kiss the cut as I have kissed countless other bumps and scratches on her over the past nineteen years. I kiss it again and again. *Katie, honey, I am so sorry.*

A white sheet covers her legs. I yank it back. Underneath, her skirt, leggings, and boots leave no skin exposed—but her legs don't look . . . natural. I adjust them to lie more comfortably, then tuck the sheet back in its place and look again at my daughter's face.

I have grossly underestimated today's task. I shudder and another wave of nausea sweeps over me. *What was I thinking? Who do I think I am?* This experience is much more horrible than I ever imagined. I cup Katie's shoulders in my hands, draw myself near to her, lay my head on her chest, and sob.

Life is not about our bodies. There is a big difference between being brain-dead and being *dead* dead. I assumed a dead Katie would look roughly the same as a comatose Katie. Wrong! The body lying in front of me is as different from the beautiful girl in the hospital room as an empty cocoon is from the butterfly that once inhabited it. The shell is hers, but Katie has flown. That vision from the accident plays again in my mind—Katie being scooped up into the arms of Jesus and soaring through the trees—utter joy on her face and radiance in her eyes. *That was Katie.* This is nothing but her vacated cocoon.

I don't know how many minutes have passed as I stand there, bent over my daughter, crying, but suddenly I remember Sandy. How long has she been waiting? *I cannot put Sandy through this,* I realize. *I cannot let her see Katie like this.* Partly, I am embarrassed for Katie—I don't want anyone to see her in this condition. Partly, I want to protect my sweet friend.

Tears and snot wetting my face, I rush toward the door and yank it open. "Sandy—never mind! I don't want you to go in there!" I say. "It's awful. She looks awful. It is so much worse than I imagined. Thank you for being so willing to help, but just wait out here. I'll do her makeup myself, and then we'll go. Give me the bags. I don't want you to see. It's horrible, horrible." I wipe my face with my sleeve.

Sandy stands and wraps me up in her arms. She holds me for a few brief seconds, and then she steps back and plants her hands firmly on my shoulders, looking me straight in the eye.

"You are not doing this alone," she says, flecks of iron in her lilting voice. "I will be fine. I can handle it. You are not going back into that room by yourself. I am going with you, and we are going to make Katie look as cute as possible. We are doing this together. And that's all there is to it."

She picks up one of the sacks and thrusts it into my arms. She grabs the other sack and nods toward the door. "Let's go."

I blink, turn, and follow her into the room.

"Well, we have our work cut out for us," Sandy agrees upon seeing Katie. She wipes her eyes. Then we dive in. We pull a podium over and set up an art station. And for the next ninety minutes, we partner together. We apply Katie's makeup, style her hair, add her jewelry, place her pillow under her head, and snuggle her blue-and-white quilt around her.

Like an art critic examining a statue, Sandy steps back to survey our work. "This is not Katie's best angle," she says matter-of-factly. She crosses to the other side of the gurney and takes a look. "Much better. Her neck looks less swollen from over here. And her incision won't show as much. Dan should see her first from this side. Let's turn her gurney around."

"Do we have permission to move her?"

"Do we care?"

"Works for me."

We grab the gurney and begin to rotate it. "Hang on, Katie!" I say. "Road trip!"

Is it wrong to create levity in the depths of life's pain? Is it irreverent? I don't think it is. Sometimes—not every time, but sometimes—it's okay to laugh to keep from crying, laugh in order to breathe, laugh to survive the moment. And if anyone would've given us permission for a brief flicker of laughter on this heavy day, it would be our girl who regularly laughed herself into a giggling heap on the floor. She would not take offense at our coming up to breathe.

We step back. "Her lips are too white," I say. Katie never wore lipstick because her lips were naturally red, and I hadn't foreseen the ashen hue they would have today. I packed only her clear lip gloss. "Crap. I have no lip color with me. And Katie would just die if we left her lips so—"

My words catch in my throat. I shoot a glance at Sandy. She grins at my poor choice of words.

I shrug. "Too late!" I say, and we laugh again.

Forgive us. We are coming up for air.

"I have a red lip gloss with me," Sandy says. She pulls a rosy-red tube from her purse. We apply the gloss to Katie's lips, and it adds just the right amount of color.

The final touch is Kati Harkin's newsboy cap. I lift her head, and Sandy slips the cap in place. She cocks it jauntily across Katie's forehead, dipping it low enough over her right temple to cover any evidence of the surgery. Katie has always looked good in hats. Today is no different.

I pull out her favorite perfume, something from Victoria's Secret. A few light sprays mask any lingering scent of hospital or funeral home. I breathe in, savoring that familiar Katie smell of her perfume mingling with her skin, her hair.

We stand back and survey our handiwork.

"She looks darn cute, September," Sandy says.

"Compared to where we started, she looks terrific," I say. "I think we're done." I look at my watch. It is pushing two o'clock. Almost three hours have passed. It is time to go.

We gather our things and stand for a moment at the head of Katie's bed, two sentinels who have fought together against the ugliness of death. Tears pool in Sandy's eyes. She kisses Katie's head. "I love you, girl," she says and walks out of the room. The door clicks behind her, and I am alone again with my daughter.

What now?

This is my last chance to see Katie, to capture her in my mind's eye. I want to memorize every detail of her face, her hands, her body. I pull out my cell phone and aim its camera toward her. Is this morbid? Perhaps. Probably. In the 1800s, it was common for people to have a tintype photo taken of their loved ones in death. But it seems border-line creepy today. *Once I walk out of this room, I will never see her again. I may choose to never look at these photos, but at least I have the option. No regrets.*

Click. Click.

Like the last swirls of water draining from a tub, my moments with Katie are drawing to a close. Irrational, panicky thoughts begin to spin: *I don't have to leave just yet. I could stay with her all afternoon, right up until she is cremated. I could just sit here and keep her company until the very last minute. I could hold her hand and . . . and . . .* And what? *Are there perfect words I should be saying? If so, what are they?*

Katie had already said her goodbye to me. "Love you, Mom," she'd told me over the phone on Saturday as she was driving to work, just moments before she died. This body that my eyes now hungrily memorize is where my daughter lived out her nineteen years, but life is in the soul. Before me lies her empty cocoon. Katie is gone.

I reach out and stroke her hand. "Goodbye, Katiebug. I love you. Goodbye."

I kiss her hands, her forehead, then her lips. I turn and with automated steps walk out of the room.

~�~

We pull into the driveway at home and find Matt, Adam, and Jeremiah (the grad-school intern who is living with us) hauling bags of river stone to the front flower bed. They are putting the finishing touches on the interrupted landscape project Scott began last week.

"We introverts need a break from all those people," Matt says, thumbing toward the house. This isn't the first time I've found the three of them hanging together outside, talking or just sitting in the shade, sipping Cokes. What must it be like for introverts, trying to process their grief amid the bustle inside? How do they refuel their over-stimulated souls? This landscaping project probably helps. Something physical they can put their hands to, expressing love to Scott in a tangible, practical way.

"Your dad will be so grateful," I say.

"Yep!" Matt says, and I smile at that familiar expression of his, which reveals the little-boy mixture of pride and delight he feels whenever he's helping others. His joy in being helpful is one of the things people love most about my firstborn son—myself included. Sandy and I leave them alone, and they resume hauling bags of rock to the flowerbed.

~�~

That afternoon, Dan calls. He has paid his final visit to my daughter.

"Mrs. Vaudrey, she looked so beautiful," he says. "Thank you."

No regrets.

~�~

Evening comes. Our house is a haven of friends and family enjoying good food and savoring one another's company. If it wasn't for the horrid reason everyone has gathered, these would be the grandest of days—reminiscent of Matt and Andrea's wedding last summer, when these very same people were in town, gathered at our home.

Here we are again, the house filled to capacity. Last year, unabashed joy was the dominant emotion of the day. Now, though we cling to one another in sorrow, flickers of joy are present. We are utterly real. We cry, but we also laugh, hug, and tell stories, just as we have done before. The kids play and cry and sit together in stillness—and make us laugh as they always have. They find solace among their peers that no grown-up can provide. The paradox of laughter at one end of the kitchen and tears at the other—and no one thinking this is odd—captures the authenticity we feel with one another.

This is life in its fullest—true community as God likely dreamed it to be. Our shared pain is softened by one another's presence, and our friendships are deepened by the piercing presence of the pain.

27

FRIDAY

Katie was dedicated to her uncle Greg. Just two months ago, she spent spring break in Seattle with my parents, in part to visit him. It added a bit of light to his small world, and he loved her deeply.

The unfairness of life handing my brother yet another sadness is crazy-making to me. Greg has cerebral palsy. He has an IQ of 69 and has epilepsy. He is wheelchair bound. He has such bad arthritis that he takes pain meds 24/7, and yet his joints remain red and swollen. He's often grouchy (any wonder?) and paranoid and self-focused.

Why does life cast rays of sunshine upon some and send storm after storm to others? Even with the death of my daughter, I feel guilty for the blessings in my life compared to his. Since Saturday, every time I've thought of Greg, I have shoved the image from my mind. Too much. Too much guilt, too much pain. I have not spoken with him since Mom told him about Katie. I can't go there, not yet.

But on Friday morning, my kid brother, now forty-two, reaches out to me. He has typed an e-mail, striking each key of his computer keyboard with the contracted index finger of his right hand—the only finger he can commandeer to obey. I click to open his note:

Hi sis, how are you feeling and doing today? I'm really sorry to here about your loss your daughter was a very kind hearted loving caring person I to feel your pain I surrow with all of you

I spoke with Katie before she went to work via skype I told her
I love you and she said that she loved me I thought you should
know if you guys need anything I mean anything please give me
a call at 555-640-0765 anytime day or night I'm praying deeply
for all of you please give my love to the whole family and Dan
and lots of hugs and kiss's to I love you all very very much god
bless love Greg jr

Such a beautiful, selfless note. Beneath the bristly, irritable ways of
my brother beats a deeply loving heart. *Father, soothe his troubled soul.
Bring comfort to my brother.*

I hit reply and answer his e-mail:

Greg,

Thank you for such a nice letter. Katie really loved you, and she
enjoyed exchanging Facebook and e-mail notes with you. Glad
you got to talk with her via Skype on Saturday. I love you, Greg.

September

My words pale in comparison to his. Me, the writer. It is all I can
muster, and I know it isn't enough. I feel ashamed that I can't offer him
more. *Cover him, Father.* I hit send.

By nine, the house is buzzing. Sam offers to run errands for me. He picks
up Katie's art at the high school, where every piece has been gallery-
matted with precision—and Curt Pinley not only restored Katie's final
work of art but also triple-matted and framed it. A small brass plaque
that reads *The Bleeding Tree* glistens on the bottom crossbar. Rough draft
though it is, this watercolor becomes a treasure to me, and I can't help
but wonder about its intended meaning.

I gather a box of mementos from Katie's room for my friend Susan
to display in the Life Exhibit. Bethany and Tember add a few things as
well, and Sam takes the box and artwork to the church.

When he arrives home an hour later, he finds me.

"Mom, you can't imagine what's happening over there," he says. "There are dozens of staff people helping Susan set up the Life Exhibit, and a ton of Katie's friends—Whitney, Ester, Melissa, Darla, the whole gang—are pitching in. It's amazing. Can't wait for you to see it."

∽◈∾

"I still need to buy funeral clothes," I tell Scott.

"I need to go to Costco to print off a photo for Tember's eulogy," he says. "Let's each run our errands and then meet back here at the house."

Scott heads to Costco, and twenty minutes later, Sandy and I set out for Kohl's.

Halfway there, my cell phone rings. I pick up and hear choked-back sobs on the other end.

"Scott? Are you okay?"

"I . . . I can't get Costco's photo machine to work," he says.

My tech-savvy husband, stumped by a simple photo machine? No. This is not about the machine. Stalwart Scott has hit a wall. "I'll be right there, honey," I say.

Sandy turns the car toward Costco, and a few minutes later, she drops me off at the main entrance.

"Scott can drive me home," I tell her.

"We'll hit Kohl's as soon as you get back," she says.

Scott is standing just outside the store, a little more pulled together than he sounded on the phone, but with reddened eyes and trembling hands. I wrap my arms around him and cradle the back of his head with my hand. He begins to sob. People streaming past us stare, but we don't care. Katie's death has rightsized what things to worry about and what to let go.

"I am so sorry, honey," I whisper in his ear. "I'm so, so sorry for your loss."

You might think it is weird for me to express sorrow for his loss—when I lost a daughter too. Yet it makes perfect sense, really. No one knows what Scott is going through better than I do, so I am the best person to offer him sympathy. And no one understands what I lost as well as he does, so who better to empathize with me? We are learning to give our fullest sympathies to each other in our own unique down-pourings of grief. Right now, it's Scott's turn. No doubt before the day is out, it will be mine.

We pull it together, grab a shopping cart, and head inside the store, where we quickly master the photo machine and retrieve Tember's picture—an eight-by-ten-inch print of the last photograph ever taken of Katie—the one she requested we take of her with Tember all dolled up last Friday for her eighth-grade dance.

"Is there anything we need to buy?" Scott asks.

"I dunno. I can't think."

"Me neither."

But out of habit, we turn our cart up the main aisle. We wander, dazed, hoping we'll remember something we should purchase.

The other shoppers act as if this were just a regular day—chatting, browsing the merchandise, and loading stuff into their carts with such normalcy I want to scream. *What is wrong with you people? Katie is dead. Everything has changed!* The scene plays like a warped wide-angle video. I feel dizzy.

"Everyone's acting normal," I whisper.

"I know. It's bizarre."

We continue toward the back of the store and find ourselves in front of the liquor section. We have lots of relatives and guests in town, and even in our dazed state, Scott and I want to make them feel at home. Some of them drink rum and Cokes, and maybe gin and tonics. Scott finds a bottle of rum and another of gin. He lays them in the cart, and we continue on our way. But we cannot think of anything else to buy, and we can't shake the bizarre feeling of shopping at our normal Costco as if everything were actually normal.

"This is giving me the creeps," Scott says. "Let's get out of here." We head toward the front of the store, the bottles clanking together in our basket.

I point to the two lonely bottles of liquor. Nothing else in our cart. No food, no snacks, no toilet paper—just booze. "What will our friends think if they see us?"

Scott grins. "They'll assume we're drowning our sorrows." Like small-town teenagers not wanting to get caught buying beer, we scan the crowded lines for familiar faces. We get through checkout undetected and make a break for the car, each of us swinging a fifth of liquor at our side.

⌒◈⌒

Back at home, Sandy shows me an article about Katie from today's *Daily Herald*. It is a flattering story about her role as a local artist. *A newspaper reporter found her death to be newsworthy. Does every dead teenager get an article like this?* The article validates my loss—and then I quickly feel ashamed for feeling validated. My dead teenager might have been somehow newsworthy as a local artist, but she was no more priceless or irreplaceable than anyone else's child who has died.

Yet I clip the article and tuck it safely in my desk drawer. Then Sandy and our friend Kristin, in town from Spokane, run me to Kohl's and help me choose a simple black-print dress with small flowers, along with a pair of black flats. Kristin insists on picking up the tab.

28

AT SUSAN'S REQUEST, our family arrives an hour early to the Life Exhibit. "I want you to experience this unrushed, before the doors open," she told me on the phone that morning.

We walk into church and are greeted by a giant three-by-four-foot black-and-white photo in the lobby—a recent snapshot of Katie's smiling face. She is winking at the camera—a gleam in her eye as if she is privy to the best secret ever and can't wait for others to find out what she already knows. On either side of the photo board stand three huge white-and-cream floral bouquets: one from us, one from Dan's family, and a third—a heart-shaped arrangement of white roses—from my parents. Next to this display, three of Katie's large, abstract acrylics pose artfully on easels, a preview of what we are about to experience inside.

Susan opens the door and we step into the Life Exhibit: Katie's entire life's portfolio is displayed on easels draped with fabric in tan, cream, or black. *New York style art exhibit!* The spectacle of color that fills this room through Katie's art takes my breath away. Beautifully designed black-and-cream placards provide details about each piece: the date, medium, Katie's age when she made it, and a short backstory. A maze of tables holds smaller pieces of art, her childhood mementos that Sam brought to the church for me, flowers and plants that people have sent, and the half-dozen photo boards that Katie's friends and siblings have created in her memory. Everything is elegantly arranged—and with an artsy edge that seems pure Katie. Susan and her army of helpers—Katie's friends—have hit a home run. They stand unobtrusively against a back wall, witnessing our family's first reactions. We are speechless and flooded with gratitude. It is lovely, lovely—the art show of Katie's dreams. If she is watching, she must be wriggling with delight as we wander through her former world, admiring her skill and her life.

Each of us walks in silence through the exhibit, free to drift in our own thoughts. Seeing her portfolio in its entirety moves me deeply. *How could one person have produced such a diverse and vast body of work in so little time?* On display are acrylic abstracts in crimson, indigo-purple, yellow, and black; delicate floral watercolors in lavender and sage; life-like landscapes done with oil pastels in rich blues, browns, and greens; ebony-on-paper sketches; contour drawings in pen and ink; graphic designs rooted in original photographs; architectural sketches; simple freehand sketches of friends; and several pieces she made with found objects. There are vivid watercolor portraits and a pen-and-ink pointil-lism homework assignment, which she detested creating ("I hate making all these stupid little dots!" she had complained to me over the phone). There are two master-style oils in earthy browns and gold on unstretched canvas, ceramic sculptures, the un-kidnapped pewter penguin, and even her first 3-D creations from about age eight—chubby babies formed from Sculpey clay with tiny black glass-bead eyes. Her works easily fill this vast room.

Making art was what Katie was created to do, and she felt God's delight in it. Viewing her portfolio in its totality, I am swept into a bizarre dichotomy of sadness and awe. *My daughter did what she was created to do. What was I created to do? Am I doing it?*

On the final table of the exhibit lies Katie's faded-pink baby blanket—the kind made of thermal fabric with a satiny border. It had been her superhero cape, a picnic blanket, the roof of a fort, and her bedtime companion. *Does it still smell like her?* I lift the blanket to my nose, bury my face in its softness, and breathe deep, but it smells mostly of closet shelf.

Nearby sits a shoebox covered in brown packaging paper and decorated with Katie's characteristic swirls and doodles. "To My Future Husband" the box top reads in the artsy scrawl of thirteen-year-old Katie. Inside are notes she wrote over the past six years to her future husband, the anonymous man who would someday capture her heart.

"I'll give this box to my husband on our wedding night," Katie told me when she created it. Through the years, she added notes for this future love-of-her-life, dreaming of the kind of wife and mama she hoped to be someday. Earlier this week, I pulled the box down from the top shelf of her closet and peeked under the lid. It was three-quarters filled with folded notes and fat envelopes. I didn't read the notes. I was not the intended audience. For privacy's sake, I tied the box shut with a bow of hemp twine before letting it be displayed for this exhibit. Now I pick it up and notice the faint imprint of a lip-gloss kiss she'd planted on one end. Vanilla Swirl, perhaps? Such a romantic.

In losing Katie, I have lost a future son-in-law—the intended target of these notes—and the babies he and Katie might have had. The box is too tragic for words. I set it down and move on.

Next to the box sit her bronzed baby shoes. *Could her feet ever have been this tiny?* She learned to walk in those little shoes. And next to the baby shoes are her pirate boots—the suede boots she wore everywhere, including at yesterday's viewing in the funeral home.

Boots bear symbolism. When a soldier falls, his comrades use his boots to form the base of the Fallen Soldier Battle Cross commemorating him on the battlefield. When a cowboy dies, a riderless horse escorts the casket from church to graveyard, and the cowboy's boots are placed backward in the stirrups. To me, these pirate boots bear the same kind of symbolism. In recent years, Katie fulfilled her mission, touching people's lives, pouring her full self into each day, often while wearing these boots. It is fitting that they conclude the exhibit.

Never another brushstroke, never another piece of clay to be formed. Never another coffee date with her friends, or story shared with a sibling, or batch of jam made with her mama, or pirouette danced beneath her daddy's hand. Any fingerprints Katie was to leave upon this world have been left, and no more will be added. The portfolio of her life is complete.

∽◎∾

On the wall above one of the tables, our friends have projected a short essay Katie wrote for her senior exhibit in high school:

On Beauty and Art

The relative beauty that is cultivated by pain—the growth, insight, and strength—compels me. I am learning never to waste pain, but to experience it fully, and my work is a reflection of that growth. This formation of thought has also inspired me to delight in things that are relatively lovely, like blushing cheeks and birthmarks. I want my work to be indicative of the beauty within struggle in a cover-your-freckles culture.

As a lover of the human form, I appreciate the drawings and paintings of Degas, who depicted women simultaneously as imperfect and beautiful. Many were flawed, with skin that was grey; still, their form as a human in the Imago Dei made them lovely. Degas's figurative work really compels me to interpret the human form as something lovely in spite of, even because of, its flawed nature.

All art, whether it intends to or not, communicates. I want mine to communicate this.

Katie Vaudrey

"Beauty . . . cultivated by pain."
"Beauty within struggle."

"Never to waste pain, but to experience it fully."

The irony of her words strike me. She sought to draw—literally—the beauty found within struggle and pain. And I wonder, *What beauty can possibly be cultivated by* this *level of pain?*

At five o'clock, someone arranges us into a receiving line and then opens the doors of the Life Exhibit. For the next several hours, people stand in line to express their condolences and pay their respects to Katie. It is heartrending to see everyone we love in such sorrow, yet I am struck by how their faces, white with shock and pain as they approach us, turn rosy for just a moment as they tell a story of how they knew our daughter or how she or one of our other kids has impacted their lives.

The junior high girls whom Katie mentored when she was in high school approach, their parents at their sides. A handful of memories flash through my mind: Katie at the kitchen table painting canvas tote bags for each girl for summer camp, Katie painting their names on chunky pillar candles as gifts, Katie telling me about challenging questions the girls asked and how she helped them navigate the wilds of middle school. Several of these girls committed to following Christ as a result of Katie's years with them. Now here they stand, freshmen in high school with tears streaming down their cheeks, telling us fresh stories about Katie and their parents telling us how she marked their daughters' lives. *She invested those years well.*

Katie's art teacher from her years at Jacobs High School, Ms. Ellis, approaches, carrying a manila folder. She is crying.

"When I heard the news," she says, "I was so shocked. I went to school and pulled out Katie's old file—and look what I found." She opens the folder and hands me a tiny colored-pencil sketch I've never seen before—a four-by-five-inch drawing of a small Asian boy in a refugee camp, his little fingers laced through a wire fence, a haunting look in his eyes. The detail and realism of the tiny drawing are remarkable. I recognize Katie's touch immediately.

"She was only fifteen when she drew this," Ms. Ellis says, her eyes brimming. "What a talent she was. I've never seen the likes of her. And what an accomplished artist she became in these past three years. I will *never* forget your daughter." She hands me the drawing.

"Thank you, thank you," I say as we hug.

The line seems endless. Teachers from Fremd are here—including Curt Pinley—and the manager and owner from Bandito Barney's have come.

"I have never interviewed anyone like your daughter," the manager tells us. "She was all energy and joy. I knew within a few minutes I was going to hire her, but she was so much fun that we kept talking for another half hour. What a loss."

Bethany, ever the mother hen of the sibs, keeps an eye on Tember and Sam, comforting them as needed. Adam, in turn, is supporting Bethany, and Andrea is providing strength and comfort to Matt. For nearly four hours, we hug and cry and listen to kind words from so many incredible people. I steal glances at those who are weaving their way through the Life Exhibit, and I feel a surge of pride at their expressions of amazement upon seeing my daughter's art. But it is their words and stories in line that touch me most.

One friend shares how earlier this month, Katie spotted her sitting alone at a table at church. "As she walked by," the friend tells us, "she simply stroked my face with a single finger and said, 'You're lovely.' And as I watched her continue on her way, that is just how I felt—lovely. I saw myself as she saw me." Just a simple, reflexive gesture—another chance to help a fellow woman see her beauty.

Several of her friends mention that Katie had a safe way of mixing unconditional love with high challenge. "She wasn't shy about calling me out on stuff when I was not being my best self" was a common thread we heard—paired with "but I knew she did it because she wanted what was best for me. It made me feel loved." Others share funny stories or poignant moments, or they simply hold us and weep. But the most common refrain Scott and I hear is this: "Your daughter squeezed more life out of nineteen years than most people squeeze out of a lifetime." We can't help but agree.

By the time we greet the last people in line, it's almost nine o'clock. Scott and I gather the kids and thank Susan and her army of helpers who created this exhibit. What a gift they have given us. May I never forget what it feels like to be on the receiving end of such kindness in a time of loss.

We step outside to the parking lot. The sun's golden rays cast long, velvet shadows as we walk in silence toward the minivan. I don't know what I expected from a wake, but what we just experienced was beyond my wildest imagination. My sorrow begins to mingle with a dawning awareness that God is doing something powerful through Katie's death, something moving and holy and—dare I say—something stunningly beautiful. *Beauty cultivated by pain.*

29

By seven the next morning, everyone is up and moving. Over a scattered breakfast, Scott announces, "Family meeting in the Bug Room at eight thirty. All Vaudreys dressed and ready to walk out the door by that time. We'll load up at nine o'clock." The memorial isn't until ten, but we will meet with our pastor, Bill, at nine fifteen.

We crank everyone through quick showers. The ironing board comes out. The guys scramble for dress socks, belts, and ties, and the women crowd around bathroom mirrors, sharing curling irons and hair spray. At eight thirty, we assemble in the Bug Room. The kids, freshly scrubbed, sit motionless, eyes alert, faces pale. Matt and Sam wear their new funeral suits, but the girls have put on two of Katie's dresses. Their newly purchased funeral dresses from Kohl's hang in closets upstairs, untouched. A better plan, truly.

"Kids, this is it," Scott says. "I am so proud of each one of you, and I know Katie would be proud of you too. Are you ready? Do you know what you want to say?"

They nod. Over the past five days, each has found time to assemble some thoughts on paper and print copies of their eulogies, which they now hold in nervous hands. Tember also holds the enlarged Costco photo.

"Hopefully we aren't all going to tell the exact same Katie-stories or say the exact same things," Bethany says. "What if we repeat?" I'd had the same worries myself. *And I probably should have read the kids' eulogies. Too late now.*

"It can't be helped," says Matt. "We haven't had time to coordinate or double-check with each other about stories. It'll all work out."

"And let's face it," Sam adds. "People will cut us some slack today. No one's gonna say, 'Hey, I've heard that story before!'"

"It will be fine," Scott says. "We'll just have to trust that whatever needs to be heard today will be said."

Scott walks us through the order of when each of us is speaking, and then we all hold hands as he prays. "Father, never did we imagine such a morning as this. Thank you for these kids. I am so proud of each one. Help us get through these next hours, and may everything in Katie's memorial point to You. Amen."

~◦◦◦~

We pile into the minivan and pull onto the road. The McConkeys, Adam, and the rest of our friends and family will follow later. The kids talk quietly in the backseats, but Scott and I are silent. My eulogy trembles in my hands, and I fight tears. Scott sets his hand on my knee and squeezes. We are one in this.

I rest my forehead against the cool glass window next to me. Familiar neighborhood scenes slip by, but the same wide-angle-video feeling I had in Costco washes over me once again. I close my eyes. *I cannot freaking believe we are driving to Katie's funeral.*

All week long, we've been racing toward this morning, toward this event. Always there was something else—a task yet undone—that stood between me and, and . . . this. Now here it is. No more planning, no more blessed details to shield me from the finality we are about to face.

The church parking lot is already filling with cars as we pull in. I think of my brother, alone in his wheelchair this morning. *Please, Lord, send someone to be with him today.*

~◦◦◦~

Scott parks the van, and before he can turn off the engine, Pastor Chris Hurta approaches from the side door. Dressed in a black suit and smiling, he exudes a comforting mixture of professionalism and warmth, opening doors, helping everyone out, taking command. "Hey, everyone," he says, tenderness in his voice. "Good to see you guys. Follow me." I take a deep breath and follow.

Chris leads us to the senior pastor's office, where Bill and his wife, Lynne, greet us. Lynne slips me some Kleenex and wraps her warm hand around mine. Bill checks in with each of us, then addresses us as a family.

"I can't imagine what you are going through, with this kind of loss," he says. "But I know a little bit about God's character—and Scripture tells us He draws near to those who are brokenhearted. Today you would qualify for that definition, I think." Everyone smiles. "He shows up the strongest when we need Him most. And I fully believe He is up to something powerful in your situation. I sensed it at the Life Exhibit last night—and I think you will sense it, too, when you walk into that auditorium in a few minutes."

Bill prays for each of us, one at a time, and then prays for each person who has come today to remember our girl. "God, may You use our words today to bring comfort and a deeper understanding of Your presence in this broken, often pain-filled world."

After "amen," Chris hands each of us a program and reviews the order of the service one last time. "Friends, you will make it through this," he says, "but it will be exhausting, and when it's over, you will need some time alone to regroup. Exit with me during the closing prayer. We have a room set aside for you." We nod obediently. At ten o'clock, Chris leads us to the doors at the back of the Lakeside Auditorium. He opens them, and we follow him in. Lynne and Bill are already seated down front.

A slide show—the handiwork of Matt's friend Bowman—is projecting Katie's life onto the big screen above the stage. My eyes adjust to the dark as we follow Chris down the aisle, and the magnitude of this event begins to sink in.

The auditorium is near capacity with familiar faces—reddened, grief-stricken faces, each one precious to our family or our daughter. Chris guides us to our row up front, and we take our seats. Videos and photos on the screen show Katie growing from toddler to teen to young adult. A photo of her with my brother, her arm draped around his wheelchair as both of them grin, prompts an unexpected sob from my throat.

Jon, the college pastor, welcomes everyone and shares beautiful words about Katie. Then Kati Harkin and Dan take the stage.

"Katie is not a friend who lets you stay the same," Kati shares from a college essay she wrote about Katie earlier this year. "She helps you grow, she holds you accountable . . ."

"She didn't settle for the people who were easiest to love," Dan says when it is his turn to speak. "She actively sought out the overlooked and the underdogs. She searched with great passion for the people most desperate for God's love. She had eyes that allowed her to see Jesus in all His distressing disguises, to find beauty in brokenness, and to shine light in dark places. She loved you *first*, no matter who you were . . ."

❧

Our kids then take the stage. One by one, from youngest to oldest, they speak of the sister they loved and lost.

"I'm September, Katie's younger sister," Tember begins. "Katie and I share an infinite number of little inside jokes and memories that crack us up. And I thought of one I could share with you.

"Our family would go camping in our motor home, and we'd get to know the other families at the campgrounds. But in the back of our minds, we kids would think, 'We're never gonna see these people again . . .'" She smiles mischievously at the crowd, and they laugh.

"So one day opportunity struck, and we sisters made up fake names and Southern accents. Bethany was 'Mary Sue,' Katie was 'Anna Jo,' and I was 'Louise.' And we walked around the campground, talking obnoxiously loud so other people would overhear us in our fake Southern accents.

"But my accent was so bad Bethany and Katie wouldn't let me talk in public. I begged them, 'I can totally do the accent!' They wouldn't budge. So I was the mute, weird sister. They would talk and laugh in their little Southern accents, and I would just stand there, mute, kicking dirt at them. Finally, Katie turned and said in her cute Southern accent, 'Louise! Stop kickin'!'

"And that phrase just stuck. Today if one of us is being annoying, someone will say, 'Louise! Stop kickin'!' I will always remember Katie putting her hand on her hip, tellin' me to 'stop kickin'!'

"Katie loved dressing up and makeup. I would always watch her getting ready for her school dances and for prom, and I'd do whatever it is that sisters do to help. Because I am the youngest, I worried no one would be around for my prom. Neither of my sisters would be living at home to help me get ready. And Katie promised she would fly home for prom, just to help me get ready."

A murmur of quiet groans ripples through the audience. I glance down the row at Bethany and Andrea. I see a pair of big-sister plane tickets in my future.

"The night before her accident," Tember continues, "I had my eighth-grade dance. When I got home from school that day, Katie was waiting to help me get ready. She had set out her earrings and a necklace that she thought would be pretty with my dress, and she put a little ribbon on her purse and lent it to me. She painted my nails and did my hair, and she found my missing stiletto. The last photograph we have of Katie is of the two of us, with me all ready for my dance." She holds up the eight-by-ten-inch photo from Costco.

Tember's eyes fill and her voice cracks. "Katie is so special to me. I really miss her." She gathers her papers and the photo and turns from the podium.

Sam steps to the mic. "I'm Sam, Katie's younger brother. My sister led the most laughter-filled life of anybody I know," he says. "She also found time for seriousness and thought and even pain, but most of her days were simply spent in joy. Whether she was singing, baking, drawing, or laughing, she dispensed love over anybody near her. She used her persistence to demonstrate kindness and acceptance to just about anyone—and believe me, not many people were more persistent than Katie when it came to something she really believed in.

"When Katie was in the eighth grade and I was in fifth, we played a game of Monopoly one Saturday morning in the basement. I don't usually win at Monopoly, but for some reason that day, everything was going my way. I owned Park Place, Boardwalk, and six other monopolies—and Katie was $4,000 indebted to me. But she was still smiling and laughing at every roll of the dice, as if she were about to win some sort of $5,000 bonus roll. She drew her loss out for so long that eventually we got called upstairs for lunch and had to call the game a tie.

"She just wasn't willing to quit. She fought for things she really wanted or things she thought were right, and she demonstrated that kind of fight, over and over, throughout her life—right up to her last day when her heart restarted three times, against all medical odds.

"Katie greeted me with a hug every day this past month when I got home from school. She woke up early to make us warm breakfasts. She painted in the sun, and played games, and sang, and watched movies, and fell on the floor laughing, and listened to good music, and journaled, and she just loved like crazy. She squeezed every drop of life out of every day. There is nobody I know with that much charisma, laughter, encouragement, and affection all in one body, and I cannot express how much I love and will miss my sister."

Bethany is next.

"When my sister died," Bethany says, "she was wearing thick white ankle socks with purple stripes."

Ah, the hospital footies!

"These were the very same socks that had been 'borrowed' from a clothing donation bin at APU a month ago by two sisters laughing so hard they had to drop the boxes they were carrying. It ended up being one of my best memories with my kid sister, even though I didn't realize at the time that it would be my last.

"It was move-out day at APU. Katie had called me frantically the day before. 'I don't have anywhere to store my stuff for the summer! Can you keep it in your apartment?' I agreed to put her stuff in my tiny bedroom closet but asked her to please compact it so it would be easy to move and store. She said, 'Sure, sure . . . oh, and oops! I don't have a ride to the airport in the morning! Help!' Classic Katie.

"I told her, 'Okay, sure, I can drive you,' and we arranged that I'd pick her up in front of Trinity Hall at ten o'clock to load her stuff into my car.

"When I arrived at Trinity the next morning, Katie was not out front. I found her standing outside her dorm room door looking frazzled, next to about nine thousand pounds of her 'most prized possessions.' This, she assured me, *was* the compacted version of her stuff!

"So the two of us spent the next hour trying to get everything she owned down four flights of stairs, across Trinity's lawn, and into my Honda Civic! It was one of the most hilarious undertakings we ever shared.

"She had this one huge, flimsy set of plastic drawers that was packed full and was unbelievably heavy. It took two of us to carry it down the stairs, and its sharp edges started digging into our fingers as we walked. We must have been a sight, these two girls carrying this heavy box, shouting, 'Ow! Ow! Ow!'

"By the time we finally got to the front door of Trinity, our hands were killing us, and we spotted this donation box full of clothes. Katie got an idea, and her face lit up. 'We can take donation socks and put 'em on our hands!' So there we were, laughing like idiots, pulling someone else's used socks onto our hands, then waddling across Trinity lawn with this heavy box, yelling, 'Ow! Ow! Ow!'

"I don't know anyone else but my sister who could have turned the task of moving heavy boxes into a hilarious memory like that.

"I brought those stolen charity socks with me from Azusa to Chicago this week, and Katie wore them—on her feet this time—as she went into her organ donation surgery. I share this story with you because it illustrates the two things I love most about Katie: She brought life to everyone she met, and she was one of the most hilarious people I ever had the privilege of knowing. She had the unique ability to make absolutely anything into something fun. She was hysterically funny and intensely creative. Her laugh was contagious, and I am going to miss hearing it all across the parking lot at APU, at the Starbucks where I work—I could hear her coming from a mile away—and at home in Chicago. I am only beginning to understand the deep sorrow of losing my sister, but I feel so privileged to have known her from her birth to her death."

❧

Matt steps to the podium with Andrea at his side. "I'm Matt, Katie's older brother," he says, "and this is my wife, Andrea, Katie's newest sister.

"Our dad always encouraged my sister to be as 'Katie' as possible, but she didn't really need any coaxing to be fully Katie all the time. She had no setting between 'sleep' and 'Katie.' Growing up, on Christmas morning she would wake up before dawn and come jump on my bed, screaming, 'How can you be sleeping? It's Christmas!' . . . And that happened again *this* year!"

The auditorium erupts in laughter and then quiets as Matt continues. "I have a head full of memories and conversations and pictures, all of which form the Katie we knew as an adult. This Katie showed little restraint toward laughter or beauty or art or hugs or—especially— intentional conversation. Katie was relentless in her pursuits of beauty and of people.

"While I accept the dreadful truth that Katie is not coming back, I am faced with a decision of how I am going to honor and remember her. My sister accomplished much in her short nineteen years, but life is too short to accomplish all the desires of the heart. Perhaps the best tribute to Katie would be to live as she learned to live: by treating each relationship with relentless interest, to treat each conversation as if it matters for eternity.

"If my sister's life were a lesson, the charge might have been this: Speak kind words to people who are still present to hear them. Take a friend out to coffee and listen to them. Spend your lunch break with a coworker. Leave a note on a roommate's desk. Call your parents to check in. Make relationships your relentless pursuit.

"Katie posted this Vincent van Gogh quote on her Facebook page, and it summarizes her life as much as one phrase can: 'There is nothing more artistic than to love people.'

"Katie, rest in peace. To the rest of us, live in purpose."

~⊚~

As our kids step off the stage, I have never felt more proud as a mama. They have painted such a vivid portrait of our family and of Katie's role in it, her character and personality, the love they share for one another, and the fun that erupts whenever they are together. This is our family.

And not one story was a repeat.

~⊚~

I speak next: "I'm September, Katie's mama. Katie and I shared the same heart for family and motherhood. I love that she someday wanted to do what I have so loved doing: being a wife to an amazing man and raising a big family. She told me again last week, 'I am so glad we have a big family. I love each of my siblings so much.'

"For all her gracefulness, Katie was comically clumsy. Falling down the stairs became so commonplace for her that when we'd hear a series of thumps and bumps, followed by a quick, 'I'm okay!' we wouldn't even look up. It would startle dinner guests, but we'd explain, 'That's only Katie, falling down the stairs.' What a paradox that someone so clumsy was also so graceful and artistic."

I spoke of those hours at the hospital: "We begged God for a miracle that night. He gave us three. Katie's body was revived three different times for a total 'downtime' of more than forty-five minutes.

"Her brain was in grave condition. I begged God, 'Please, please, make her mind whole.' And He did. It wasn't in the way we wanted, but Katie is now living in eternity, fully whole.

"God did three miracles that night, and we desperately wanted those miracles to be for our family. But those miracles were for the families of the people who received her organs, and we celebrate with them.

"In the moment that the neurosurgeon told us Katie was brain-dead, a mental picture—some kind of a vision?—flooded my mind: Katie's car, barreling down Route 68 under the canopy of ancient oaks, her lifeless body slumped over the wheel, unconscious. And right before impact, God just swoops down and scoops her up into His arms. And together they soar through the trees. He just scooped her up. I don't blame Him. I'd have scooped her up too.

"God tells us in His Word that our days are numbered, and I have been struck by the intentionality with which Katie lived each day. Her first priority was her relationship with God. After that came people. She poured herself into her relationships. I want to do a better job of living my days with such focus.

"For Katie, painting was a form of worship, and her art couldn't be contained. She filled closet walls, the insides of cupboard doors, and the backs of dressers with her art. The bigger the canvas, the better. Last summer, Katie built a giant stretched canvas—four feet by four feet—to paint her largest acrylic piece to date. The canvas was much too big for her easel, so she found the perfect place to set up shop and paint: in our rec room, where only the week before we had installed brand-new carpeting. Sure enough, her rinse water spilled. I guess you could say we got *two* paintings from our daughter that day. Well, Katie, at last you have a canvas big enough, and if you spill, you won't ruin the carpet!

"In the days and years to come, when a beautiful sky catches my eye, I will think of the girl who loved beauty and loved people. And I will be washed anew with the unending goodness of God, the Inventor of beauty, the Creator of people, the One whom Katie loved most of all."

Scott closes out the eulogies with a powerful tribute to his Katiebug, and he shares a part of his journey that he hasn't yet shared with me.

"From the time we got the first phone call," he says, "I've felt this tight band around my chest—a sense that there was something for me to do as a dad. And sometimes it got so bad it felt like I couldn't get air. But on Thursday, I got this image I sensed was from God. Jesus was holding Katie, reminding her of her legacy—how she had loved people, fought for people who were voiceless, and cared for and nurtured so many; how she had created dozens of pieces of art, each with a specific spiritual purpose; how she had loved her siblings well. And then Jesus looked in her eyes and said, 'Well done.'

"And in that moment, I realized Katie no longer needed her earthly daddy, that I had been released from my role of protecting her and advocating for her and guiding her. And knowing where her guidance and nurture were now coming from, I could let her go. And at that point, my breathing came easier. I exhaled and I relaxed.

"If she could hear me today," he concludes, his voice quivering ever so slightly, "I would tell her that I love her so much. I will miss her every day. And I have no doubt she has heard, 'Well done.'"

~⊙~

As Brandon and our musician friends take the stage to lead everyone in singing the songs Bethany selected, I catch a glimpse of my kids, sitting down the row from me. Tears stream over Sam's reddened cheeks, and beyond him, Andrea holds tightly to Matt's arm. Bethany's and Tember's faces lift upward—tears escaping through dark, wet lashes—and all of the kids join Brandon and this amazing roomful of people in singing together, "Lord, You never let go of me."

Bill closes out the service with a message rooted in Hebrews 6:19—"We have this hope as an anchor for the soul, firm and secure." He describes how, for first-century mariners facing a storm, an anchor "firm and secure" meant the difference between life and death—and how our family has faced a force-ten gale these past seven days.

"It's only human to wonder if the Vaudreys' anchor is really holding," he says. "Those of us who have walked closely with them this week, we know up close and personally that they have an anchor that is more than adequate, even for this storm."

He is right. My anchor is holding—for now. But in a month? A year? Will my anchor hold when this numbness and shock wear off? When I am facing the rest of my life without Katie?

"Katie lived in vital relationship with God until her final breath," Bill continues. "She may well have passed into His presence with His name on her lips. He was not ancillary to her life. He was central; He was fundamental; He was true north. And He brought to her experience what Jesus promised in John 10:10—and what you heard so often relayed from family members on this stage—life in all its fullness.

"Katie's confidence in the person and work of Jesus Christ was unshakable. She actually believed that everyone she knew would be better off if they would live their lives with God at the center. And if some here today are looking for a way to honor Katie's short life, one appropriate way would be to explore the God who meant so much to her. She would be delighted. Maybe Katie's life would inspire you to taste, to see, and to experience the goodness and grace of our great God."

Bill says some kind words about our family and then adds a final thought. "Katie's death was not the end of her. Her current absence is not the final reality. You're going to be reunited with her someday, and every chair around the Vaudrey dinner table will be filled again. The Scripture says that on the other side, there will be no more tears, and no more sorrow, no more separation, and no more funerals.

"And I know you'll hang on to that hope between this day and that day, because you 'have this hope as an anchor' for your souls."

30

As Jon closes the service in prayer, we follow Chris, Bill, and Lynne out of the auditorium and into a private room off the main lobby. As the doors close behind us, Scott stops in his tracks, covers his face with his hands, and breaks down in deep, guttural sobs. We gather around him—the sequoia of our family, the one who has stood so tall for each of us this past week and throughout our lives. Released at last to express the full depth of his own sorrow, he weeps. Sam wraps his arm around his dad and holds him—a poignant role reversal of the ER trauma room scene just a week prior.

"I hate it," Scott finally says, wiping his eyes and looking up. "I just hate that she is gone."

～❧～

We've done it. We have crossed the finish line and made it through the funeral. A rolling surge of lightness sweeps through the room. We begin to chatter with relief.

"You kids were incredible," Scott says. Tember and Sam get high-fives from their older sibs.

"And you all had original material!" I say, winking at Bethany. "No repeats!"

"There was something powerful happening in that room," Bill says. "In my forty years of being a pastor, I've spoken at a lot of funerals, but I've never experienced anything quite like this. And your kids are amazing speakers, every last one of them!"

"Your message, Bill, was just what Katie would have wanted," Scott says. "'An anchor for the soul . . .'"

"I have long wanted to teach on that particular passage of Scripture because of my love of boating and the water. I don't know why I've saved it this long. But this seemed like the right time."

"It was perfect. Thank you."

"It was an honor."

The kids begin joking and laughing, which is like salve on my battered mother-soul. Tember's face lights up when she notices the table of snacks and drinks set out for us: bottles of Snapple, full-size candy bars, and SunChips—name-brand stuff, not the cheap house-brand snacks I occasionally stock in our pantry.

"Are all these for us?" she asks, wide-eyed. No one has eaten since early this morning.

"Yes, I think so, honey," I say. "Help yourself."

"Wow!" Her eyes pop, and she reaches for a bag of chips.

When we load into the minivan to head home, I notice my purse seems unusually heavy. Looking inside, I discover a Snickers bar, a bag of M&M's, a pack of SunChips, and two bottles of Snapple lemonade. My youngest daughter has smuggled out the fancy snacks!

"Tember!" I say, holding up the Snickers.

She grins impishly and snatches the candy from my hand. "You said they were for us."

On the ride home, the kids begin to emerge from the hazy fog of this hellish week. Their conversation grows livelier, and they begin to make jokes about which parts of the service Katie would have loved the most. Suddenly Bethany has a revelation.

"Hey, wait! Katie's favorite baby name is now up for grabs! I shotgun 'Jael'!"

I burst out laughing. With her typical irreverent humor, Bethany has not only laid claim on her sister's favorite name for a daughter but also trailblazed new territory for us. Post-Katie territory. She demonstrates that it can still be okay for us to laugh, tease, and joke about Katie, who isn't here to defend herself or tease back. This sort of irreverent humor is the Vaudrey way.

It is new territory for all of us. How will we choose to remember Katie in the future? Will we speak of her only in hushed and reverent tones? The laughter in the van—less than an hour after her memorial, no less—reassures me that we will not turn Katie into some sort of sterile, off-limits idol. For us, she will always be the same lively, impulsive, imperfect, delightful girl we knew and loved—and she will remain fair game for family teasing. She is a Vaudrey, after all, and she will remain so.

Bethany's placing dibs on "Jael" unleashes everyone's goofy remembrances of Katie's quirks—her pretending not to notice (but still posing) whenever someone was taking her photo, her propensity for falling down the stairs, and how, after having lost a brand-new pair of knitting needles to airport security, she made it her mission to sneak harmless "contraband" past them whenever she flew. She kept a running tally and would text us from the gate: "Ha! Fingernail file! Katie, 4. TSA, 1." We recall her habit of "accidentally" wriggling her way into family videos (her childhood refrain, "Are you *filming* me?" had long been a running joke). The kids tell tales of what a restless sleeper she was and recount the hazards of being the sibling who drew the short straw—and had to share a motel or motor home bed with her. And they vie for who should be awarded their middle sister's favorite game pieces from The Settlers of Catan—the red ones—now that Katie won't be there to snatch them up as soon as the box is opened.

By the time we arrive home, we are in good spirits, and the house and yard are overflowing with family and friends. As we step into the kitchen, the hearty aroma of Italian sausages, pasta, and marinara hits me. The meal is a gift from the parents of Katie's friend Marie, whose family owns an Italian restaurant. It pays to have Italian friends! I breathe deeply and feel a familiar twinge in my belly: the pangs of hunger.

But first, I have a phone call to make.

I step onto the back deck. A few tufts of cottonwood drift across the cerulean June sky, and the songs of scarlet cardinals announce the coming of summer. I sit down on the stairs, pull out my cell phone, and dial my brother.

"Hiya, sis," he says, recognizing my number on his caller ID. "Sorry about Katie."

"Thanks, Greg. She loved you very much."

"I know. She told me she loved me when I was Skyping her on Saturday. And I figured you'd want to know I said, 'I love you' back."

"Yes, I did want to know, Greg. I'm glad you told me. Thank you."

Has he been all alone during the funeral? How is he doing? I begin fishing for clues: "So, Greg, how was your morning? What have you been up to?"

"Not much, not much," he says. "I had oatmeal and coffee for breakfast at 9:30, and then Wendy stopped by for a visit. She's the new CNA." *Nicely done, Wendy.*

"Hey, did your e-mail get hacked yesterday?" he asks, switching gears. "My friend David got his e-mail hacked. And I thought you'd want to know. I told him to report it. And I warned Dad. And Mom. Maybe you should warn the kids. You better check your e-mail because there is a hacker out there. Do you think I should change Internet providers?"

Ahhh . . . computer paranoia. One of Greg's baseline topics of discussion. He never tires of talking about two things: computer security and his own aches and pains, which are many.

I exhale. My brother will be all right. He has already moved on. Perhaps this is one upside to his limited intellectual capacity. We talk about computer hackers for another few minutes, and then I say goodbye.

The kids and their friends have been streaming past me on the deck, their plates piled high with food. They sprawl on the grass under the hawthorn tree, talking and eating. Someone grabs a volleyball from the sports bin on the deck, and a crowd gathers on either side of the net on our back lawn. *Katie would have loved today—warmth and sunshine, incredible food, and all her favorite people. She would be playing volleyball and talking and collapsing on the grass, laughing.*

As I stand to head inside, an old friend of Scott's from Spokane approaches me. "September, you know that image you shared in your eulogy—about God scooping Katie up before the car crash?" he says.

I cringe inside. *Should I have shared that vision?* It's a little bizarre to sense that the God of the universe might be communicating to you in such a direct way—and only a weirdo would then tell an auditorium of people about it at her daughter's funeral. I am that weirdo.

"When my wife and I got the phone call about Katie being in the hospital last Saturday," he continues, "we were only told she was in a coma, but we didn't know why. We hadn't heard that it was a car wreck, and we knew nothing about the aneurysm until today. But when my wife prayed for Katie that day, she experienced the exact same image as you did—Katie's car driving down a tree-lined road, with her body slumped over the wheel, unconscious, and God scooping her up, right before the crash. The image made no sense to my wife. Had Katie been in a car accident? If so, why would she be unconscious before the crash? But now it makes perfect sense. I can't wait to call and tell her!"

Incredible! A woman I haven't seen or spoken with in years, who had known nothing about the aneurysm—or even the car accident—had experienced the exact same vision as I had. I have no idea how such things work, but it seems like more than just a coincidence to me. I am more certain than ever that this image—or vision, or whatever it was—depicted what happened to my girl.

The house is filled with all the people I love most in the world, and I want to speak with each one. But my stomach growls. I grab a plate and serve myself a scoop of pasta, half an Italian sausage, and three strawberries. Then I find a seat alone and take a bite of the sausage. The oregano and fennel come alive in my mouth—delicious. I eat a strawberry. Not a hint of sawdust.

How the world had changed in seven days. It had been the most horrid-beautiful week of my life—a week of stunning contrasts. Never could I have imagined such pain. Nor could I have foreseen such beauty through these good and loving people. God had indeed provided the strength our family needed thus far. He had carried us through—in the arms of these people.

Tomorrow, our friends and family would begin heading home to resume their normal lives. And it hit me: Today was not the finish line. It was the starting line.

Tomorrow our new normal would begin.

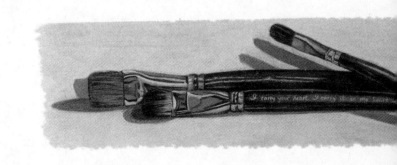

164

burnt sienna

[burnt see-'en-uh] / an intense, dark-roasted reddish-brown

A freshly turned field

is a stark wasteland to the untrained eye.

But given seed, water, sun, and time,

the rich farmland sod produces life and growth.

The stark was merely setting the stage.

Learn not to be afraid of pain. Grit your teeth and let it hurt. Don't deny it, don't be overwhelmed by it. It will not last forever.

HAROLD KUSHNER

Suffering will change us—but not necessarily for the better. We have to choose that.

WAYNE CORDEIRO

31

A FOG OF SHOCK AND NUMBNESS settled over me in the days following the funeral. Our entire world had been severed into "Before Katie" and "After Katie." How does a family move forward after such a life-altering loss?

I'd heard of families who lost a child and never moved on. The one who died became the centerpiece of the family, and those left behind were mere afterthoughts. I worried I might be prone to do this to my family, and I was determined to not let this tragedy wreck my kids—or my marriage.

Perhaps these worries prompted the vivid dream I had just two nights after the funeral: I saw an aerial view of a rural homestead that had been devastated by a tornado. The house was ripped in two, the barn nearly flattened. A deep-brown scar cut its way through the rich sod of the surrounding fields of green wheat. But the family vegetable garden next to the house was untouched.

When I awoke, I sensed I knew the dream's meaning. That homestead was our family, and that garden was my marriage. The message was this: As we began picking up our lives after this devastating tornado, first and foremost we must tend to that garden because it would provide the sustenance and strength needed for the rebuilding.

Friends and acquaintances alike had already been dropping well-intentioned little hints about the terrible divorce statistics for couples following the death of a child. I knew they were watching us, looking for chinks in our marital armor. I was not too worried—our marriage was a strong one, seasoned by all we had learned through our own struggles in years past. Our family knew how to do pain. We knew commitment and healing and forgiveness and God's faithfulness. We had learned firsthand to say yes to pain; we knew the surest way through hardships was to face them head-on.

My guess was that many of the marriages from those daunting statistics crumbled because the partners felt the same kind of certainty I now sensed about Scott and me—a "surely not us" overconfidence that had contributed to their downfall. Surviving a blow like this would take intentionality. And skill. And a lot of grace.

So Scott and I took everyone's worry seriously. We made a commitment to support each other fully as we navigated this uncharted territory. We reminded ourselves that our grief would not look the same, that even though we had both lost the same person—our daughter—our individual journeys toward healing would look vastly unique. (We are opposites in every other area of our lives; why would our grief be any different?) I needed to trust that Scott's nonverbal way of processing didn't necessarily mean he was suppressing or avoiding his grief. And he needed to let me talk about Katie's death, even when it pained him. We made a deal to tend to what our own souls needed if we were really in the ditch and to tend to what the other's soul needed when we were feeling strong enough to help—and when we were both in the ditch at the same time, to cling tightly to each other until the wave of grief passed. We prioritized those things that had always worked for us—time together alone, long conversations, and sex.

So I felt fairly confident our marriage could make it. What worried me more was my capacity as a mom. I desperately wanted to wipe away our kids' pain, but I didn't know how—or if—I could help. Just as Scott and I had differing needs in grief, so did each of our kids. The complexity of what we were facing as a family felt paralyzing.

I was also concerned that I would place too much focus on the child we had lost. She was ever present before my eyes. But I didn't want to be a "centerpiecing" type of parent, nor did I want my other kids to feel they were somehow less important than Katie. How could I stay balanced—honoring and remembering my dead daughter, yet helping my living family move forward? How could I hold in one hand this devastating tornado, and in the other hand my family, our future, and our lives?

With no clue how to pull this off, but with an earnest desire to do so, I entered year one of our new normal.

32

NOT LONG BEFORE HER FATAL ACCIDENT, Katie had had a vivid dream, yet another in a series she had been having. She and I were making apricot jam together in the kitchen when she said, "Mom, I had another nightmare last night. Second one this week."

"What about?"

"Both dreams were the same: I was lying on a long white table, and a man cut me from the top of my chest all the way down my belly. He opened me up and took out my organs. Creepy, right?"

I stopped chopping the apricots. "Ewww. Yes, creepy."

"What does it mean?"

Dreams again—and such a graphic image. A few of Katie's dreams over the years had held almost a prophetic element—images that made sense or events that had come to pass. Should I dig deeper? Or should I play the reassuring mom?

"I'm no expert on dreams, babe," I said. "But often nightmares don't mean anything—they're just weird images that float through our minds while we sleep. I wouldn't worry about it."

With her dark dreams on the increase, Scott and I had suggested that she talk with a counselor about them. "Did you make an appointment with Andy yet?" I asked Katie.

"I called and left a message this morning, but I haven't heard back. Maybe tonight."

"I'd go ahead and set something up, and tell him about your dreams. He's a sharp guy. Perhaps he can give you some insight. In the meantime, I wouldn't let it worry you."

She seemed satisfied, and our talk turned to her hopes for the future. But just nine days after this dream, Katie in fact had lain on top of a long white table, and a doctor had cut her open.

When one of your children has had premonitions of trauma, and then the unthinkable happens and that child actually dies, it's hard to fight a panicky instinct to protect the rest of your kids at any cost. It envelops you. I am not a worrier by nature, but both Scott and I fought the urge to simply lock our remaining kids in a cage to be certain they would remain safe forever. Of course, this is both impossible and illogical (a cage would not have protected Katie). Also, it's illegal in most states.

One night shortly after Katie died, Tember went to the movies with some girlfriends. Another mom was on deck to drive them, and Tember had her cell phone with her. What could be safer, right?

But when the unpredictable Midwest weather turned from sunny to dark and our village's tornado siren blared, Scott and I freaked. I called Tember's phone, but it was turned off (thank you, annoying movie theater ads about shutting off your cell so as not to disturb fellow moviegoers). I left quavering messages for her to call and let us know she was all right. For the next few hours as the impressive storm raged outside, Scott paced in our bedroom, repeatedly looking out our front window and checking for cars. I sat up in bed, motionless, staring at the clock, waiting for Tember to get home.

At last, around midnight, a minivan pulled into our drive, delivering Tember home safe and sound, despite the storm. I burst into tears.

The kids understood our obsessive protection over their safety that summer—but it still annoyed them. The compulsion to worry has calmed over the years but not disappeared. I suspect Scott and I will always have to work on managing our hairpin triggers.

∽◌∾

With the funeral behind us and all the guests gone home, the frenetic pace of the past eight days came to a screeching halt. The silence was deafening. I wasn't yet ready to feel as if Katie's death was over. It was too soon.

So I busied myself with "death chores"—writing thank-you notes, throwing away the bouquets of dying flowers (the symbolism behind this chore did not escape me), picking up Katie's wallet and phone from the police station, getting copies of the accident report, settling matters with the auto insurance company, and poring through the first of the medical bills that showed up in our mailbox.

One death chore I wanted out of the way was picking up my daughter's ashes. I stopped by Ahlgrim, where Karl the funeral director greeted me kindly and had me sign for a shiny, mahogany-colored wooden urn—sort of like a minicasket—that Scott had selected when he dropped off Katie's clothing the week before the funeral.

"The lid is screwed on tightly," Karl assured me, "and Katherine's ashes are secured inside the urn in a can with a pop-off lid."

A pop-top can inside an urn. These are the things you learn when your loved one dies. But I appreciated Karl's explanation, as I had been worried that if I needed to slam on the brakes on my drive home, I might send Katie flying everywhere.

We didn't yet know what we wanted to do with Katie's ashes. We didn't know whether to scatter them or bury them, and Scott and the kids were unified in not wanting the urn to go on display in the house. So when I got home, I wrapped the urn in Katie's pink baby blanket and tucked it on a shelf in my closet.

For many months, no one asked what I had done with Katie's ashes. Not even Scott. I liked the private coziness of having Katie all to myself, nearby, where I could take her urn and hold it close to my heart, unobserved.

And yes, I am aware that some might find this creepy. If I ever spotted a lady sitting inside her closet snuggling an urn that was swaddled in a pink baby blanket, I might have called the authorities. Never thought I'd be that lady!

One of the more pressing death chores was Katie's car, which had been totaled in the crash and taken to a wrecking yard where it waited for someone to sign over the title and pay a hundred bucks for the towing. I handled this chore partly out of duty—but partly out of desire: I wanted to see if any of Katie's personal effects were still in the car, and I just needed to see the vehicle for myself. She loved her Taurus, and it was the last place my daughter had been alive.

The man in the towing office helped me sign over the title and took my check. Then he handed me a screwdriver and pointed to the yard.

"Remove the license plate before you go," he said.

I spotted Katie's gold Taurus immediately amid the sea of crashed cars, and a wave of nausea hit me. The other car in her wreck, a Mercedes, had impaled her front passenger door, leaving an indentation so deep that the nose of the Mercedes would fit perfectly into the side of Katie's car like a giant 3-D puzzle piece. The outside of Katie's passenger door was now just twelve inches from her driver's seat. I shuddered, thinking again of how easily Tember might have bummed a ride with Katie that day and been sitting in that seat when the crash occurred.

The back of the car was also caved in, crushed like a tin can. Even the backseat was squashed. Broken glass was everywhere. But amazingly, the driver's door was untouched. It popped open with little more than a tug. The front driver's seat where Katie had been sitting was perfectly intact. It looked as if God had cupped two giant hands around her, creating a little bubble of safety that had protected her body during the crash.

If it hadn't been for this den of protection, Katie would have never made it to the hospital. The paramedics would have taken her straight to the morgue, and this story would have ended much differently for the people who received her organs.

I looked for any belongings on the floor and around the seats. The cops, however, had done a good job of clearing things out. I tried to lift the lid to the center console, where Katie would often set a piece of jewelry or other odds and ends, but the console was now crushed, pinned beneath the mangled passenger's seat. What connections to my daughter did it hide?

The guy in the towing office loaned me more tools—a box cutter, a hammer, and a crowbar. With the box cutter I was able to slice away the seat cushion, but beneath the velour fabric and padding lay a quarter-inch-thick slab of raw metal from the passenger's door that had wrapped over the edge of the console's lid. Despite another twenty minutes of effort—and dozens of miniscule, pinprick cuts on my hands and arms from brushing against the shattered cubes of glass—the hammer and crowbar did nothing to move that metal. Short of a blowtorch, this lid was not going to open. The Taurus would be taken to a metal-recycling plant and crushed by a giant crane. Whatever treasures were entombed inside the console would be destroyed along with it.

I moved to the trunk. Maybe something inside would make up for the uncrackable safe that was the console. The trunk lid was smashed, but there was a gap on both sides almost wide enough for my arm. I wedged the crowbar under it and widened the first gap just enough to slide my arm through. I felt around and pulled out a few pens, a spiral notebook, a hairbrush. No jewelry, nothing of significance. I tried on the other side of the trunk, to the same effect. I had hoped to find something—anything—that would further connect me to my child. Every memento now had the potential to expand my memory bank and remind me of a story I might have forgotten. No new stories here. I pulled my arm out and swallowed hard.

I removed the license plates with the screwdriver as instructed, then headed to the office to return the tools, weaving my way among the rows of smashed vehicles. I wondered about each car. I had been to wrecking yards before, but I had only ever thought of them as salvage opportunities—places where you went to find a replacement knob for your dashboard or the engine part that was too overpriced to buy new.

But then it hit me: These cars were more than just metal. Many had been temporary tombs, places a daughter or father or friend had exited this world. I wanted to bow my head in reverence for each one, to hear each story, to pay tribute to someone's tragedy besides my own.

I handed the towing office guy his tools and thanked him.

"Find what you were looking for?" he asked.

"No," I said. "Not today."

I climbed into my minivan and started the engine. Before I pulled onto the road, my eyes lingered on Katie's Taurus. I thought about the energetic girl who had driven that car all around town, meeting friends, driving to work, sitting in the driveway long past midnight engrossed in meaningful conversation with a friend. She'd loved that car. She was so proud of the fact that she had paid for half of it with her own money. The last time I had seen her alive, she was driving off to work in that Taurus, full of life, her foot a little heavy on the pedal, with places to go and people to see. Now there it sat, crushed and abandoned, simply another smashed car in a wrecking yard, its broken glass glistening in the summer sun.

～∾⌇∾～

Tember approached us nervously one morning at breakfast. "Can I move into Katie's room?" she asked.

Many times over the past week, I'd found Tember just lying on her sister's bed, tears rolling down her cheeks onto Katie's pillow. I, too, had savored time in that bedroom, just touching my middle daughter's belongings, looking at all the physical details of the life she'd left so unfinished inside those four walls.

"I just feel close to her when I am in there," Tember explained. "She loved her room, and I just sort of want that to be my place now, like it was for her. Plus . . ."

"Plus what, beautiful?" Scott asked.

"Well, every time I walk by her room, her absence just seems so glaring, like it's screaming at me. I know you guys must feel it too."

I nodded.

"She should be in there!" Tember said, pointing in the direction of Katie's room. "And she's not. And she won't ever be. I don't want her room to become something we hate walking past. I want it to be a happy place, full of life. I want to sleep in her bed at night and have sleepovers with my girlfriends on weekends, just like she did. I want her room to be lived in and loved—the way she lived in it and loved it."

How could we argue with that? Absolutely she should have Katie's room. But giving Tember that space as her bedroom would mean losing the sanctuary I had been finding there for myself.

I didn't want us to leave Katie's room untouched—mostly out of my fear that if we left it as is, I would have a propensity to turn it into a shrine. I'd had fleeting thoughts about transforming it into an art room for my own projects but hadn't made any concrete plans. The timing of Tember's request caught me off guard. I wasn't ready.

She waited uneasily for a response.

"Sure," I said, trying to sound nonchalant.

"If you want to leave it alone, I totally understand," she said, beginning to backtrack. "Or if it's too soon . . ."

"We'll think about it," Scott said. "We like your idea, but we need to discuss it first."

Later, the two of us talked.

"I am all for anything that would be helpful to one of our heartbroken kids," I said. "And her reasons are good."

"I agree," he said, "but the kids aren't the only ones who are heartbroken. You spend quite a bit of time in that room yourself. Are you ready for a move like this?"

"No," I said. "But I never will be, and it's the right thing to do, I think. So we might as well do it."

"If you're sure, then fine," Scott said. "If you change your mind, though—if it's too hard or too soon—it can wait. Tember will understand. No shame in that. And there's no rush."

I wanted to do what was best for my daughter. That's what we moms are here for, right?

Tember and I decided to tackle Katie's room the next day. Bethany was still in town, and we called Kati Harkin to join us for yet another death chore.

We went through Katie's closet first, bequeathing to Bethany, Tember, Andrea (who had already flown back to California), and Kati whatever clothes or shoes fit. We did the same with her jewelry, and I kept a lot of pieces for myself—including a sterling ring and a pewter pendant, both of which she had cast by hand in her 3-D art class at Fremd.

The simple act of going through Katie's clothes should have been tremendously difficult, but perhaps because we expected it to be hard and had emotionally geared ourselves up for it, we were all pleasantly surprised when it actually turned out to be not that bad. Bethany brought her levity to the game, which helped. At five feet ten, Bethany was too long legged for most of Katie's pants and skirts. And let's face it—Katie's taste in clothes was a little quirky. Bethany came across one pair of long, wide-legged palazzo pants that were about a foot too short for Bethany's thirty-seven-inch inseams. She slipped them on over her shorts.

"Look at me! I'm a stilt man!" she said. We all looked—and laughed. Her thin legs protruded from the bottom of Katie's pants like stilts. She began humming a circus song and doing a dorky dance around the room, her arms flailing and knees prancing high. How I love this girl and her wacky humor!

With laughter and warmth, we finished our chore. I found solace in slipping into one of Katie's cardigan sweaters—it was as if she were wrapping her arms around me. It still held a faint smell of her perfume.

After everyone had taken the items they wanted, I wasn't sure what to do with the leftovers. I couldn't bear to give anything of hers to Goodwill. Maybe I would make a quilt for each of the kids someday. So I loaded everything into bags and stored them on a shelf in our basement.

I tackled the rest of the room by myself the next morning. Bookshelves, desk drawers crammed with art supplies, and closet shelves piled high with childhood treasures—each item warranted a decision. Despite my best intentions, it proved too much. Tember found me an hour later, sitting on the floor of Katie's room in a puddle of tears.

"I just can't do it—not yet," I confessed.

She put her arms around me and hugged me. "It's all right, Mom. There is no hurry. And I don't ever need to move in here if it's too hard. Do whatever you think is best. No pressure. No pressure at all."

I sat there and thought. "Tem, I really think you should have this room. I want you in here. It's just a little harder than I thought. Give me until after the weekend."

"Take as long as you want."

"Just the weekend."

I took the weekend. And on Monday, I tried again. This time, I finished organizing and storing Katie's belongings. And when the room was empty and ready, I was genuinely happy to help Tember make the move. Katie would have loved seeing her kid sister snuggling into her old bed, where they had shared countless sister sleepovers on so many nights.

There was another sorting project that proved too difficult the first time around. A friend had gathered all of Katie's art supplies from her studio space at APU and shipped them to our home. When I pulled her artist's toolbox from the cardboard FedEx package, my throat tightened. But I was hell-bent on not avoiding the task in front of me. I wanted to say yes to the pain rather than pull back from it—not out of bravado or masochism, but because of my growing conviction that "through" was the quickest way out and because I feared that avoiding the difficult tasks would later leave me stuck in my grief.

So I opened the toolbox. The memorable smell of her oil paint and turpentine wafted into the air. I looked through her brushes, picking up a few of her favorites and stroking their soft bristles against my cheek. Then I spotted that favorite paint-stained apron of hers—a green Starbucks apron from her high school barista job. I held it up. It bore splatters of new, unfamiliar paint from the pieces she had completed at college this spring. One of the new splatters showed a partial fingerprint . . .

Too much. I bundled the apron, stuffed it inside, shut the lid, and stored the toolbox on a shelf in the basement, next to the bags of her clothes.

A friend paid a professional housecleaner to come over and give the whole house a good deep clean—which was a tremendous relief, as it was long overdue but I had zero energy. The woman did an excellent job. And the next morning, I discovered she had washed the girls' bathroom mirror. Katie's message, "72 days," was gone.

I wanted to throw up.

But then again, what was I to have done—never wash that bathroom mirror again? I'd give anything to have a photo of that mirror before the number was washed away. But we don't always get what we want.

Sympathy cards from friends and loved ones continued to trickle in with the daily mail, and they lifted my spirits immensely.

A delightful twist: Many people tucked restaurant gift cards into their envelopes. Evidently Scott's administrative assistant at work had suggested this idea to people who asked her how they could help. One family gave us free pizza for a year from the restaurant chain they owned, Lou Malnati's.

These gift cards proved invaluable in the weeks and months to come. On nights when the idea of cooking felt insurmountable, we could drive to Panera Bread or Portillo's or Macaroni Grill for dinner. And on nights when even leaving the house was too overwhelming, we could order the best deep-dish pizza in Chicago. These generous gifts helped us discover we could still laugh and tell stories around a table and make new family memories—memories without our middle daughter.

33

TWO WEEKS AFTER THE FUNERAL, our friends in Spokane hosted a memorial service for Katie at our old church. They flew us out and we stayed with Sandy McConkey and her family. Her husband, Bobby, gave a beautiful eulogy; our friend Greg led worship; and we showed the DVD of the Willow Creek service.

In the receiving line afterward, we were greeted by the kids' schoolteachers, Scott's former ER partners and nurses, church friends, and neighbors—many of whom we hadn't seen in more than six years. Katie's fifth- and sixth-grade teacher, Mr. Rae, was so shaken when he greeted me that he couldn't speak. We simply hugged, and he wept on my shoulder. It moved me deeply. Katie's third-grade teacher, Mrs. Metcalf, held me close. Her fourteen-year-old son had died the year after Katie had been her student, and I had attended her son's funeral. Now here she was for my daughter's.

"Will I survive?" I whispered in her ear.

"Yes," she said. "But not for a while. You won't feel human again for at least a year."

Her honest answer gave me hope, actually, because from my vantage point I wondered if I'd *ever* feel human again.

~⦿~

During that trip to Washington, we savored a few days with the McConkeys, who live on the Palouse Prairie—rolling wheat fields southeast of Spokane, nestled against the western foothills of the Rockies. These were the same farmlands where Scott and I had lived when the kids were young. Katie had rescued Bethany from the yellow jackets at the house located just a few miles down the winding country road.

Before anyone else stirred on the morning after the memorial, I made coffee, poured a cup, and took a walk in the fields beside the house. The Palouse is dryland farming country, and winter wheat blanketed the rolling hills as far as my eyes could see. The air was arid and hot, and already the vibration of grasshoppers' wings buzzed from the wheat stubble around my feet. The dawn breeze smelled like warm, unbuttered toast. I picked some wildflowers—black-eyed Susans, blue bachelor's buttons, yarrow. In the distance, a pheasant's staccato call broke the stillness. *These sights and sounds and smells filled our kids' childhoods, their endless summer mornings long ago. Did I treasure those days enough? I can never have them back.*

I sat down among the stubble, sipping my coffee and taking in the expanse of the horizon. I replayed scenes in my mind—the children building forts in the ravine, catching garter snakes along the drive, poking the giant anthill in our pasture with sticks, eating cherry tomatoes and snow peas straight off the vine from my garden, and playing fetch in the hay field with our dogs, Lloyd the Wonder Dog and Betty. *I am rich beyond measure.*

The toasted summer breeze dried the tears on my cheeks. The house would be stirring soon. Flowers and empty cup in hand, I stood, stretched, and retraced my steps, ready to savor the new day.

When we got back home to Chicago, I did a mental recap of the past few weeks—and looked ahead to the weeks and months to come.

We had navigated Scott's first Father's Day and birthday without Katie, and it had been an inner agony for him. Katie had purchased two shirts for her papa's birthday a week or so before she died, and I had wrapped them for her and given them to him. I gave him fair warning, too, but there was no protecting his heart against opening these final gifts from this daughter who loved him so.

We had hosted Tember's eighth-grade graduation party in our back-yard, and adding to Katie's glaring absence was the fact that she had preordered the "Congratulations!" cake—a Vaudrey tradition—from Costco. Katie had chosen the flavor, the colors, the filling. I had picked up the cake the morning of the party and gently told Tember its story. There was a "make a memory" look in Tember's eyes as she cut into the cake her sister had planned for her big day. Then it was eaten, and then it was gone.

These milestones were excruciating, but they could not be stopped. I scanned the calendar pages, looking ahead for other such milestones still looming. I didn't want to be blindsided. I wanted to see these "firsts" coming and to prepare.

Our summer vacation in August—a road trip to Massachusetts to attend a family reunion—was fast approaching, but we were a mess. I canceled our trip.

I flipped through September and October to November—Thanks-giving. No Katie at my side in the kitchen, cooking with her siblings and me. No Katie to filigree the piecrusts with her elegant swirls before sprinkling them with sugar and sliding them into the oven. No Katie to help decorate the Thanksgiving table or to write name cards for each of us in her distinctive font.

And then Christmas . . .

I could not stop these dates from coming. So I began thinking through each "Awful First," planning how our family could navigate them in a healthy, authentic way, holding sorrow in one hand and life in the other. Holding on and letting go.

The atmosphere at home during those first weeks lay thick and heavy. The older kids had flown back to California, and I felt bad for Sam and Tember, who were facing the full brunt of their own grief, plus the ripples of ours. Scott and I were caught in two roles: grieving parents and parents of grieving children. It's harder than you think to switch between roles, especially for me—the more emotive parent. So I forced myself to find time alone to get messy with my grief.

Our bathroom shower and my minivan became my "places" that summer and fall. Each morning, I would awake gasping, suffocating with our new reality. But when I stepped into the steaming shower, I could cry as hard as I wanted and not worry about the noise or the mess or ruining my makeup. I would start my morning with the slobbery release of that pent-up grief, and then I could breathe again and face the day less likely to dissolve into a puddle in front of the kids, my friends, or complete strangers.

Alone in my minivan, running errands or driving to work, I could cry—loud, uninhibited sobs. I would rail my anger or frustration or pain to God. Sometimes I would call out to Katie. I probably sounded like a crazy woman, but what did I care? No one could hear. Privacy at forty-five miles per hour. And by the time I arrived wherever I was heading, my sorrow's congestion had found its escape, and I would again feel God's presence and His calm. I would blow my nose, reapply my makeup, and move forward with my day. (Tip: If you are a woman in a season of loss, stock up on waterproof mascara!)

Scott's grief hideouts were the Bug Room, our bedroom, and his office at work—in that order. Countless times I would come upon him sitting alone with reddened eyes, wiping his tears but giving me his best smile.

"It's like an amputation," he said of the loss one day. "The wound will eventually heal, but we'll still be missing the arm."

How horrid it would be to lose a child and not be this devastated. Love comes with a price tag.

And absolutely we cried in front of the kids. It would have been phony not to. I tried hard to be the parent and let them be the kids—it wasn't their job to carry me—but sometimes I fell short. Yet even when I was a total mess, I wasn't looking for their comfort. Just knowing they understood the sadness was comfort enough.

At times the kids carried Scott or me in a way that felt healthy and beautiful, and we were grateful. In mid-July, when my birthday rolled around, Sam and Tember made me a homemade birthday cake—something that had been Katie's role in recent years. Without missing a beat, the younger kids just stepped in and filled that little gap. Best gift they could have given.

We were all looking out for one another in our own ways—not just the parents hovering over the kids, but maybe the kids hovering over the parents, too.

❦

In the state of Illinois, an unusual death like Katie's mandates a coroner's inquest to determine the cause of death. Katie's accident triggered such an inquest. This then prompted a phone call from our insurance company, since they had paid Katie's funeral home bill under our policy's accidental death clause. They wanted to know if the coroner's inquest had happened yet. They wanted to know what had caused my daughter's death.

"The inquest is in late August, I believe," I told the woman on the phone. "They said we'll get a notice in the mail."

"If the accident didn't cause Katherine's death," the woman said gently, "then it falls in the 'act of God' category, and we don't cover acts of God, so you would need to return the compensation."

"Act of God"? Never mind the money, lady. But don't pin this on God! I felt indignant.

Yet He allowed the aneurysm to happen. He didn't undo it, despite my begging. If I believe God is omnipotent, then did His failure to act mean He acted?

But He also protected Katie's body in the car. He kept Tember safely at home that day. He gave us nineteen glorious years with Katie before the aneurysm struck. Weren't these, too, acts of God?

I hung up feeling defensive of God, as if He were getting a bad rap. But the woman's words brought to light my dilemma: How could the aneurysm and Tember's safety—and the nineteen years with Katie and the million other goodnesses we had experienced—all be "acts of God"?

34

AS WE NEARED THE TWO-MONTH MARK since Katie's death, I began to feel myself sliding into a depression. Sam and Tember were at summer jobs or summer school most days, and Scott had gone back to work, so I was often home alone. Before Katie's death, I had worked as a freelance writer and had just completed a huge job, with no new assignments lined up. This was a blessing at first, but spending day after day with nowhere I needed to go was turning into a detriment. I would just lie on the couch like a slug. Merely getting dressed was a chore. Taking a shower was a major victory.

When a friend called and offered me a large freelance writing assignment at our church, I said yes.

"Only one or two meetings a week," he said. "The rest you can do from home."

So at least one day a week—sometimes two—I had to make myself shower, dress (in something besides sweatpants), and get off the dang couch. It felt good to force my grief-stalled brain into gear, to push myself to craft sentences and to find the best words. It felt good to be productive and to walk among the living once again.

～◎～

Death makes people squirm. They didn't know what to say to us, and we didn't always know what to say back. There were times when someone's comments left us speechless. And there were times when our own responses to others were inappropriate, awkward, or even funny.

"I need some material for a new song," a kid told Sam that summer, "but nothing sad ever happens to me. Sorry about your sister, man, but are you cool with me writing a song about her dying and posting it on YouTube?"

Wow. *Sure, dude. We'd love for our loss to help you be the next YouTube sensation.*

Our family, never willing to let a good story go unrepeated, found an odd comfort in regaling one another around the dinner table that summer with tales of these awkward moments.

"My first day back at work was hard for everyone," Scott told us one night. "Some people were great, but most looked scared spitless at the mere sight of me. When I walked by, they would pop their heads out of their cubes to see who it was and then pop their heads back in and pretend they hadn't seen me. Walking to and from my office, I felt like I was playing Whac-A-Mole!"

Often the person who didn't know what to do or say was me. One afternoon, I had taken Tember for an orthodontist appointment, and afterward at a red light, a man was working his way from car to car. He wore a bright orange traffic vest with the words *Homeless Shelter* scrawled across the front in faded black marker. A tub of nickel lollipops hung around his neck.

On a good day, I am apprehensive about giving cash to this type of fund-raising effort unless I am certain the money will actually go to a legitimate cause. This man with the handwritten vest didn't exactly scream legit nonprofit. I did not want to buy one of his lollipops.

Never had I hoped for a green light so badly. "Turn green! Green-green-green!"

"Chill, Mom," Tember said.

The man reached our car, and with a flashy salesman's smile, he motioned for me to roll down my window. I smiled back but shook my head no. So he hung a pouty lip and began making begging motions with his hands. Again I smiled but shook my head.

Undaunted, the man began to pantomime crying, using his pinky fingers to show invisible tears trickling down his cheeks, his lollipop bucket bouncing against his belly as he fake-sobbed, inches from my face.

World's longest red light.

Finally, he made an exaggerated brokenhearted face and began mouthing, "Please! Please! Please!"

I was being tortured by a relentless, lollipop-bearing Marcel Marceau.

"Give it up, mister," I said under my breath.

"Let it go, Mom . . . ," Tember cautioned.

Too late.

I rolled down my window. "I'm sorry," I said, real tears erupting, "but my nineteen-year-old daughter just died, and I don't want to buy your lollipop!"

"Mom!" Tember whispered.

The poor man! His jaw dropped—as did his Marcel Marceau imitation. He looked horrified.

"Oh, I am so sorry, miss. I had no idea."

I felt like I'd just kicked a puppy. "It's okay," I said, smiling and wiping my eyes. "You had no way of knowing. It's all right, really. But I just can't buy your lollipop today."

"No problem, miss. No problem. I'm so sorry about your daughter . . ."

He backed away as the light turned green, and I rolled up my window, feeling sick to my stomach. I didn't dare look over at Tember. She was so embarrassed.

"Mom," she said, "you just humiliated that guy! Sometimes you just need to let people be people."

"You're right, honey," I said. "I blew it. I really blew it."

We continued home in silence. But when we pulled in the driveway, she flashed me a forgiving smile. She knew all too well that her mother is a people too.

～❦～

The hardest moments for me often came when people failed to say anything at all about our loss.

One day I had a work meeting at church and bumped into a fellow staff member in the hall. Katie had been his kids' babysitter, and I knew he knew she had died.

"Hey, September!" he said, smiling brightly.

"Hey, Rich," I said. We continued walking, and I figured he'd at least toss me a "Sorry about your loss."

Nothing.

It felt like there was a giant elephant in the room. The longer he said nothing, the more ticked off I became. I was tempted to say something snarky like, "Oh, by the way, Katie can't babysit for your kids anymore *because she died*." But even the Lollipop-Man Attacker could show occasional restraint.

I reminded myself that this was a good man—an awkward but decent guy. He was a caring father who had been generous to our daughter. Who knows? He might have had all sorts of legit reasons for his deafening silence.

I recounted this story to our family later that night. Bethany was sympathetic toward me. "When someone is simply willing to acknowledge your loss," she said, "it gives you permission to give voice to the reality that is playing its reel over and over again in your mind. It helps you feel sane because it reminds you that this really did happen and that others outside of your house were affected by it too."

Unless you have experienced the kind of loss that freaks everyone out, you don't realize what a gift it is to have your loss acknowledged.

Navigating situations like ours isn't easy for anyone. Even since Katie's death, I have sometimes been that awkward, silent person, the one who held back from acknowledging someone else's loss. I know better than to remain silent, but it is still hard to know what to say. We are all feeling our way.

It helped our family to laugh about those awkward moments—like the time a girl told Tember, "I know *just* how you feel. My fav cat died last month." Rather than be discouraged or hurt by such comments, we shared the funny stories with one another and laughed at other people's fumbles, as well as our own. We were just doing the best we could.

We were especially grateful for friends—or even acquaintances—who were willing to be present without being overly invasive or awkwardly avoidant. Each of us could recount times when someone had simply provided space to talk if we wanted—or to be silent if we chose. Those encounters were gifts.

"For the most part, people have been remarkably sensible," Sam observed one night. "The greatest friends and companions in times of horrible sadness are the ones who don't attempt to fix or quantify your experience, but rather are simply present and willing to share only as little or as much of your life as you invite them into."

Well said.

In the stillness of summer, I became rather obsessed with Katie's art. We had dozens of finished pieces that had been matted in black by Mr. Pinley and his Fremd students. But in transit from the Life Exhibit to our home, some had been dented or scuffed up, and others had a color scheme that could be enhanced by a colored mat rather than a black one. I bought a mat cutter, several sheets of mat board, and some frames. Then I set to work at our kitchen table.

"Lots of art you got there," Scott said. "What do you plan to do with all these once they're framed?"

"Well, I won't hang them *all . . . ,*" I said, already feeling defensive.

"Okay, but how many do you plan to hang?" he asked.

"I just feel they should be protected behind glass."

He smiled. "And how many do you plan to hang?"

"Uh, probably more than you want." His gentle persistence was ticking me off.

It's dang frustrating sometimes to be married to someone who knows me so well and who can see beneath my excuses. *I pretty much want to wallpaper our whole home with Katie's art, okay? And I don't want you thwarting me. Back off, Jack.*

A testy exchange followed. And because Scott is dogged and my project took several days, we engaged in several more bouts of discussion across the kitchen table that week.

He knew me well enough to invite me in small bites to see this issue from different angles: If our home became wall-to-wall Katie art, what would it communicate to our kids? Or to our friends? And more important, what was going on inside me that was driving this?

Then there was this clincher: "You thought it was important to move Tember into Katie's room because you knew you risked making her room into a shrine if you left it empty. Is there a chance you're using Katie's art to turn our whole house into a shrine?"

Dang him.

Any family that loses a loved one faces dilemmas like this. It's not black and white, and I'm guessing it's different for everyone. But that day, it was important for Scott and me to get at the root issue. It wasn't about Katie's art. It was about finding the balance between honoring our daughter and stepping into a life without her.

In the end, I framed a bunch of her pieces, stacking several matted drawings or paintings inside each frame to protect them—and so I could swap them out if I wished. We hung more art than Scott wanted and less than I wanted—four clusters of paintings in four different rooms and a couple of single pieces here and there. Probably a good compromise. It was a small step in finding the balance between holding on and letting go.

35

Our family didn't really have a "place" to visit to remember Katie. Because we have lived in three states—Washington, Illinois, and the college kids in California—we didn't have the kind of hometown roots that make cemetery decisions easy. We didn't want to bury her ashes somewhere we couldn't readily visit, and we weren't sure whether we should sprinkle them—and if so, where. Thus, her urn sat in my closet, wrapped in her baby blanket. But I wanted a "place"—a physical location to go to and grieve my daughter.

Maybe the crash site could become that place. In early August, I picked an armful of wildflowers from the field next to our house, bought a dozen red roses from the grocery store, and set out to locate the exact spot of the crash.

Katie's friends made it easy. They had erected two crosses on the grassy bank next to the place her car had landed. One was made of rustic iron filigree, and the other was one of those white wooden highway crosses made of garden stakes. Someone had thumbtacked a laminated photo of Katie to it, a summer snapshot of her with a big grin, wisps of hair loose around her face. As I approached the site, it startled me to find her smiling up at me. *Surreal. I cannot believe I am one of "those" people leaving flowers at a marker on the side of a road—briefly bumming out all who drive by.*

I sat down on the grass and ran my hand over the sun-warmed turf. *Did Katie's body touch these very grasses as she was pulled from the wreckage?* I felt a sudden, overwhelming urge to write her a note and leave it there for her, but others who visited might read it—plus that would be littering. Then I got an idea.

I pulled a fine-tip Sharpie from my purse and picked up one of the red roses I had bought. Each stem bore two clusters of three waxen green leaves, and each leaf was like a tiny page for note writing. The bouquet would provide me seventy-two pages in all. No littering. And privacy.

At first, I wrote a single word on each leaf—adjectives that described things I loved about Katie—and her quirks, too. I said each word aloud—maybe she could hear me. *Kind, joyful, beauty, messy, funny,*

*sacred, artistic, dancer, spark, sister, flirt, authentic, daughter, baker, stub-
born, impulsive, food artist, feminine.*

The notes on the leaves were barely visible to the naked eye, so I
began writing full sentences. *I miss you. I hate that you died! I love you
beyond words. I am afraid my joy is gone forever. You were too good to be
true. I wanted to hold your babies someday. Come back! Rewind the clock!
I will never forget you. Dad is brokenhearted, Bug. I will try hard to help
Tember in her grief. Bethany loves you. I will hug Sam for you. I loved being
your mama. Matt and Andrea wish you could paint their mural. Thank
you for loving me well. I will hug Matt. I will hug Andrea. I love you. I love
you. I love you.*

When the last leaf was filled, I nestled the wildflowers around the
feet of the crosses and tucked the roses among them. The effect was
stunning. My artist daughter would have approved—though I knew I
would take a good-natured ribbing from the rest of my kids for this leaf-
writing inspiration. They might say it was a bit "Momily Dickinson" of
me—or tease me about my Laura Ingalls Wilder ways. We'd just keep
these moments to ourselves.

I breathed in deeply and exhaled as I walked back to the van. It felt
good to have a place to be purposeful about remembering my daughter.

⌒◞℗◟⌒

The miles between Illinois and our California kids tortured us that summer. Frequent e-mails and phone calls just didn't cut it. We needed to
gather as a family. We needed someplace to decompress and process
together and grieve.

Andrea's grandma owned a condo in Las Vegas, and she offered to let
us stay there for free. We bought plane tickets, booked a two-week stay,
and converged on Sin City in early August.

At first we tried to do what we normally do on vacations. We cooked
favorite meals. We read good books and played games and lounged at
the pool.

But these were just distractions, brief respites from the ache that
kept our souls as parched as the Vegas desert air. In between books
and games and the pool, we just stared at one another in disbelief, or

sat on the sofa, or sprawled motionless on the floor, or lay on our beds and cried. It was probably what we needed to do, but it was downright depressing.

The first Friday, Andrea had to drive down to LA for work. She'd be gone a couple of days. That night, the rest of us loaded up in our rented minivan and drove to Red Robin for dinner. It felt a little like the olden days: a van full of Vaudreys. The atmosphere picked up, and by the time we bounded into the restaurant's lobby, the kids were chattering away.

"How many?" the host asked.

"Seven," Scott answered reflexively.

And then it hit us.

The kids grew quiet. Sam reached over and rubbed Scott's back. We had been seven for so many years. I loved being seven. But without Katie, a van full of Vaudreys wasn't seven.

"Uh, six," he said quietly.

A deep, collective exhale sucked the air from our lungs. We were six.

Around the Red Robin table that night, we were determined to rebound. We started out pretty somber, but the kids began telling stories, and our laughter reappeared, shyly at first, but soon without apology. We were test-driving the new normal—and discovering that sorrow and joy could be decent neighbors.

For the second week of our Las Vegas vacation, the McConkeys flew down from Spokane and joined us. They saved the day! We moved from the condo to some rooms at the MGM Grand that Scott had scored at an amazing price. We floated on the lazy river in MGM's fabulous pool complex. We saw a few shows, overate at buffets, laughed too loud in restaurants, and simply played together. There were tender conversations, too, and some tears. But an aura of fun prevailed, delivering a much-needed summer shower to the deserts of our souls.

The collective sorrow that had permeated our first week in Las Vegas turned out to be a recurring vacation phenomenon. For several years to come, we would find that when we stepped away from the routine of life, the stillness of vacations gave our pent-up sorrow a chance to cut loose, and the first days of a trip were generally a bummer. We found it helped if we didn't fight it and simply scheduled some downtime up front to allow sorrow to get its release so the rejuvenating part of the vacation could begin.

Still today, for Scott and me, family trips are seasoned faintly by sadness. We miss our girl. We wish she were here to join us. While time with family brings wholehearted laughter and relaxation and fun, it's not without a slight taste of sorrow. Both/and. Never one without the other.

36

I HAD BEEN WATCHING OUR MAILBOX all summer, waiting for a letter from Gift of Hope—the organ donation nonprofit that had coordinated Katie's surgery and organ placement. We'd been told we would receive a summary of Katie's donation sometime this summer, telling us of all the people Katie's organs and tissues had helped.

Around the second week of August, the waiting paid off. I opened the mailbox one afternoon and pulled out an envelope bearing the distinct purple-and-green Gift of Hope logo in the corner. I disciplined myself to wait until Scott and the kids were home—and then I ripped open the envelope and read its contents aloud.

We learned these details about the anonymous people whose bodies now contained, in part, our daughter: A sixty-eight-year-old grandmother received Katie's liver. A twenty-six-year-old woman received her lungs. (She had been given only twenty-four hours to live—the day before Katie's accident.) A thirty-seven-year-old father of two received her pancreas and left kidney. A forty-three-year-old family man received her right kidney. A young man and a young woman received her corneas, giving them a second chance for sight. In addition to the organs and corneas, Katie's femurs contributed "bone and adjacent soft tissue" to be used for a variety of orthopedic procedures—from spinal fusions to reconstructing long bones lost to cancer or trauma. In some cases, they were used for full joint replacement. All of the transplants had been successful, and each patient was recovering at home with family and friends.

I smiled at the image of that twenty-six-year-old woman taking her first breath with Katie's vibrant, healthy lungs.

The news of our recipients brought gratitude and pride. How proud we were that our girl had cared strongly about organ donation. How grateful we were that her heart had been jolted back to life *three times* so that she could be a candidate for donation. The fact that her death had—in some cases quite literally—brought life to six different people, not to mention the many who received bone and soft tissue from her to restore their joints or legs, left a complicated surge of satisfaction in my soul. *She would be so proud. And so am I.*

Because of the confidentiality regulations around donation, Gift of Hope acts as the intermediary for donor/recipient correspondence. Our letter included a consent form to release our contact information to any of Katie's recipients who requested it, along with some guidelines for how to write a letter to our recipients.

I called the Gift of Hope family services coordinator with a few questions. She provided helpful, compassionate answers and then added, "Don't be surprised if you don't hear from your recipients for quite some time. They are recovering from major surgery. And in some cases, you may not hear from them at all. They may feel uncomfortable trying to say thank you when their gift came at such cost to you."

I guess that made sense, but I very much wanted to hear from those donors. I wanted to know how they were doing. To be honest, I wanted to hear how—hopefully—Katie's gift had been a blessing to them. When I wrote my letters to them, I tried to minimize any awkwardness they might feel by emphasizing that, although we were heartbroken at our loss, it helped immensely to know Katie's organs had helped others. I signed my letter and our consent form and mailed them back to Gift of Hope.

Then the mailbox watching resumed.

Katie's coroner's inquest, scheduled for late August, was fast approaching. We were not required by law to attend, but I wanted to go. Scott was the opposite of me in this; he had witnessed firsthand as many details of Katie's accident as he cared to stomach. He needed no extra material to haunt his dreams, thank you very much. I knew it would tank Scott to sit and hear the crash and hospital scenes replayed, and on the day of the inquest I felt up to attending alone, so that's what I did.

Why did I want to know all the details of Katie's accident? They wouldn't change the outcome, and they would be gut-wrenching to listen to. But for me, knowing all the tiny specifics—as graphic as they might be—was better than *wondering* what had happened to my daughter in those dreadful moments after the crash. The cold reality of truth, I hoped, would be less horrifying than the *CSI*-inspired scenes that played regularly in my mind.

Part of what drove me to know every detail was a maternal desire to be close to my daughter. I had been at Katie's side during every significant transition in her short life—her first day of kindergarten, middle school, and high school; the move to Chicago; her first date; her first boyfriend; every graduation; her college orientation. But on May 31, for that most significant and final of all transitions, I had not been there. She had been alone. My daughter had passed from this world to the next all by herself. In learning about the final moments of her life, this part of her story wouldn't be unknown. Someone who loves her would know all the details. Her mama would hold the details.

I drove to the courthouse in Geneva, where Kane County inquests are held, and found the correct courtroom. I took a seat on a bench against the back wall. The county coroner presided as judge over an eight-person jury for each case. When Katie's case was presented, the investigating detective and the coroner's assistant gave testimony, and I learned some details I'd not heard before: When Katie was extricated from the car, she had no pulse, her pupils were unresponsive, and she was not breathing. The paramedics started CPR, loaded her into the ambulance, and then shocked her to get her pulse back. *She must have been unconscious and possibly not breathing for several minutes before the ambulance arrived.* I learned that her seat belt had already been unbuckled when the ambulance arrived, likely by someone else at the scene. (She was maniacal about wearing her seat belt—a true child of an ER doc—and if she had been unbuckled upon impact, she would have been thrown around inside the car.)

After an hour of testimony, the jury stepped out to deliberate. As I sat on my bench and waited, some comic relief wiggled its way into the inquest in the form of a defense attorney in a polyester pin-striped suit who was there for the next trial. He reminded me of Danny DeVito in his role as the used-car-salesman dad in *Matilda*, but he was also more of a lady's man—at least in his own mind. He parked himself a little too close to me on the bench, his short legs dangling, and was very, uh, attentive.

"I got four kids—two in their thirties, a teen, plus a toddler from my third wife," he told me. "But I'm single now. So . . . how about you?"

He peppered me with questions about why I was there and offered his legal analysis of my situation, "free of charge." Lucky me.

"See, what you want here is for them to rule her death accidental, even though the aneurysm means it was technically natural," he explained, leaning in close enough for me to smell his Jōvan Musk cologne. "If it's ruled accidental, you'll get to keep all that insurance money!"

Despite the heavy circumstances of why I was sitting in that courtroom, it was all I could do to not giggle at this caricature of a man. He was ridiculous. *If only I'd brought a friend along today!* I wanted someone else to witness this.

The longer the jury deliberated, the longer I got to listen to my new friend. At long last—after about half an hour—the jury returned, and the coroner asked for a verdict. One of the jurors stood and read from a piece of paper: "In the case of Katherine Rachelle Vaudrey, we find the cause of death to be . . . accidental."

My lawyer friend jumped to his feet and did a fist pump in the air—mouthing "Yes!"—as if he'd just won a Supreme Court ruling. Turning to me, he whispered loudly, "This means you'll get to keep that funeral money—cha-ching!"

Oh. My. Gosh.

After the trial, Danny DeVito pulled out his "money clip"—a wad of one-dollar bills held together by a weary rubber band—and thumbed for a dog-eared business card, which he handed me in grand gesture.

"Ever need a little legal help (wink-wink), just give me a call."

I left the courtroom and bumped into the detective who had just given testimony. We chatted for a moment, and then I asked a question that had been bugging me.

"Why didn't you mention the witness who saw Katie passed out behind the wheel before the crash?" I asked.

"We were never able to locate him," the officer explained. "He left a voice message at the police station that told us clearly he had seen your daughter unconscious. He sounded shaken on the phone, and he didn't leave any contact information. Perhaps he had a warrant out for his arrest, or perhaps he just forgot."

"Couldn't you trace his call?" I asked.

"We worked with the phone company for two days, trying to do just that," he said. "But in the end, we were unsuccessful. That meant the witness's testimony would be inadmissible as hearsay. I couldn't use it."

I thanked him for his help and then found space down the hallway to be alone. I should have been relieved at the ruling since it meant her death wasn't an "act of God" and the insurance lady wouldn't be asking us to return the death-clause money that had paid Katie's funeral expenses. But instead I felt angry. It would have been worth the funeral money to have my daughter's death go down in the record books as "natural"—the result of the aneurysm—rather than her going on record as just another teen who died from being a careless driver.

◦◦◦

Nights were hard for Tember. In the stillness of Katie's bed, she had space to feel her loss, and every morning I would find a small mountain of spent Kleenex piled next to her bed. It broke my heart to envision her crying herself to sleep night after night, but I was relieved that she wasn't holding back. She was facing her sorrow head-on.

Sam is a reflective, deep-thinking introvert like Scott. His youth pastor and close friends were checking in on him regularly. But it fit his wiring that on many mornings I would find him seeking solace alone in his room, eyes moist, lost in thought.

When college started up in the fall, Bethany got sideswiped by the glaring absence of her kid sister. "On freshman move-in day," she told me over the phone, "I awoke to the sounds of cheering. Outside on the sidewalk, Katie's friends—the four girls she would have shared an apartment with this year—were waving signs and welcoming the new freshmen. Katie should have been down there with them, yelling and waving. She should be here, in this apartment complex with me. It's moments like these when I really miss my sister. We were so excited to be neighbors this year."

The first issue of the *Clause*, APU's college newspaper, featured a front-page story about Katie's death.

"Copies of that newspaper were all over campus," Bethany said, "and everywhere I turned, I was greeted by a photo of Katie smiling up at me. Papers on benches and tables and the sidewalk—people were stepping on photos of my sister! Walking to class was like navigating a minefield of emotions."

Ugh. I had approved the *Clause*'s story and even been interviewed for it. But it had never occurred to me how hard it would be for Bethany to see her sister's face plastered all around campus. The school's attempt to honor one of my daughters had inadvertently created a hardship for another—and probably for Katie's closest friends, too. It never occurred to me to forewarn Bethany. I had never stopped to think what it would be like for her when that article came out.

Of all the kids, Andrea was the most similar to me in how she grieved. She, too, is a verbal processor, and talking about Katie's death helped us both. She and Katie had been so close, and talking with Andrea about my middle daughter was a great relief to me. In too many ways to mention, Andrea had been a gift to our family—and in this one specific way, she continued to be a gift to me.

Matt didn't talk to me very often about his loss; he had Andrea, after all. But one day, more than three months after Katie had died, I learned about something he had been doing to cope.

Katie had been on Matt and Andrea's cell phone plan, and it was costing me forty-five dollars per month to avoid the difficult death chore of canceling her number. In late August, Matt sent our family a group e-mail:

Hey, family,

Today I called Verizon, and I discontinued Katie's phone. If you have been calling her number to hear her voice message like I have been, then I wanted to warn you not to expect her anymore.

Love you, Matt

The mental image of Matt calling Katie's number to listen to his sister's cheery message and hear the sound of her voice brought tears to my eyes. I thought I had been the only one. Perhaps it helped Matt's grief to complete this unpleasant task for me—and to take a step in his own grief process by severing this connection to his sister. It's a bit of torture to be a parent of grown kids who have wounds you can no longer fix for them. *Lord, help them, each one.*

When I finished up the freelance job at my church, I said yes to a permanent writing position on staff, twenty-five hours a week. My normal job of binge-watching episodes of *30 Rock* in sweatpants would have to wait.

Being around people regularly doing work that I loved proved good for me. I worked on the same team as Chris Hurta—the pastor who met us at the hospital and was so helpful on the funeral day.

Since Katie's death, Scott and Chris had become close friends, but I had yet to meet Chris's wife, Kaye. She and I met for a coffee date, and she was a delight. Her frank humor, tender spirit, and genuine sorrow over my loss left a lasting impression on my soul.

"September, even though I didn't know you in May when Katie died," she told me, "I will never forget the moment I learned of her accident that Saturday night. I was sitting in Culver's—the burger joint at the corner of Meacham and Algonquin Road—and Chris called me from church to tell me he was heading to the hospital to meet with you guys. And I prayed for you. Then a week later, after Katie's funeral, Chris brought home the program, and I sat on my bed and pored over every word. And I just felt a connection to you as Katie's mom. I've been praying for you ever since!" She smiled.

"Thanks! We could use it," I told her. "And your husband has been a great solace, especially to Scott. Thanks for sharing him with us!"

"September," she said, looking deep into my eyes, "I never got a chance to know your daughter. Could you help me get to know her now? What was she like?"

How can you not love a woman like Kaye? I gladly obliged her request and filled her ears with a nice assortment of Katie-stories. She listened and laughed and wept.

As we said goodbye that day and I watched Kaye walk away, I sensed I had just met a lifelong friend. And I was right.

37

I TOOK A SHORT TRIP TO CALIFORNIA that fall to connect with our college kids and see Matt and Andrea's new place. They'd moved into a duplex with a nice backyard. Kati Harkin joined us for a barbeque on the last day of my visit, and seeing her was good for my soul. She had been such a faithful friend to Katie—she was like family to us. I wondered, *Do we still hold a place in her life now that Katie is gone?*

After dinner, I walked her to her car. "Kati, I'm so glad you came out here today," I said. "It's so good to see you."

"Me too," she said. "It felt really good to be back with the Vaudreys, just like . . . before."

"You know, honey, it wasn't just because of Katie that we loved having you around all the time. We love *you*. You have always been a welcome addition to our family—you're like a daughter to Scott and me—and I hope it will stay that way, if that's what you want too . . ."

Her eyes filled. "People have been warning me to stay away from you guys because I will only remind you of Katie and make you feel sad," she said.

"What? Oh, honey, we feel just the opposite! Yes, it's true you remind us of Katie—but it brings us joy, not sadness. I love those memories you two shared. We absolutely want you around!"

"Well, this is such a relief!" she said, laughing and wiping tears from her eyes. "A much better prospect for our future! I love you guys, too, and I absolutely want to stay part of your life."

"Phew!" I said. "Glad we straightened that out!" I shuddered to think that this misunderstanding could have resulted in us losing our relationship with this remarkable young woman who had been such a great friend to our daughter.

"Can I tell you about that last night I was with Katie?" she asked.

"Yes, please."

"It was late that last Thursday night, two days before her accident, and she had invited me over to your house to catch up. I hesitated because I had stuff to do early the next morning, but as usual, the girl talked me into coming, and I found myself making the thirty-minute drive out to your house. She had found a Starbucks that stayed open till eleven, and we got in my car and drove there. We ordered coffee and talked until closing. Then we drove back to your house and parked out front and kept talking. We dove into the dreams she'd been having. She told me she planned to go to counseling for them. We planned our upcoming year at APU, and we talked about where each of us needed to get better at life. I vented about all the confusing angles of living at home and how I want to connect more with my family. She told me—and I don't even remember how we got on this topic—that she would certainly—of course—definitely be an organ donor. She tried to talk me into sleeping over for the thousandth time in the BCB [Katie's bed, or the "Big Comfy Bed," as her friends called it]. But I had plans early the next morning, so I held firm. We hugged goodnight. It was after one o'clock when I headed home, my heart full after such rich conversation.

"Then on Friday she invited me over to play Catan with you guys, but I didn't feel like playing Catan, so I stayed home." Her voice grew soft. "And this decision allowed me to keep Thursday—the holiness of it—the way it was. It is unfair to the rest of Katie's friends how perfect of a last visit I got with her. And I am forever grateful."

We hugged. "Thank you so much for sharing that night with me," I said. "I'm so glad we talked—and I'm so glad we get to keep you!"

As she drove away that night, I was struck again by the many blessings that had come to our family by way of our middle daughter—of which Kati Harkin was one of the best.

The hot-pink petunias Katie had planted in my planters in May went crazy that summer, overflowing their pots, reminding me, "Katie was here!" But petunias are warm-weather flowers. They live their short lives with robust abandon, blooming day after day no matter the heat. But they cannot take the cold. They will die at the first frost.

As the autumn days grew shorter and the temperatures at night began to drop, I felt a looming dread. I knew the first Chicago freeze would soon hit, severing this vibrant, living connection to my daughter.

About mid-October, it happened. A heavy overnight rain turned to sleet. The temperature dropped. When I stepped outside the next morning to go to work, Katie's petunias hung encased in a heavy blanket of ice, dead.

I drove to work as usual, but I couldn't get the image of those ice-covered flowers out of my mind. I kept getting weepy at my desk. That afternoon Scott stopped by to say hi, and I told him about the flowers.

"Just call it a day, honey," he said. "Go home. It'll be the first day of work you've missed because of grief. Just go home and take a nap."

I took his advice. I went home and lay down, but I couldn't sleep.

Half an hour later, the doorbell rang. Two neighbor ladies stood outside—Lois from across the street and another woman I'd never met.

"Hello, September," Lois said. "This is Kim. She lives three doors down."

The new woman hugged me. "We heard about Katie's death, and we are so sorry for your loss," she said. "We want to do something for your family. My husband and I own a landscape company, and we want to plant a tree in your yard, something living to remember her by, season after season."

Unbelievable! "What an incredible gift," I said. "Thank you!"

"I don't know why I didn't come over sooner," she said. "I've been meaning to stop by for months."

"Actually, today was the perfect day," I said, explaining about the frozen petunias. "'Something living to remember her by . . .' God's timing, I'd say!" We hugged again and I thanked them both.

Three days later, a tall, stately red maple was planted along our drive. And today, as the seasons come and go, we are reminded not only of the daughter we lost but also of a tenderhearted God who shows His love through unsuspecting neighbors on frosty autumn afternoons.

The holidays were approaching—the hardest of the Awful Firsts. How would we acknowledge Katie's absence? Is it okay to cry on a happy holiday? Is it okay to have fun when your daughter is gone? Scott and I set about planning how to navigate the conflicting styles of grief that were inevitable in a large family. At Thanksgiving, I hoped for a "moment," some sort of shared remembrance of Katie with the kids. Scott was worried I would put expectations on them, prying uninvited into their still-raw spaces of grief. Some were more reticent to share than others. Or as Scott put it, "Some want to avoid, while others want a grief-o-rama." (Any guesses which camp I fell into?)

Matt, Andrea, Bethany, and my parents flew into town for Thanksgiving weekend, which gave the house a nice fullness. The kids stepped up to take on the roles Katie had filled—namely table-setting artist and pie chef. We distracted ourselves with cooking and chatting and playing games, and then—when the turkey came out of the oven—with carving, gravy making, and the last-minute scurry of getting everything onto the table. When at last we sat down to our Thanksgiving dinner and joined hands for prayer, it hit. She was gone.

In the stillness, the gaping hole of Katie's absence could no longer be ignored. We sat in the tension between being thankful—for so much—and being horrified that this was really our life.

Scott prayed. By "amen," we were all wiping our eyes.

We got through dinner, and toward the end of the meal, Scott set down his fork.

"We're all acutely feeling Katie's absence at our table—and the pain this brings. But we're also deeply grateful for so many things. Let's go around the table twice this year: First, each of us can give a brief check-in with how we're doing with our Katie stuff. And then let's go around again and share what we are most thankful for this year."

Yes! Scott had set the stage for each of us to open up to whatever degree we wanted.

For the next hour, we took turns reflecting on the pain of this year, and also on its beauty. We were rookies at this, but each of us was practicing the balance of holding our sorrow in one hand while embracing our joy in the other.

～⟨ℰ⟩~

Christmas was the biggie of the Awful Firsts. For us, it's always been a holiday rich in Vaudrey traditions—buying gifts and wrapping them prankishly, making fudge, baking pecan-pie squares, watching *A Christmas Story*, and taking an annual family photo in front of our freshly cut Christmas tree. Our celebration always culminated in a soulful Christmas Eve service at church and a laughter-filled Christmas morning.

As the holiday approached, I didn't try to fight the tide of grief swelling inside. I invited it in and kept low expectations for myself and our family. To shore up for each day, I stole a few moments in the mornings beneath the amber glow of the Christmas tree lights. Coffee cup in hand and Johnny Mathis singing "White Christmas" in the background, I basked in the stillness of dawn, taking small sips of my grief and extending myself toward God as best I could. My prayer was two words: *Carry me.*

The weekend after Thanksgiving, I had tackled decorating the Christmas tree, which for our family is a 3-D scrapbook of family memories. The kids and I had made ornaments together every year throughout their childhoods, and each of them always hung their own ornaments when we decorated the tree. The college kids would hang theirs once they arrived home after finals.

But Katie wasn't coming home. I lifted her ornaments one by one from their boxes and hung them on our tree—her tiny hazelnut mouse in his walnut-shell bed, her macaroni angel, the wooden sled with the cheery Christmas penguin she had painted just last year, and the brass Christmas tree with the photo of Katie as a baby. Finally, I hung her sterling silver cradle, a gift from my parents on her very first Christmas. The emptiness of that cradle was illuminated by the warm glow of the tree lights, and I could just make out the inscription: "Katie, 2-4-1989."

I hung her red stocking—with its wooly Christmas lamb on the front and its white fake-fur cuff along the top—in its usual place between

Bethany's stocking with the fluffy bunny and Sam's stocking with the Christmas moose. On Christmas morning, it would hang empty when all the other stockings were packed with goodies. That wouldn't do.

I devised a plan. With money we would normally have spent on Katie's Christmas gifts, I went online and purchased gifts from World Vision's Christmas catalog for kids in developing countries. I selected items Katie might have chosen—a bicycle for a girl in India to ride safely to school, a wheelchair for a child afflicted by polio in Mexico, warm clothing for children in Mongolia, school tuition for a girl in Africa, a small flock of chickens to provide eggs for a family in South America.

And for Katie's uncle Greg, a department store gift card to buy bingo prizes for his group home. She would definitely approve.

Six gifts in all. I made certificates with descriptions of each gift, rolled them up into scrolls, and planned to sneak them into Katie's stocking early Christmas morning.

~❧~

What to do about the annual family photo in front of the Christmas tree? We'd taken this photo every year since Matt was a baby, and now twenty-four framed pictures lined our hallway. Would it be wrong to take the photo without Katie? Should we do something different this year? Should we skip the photo altogether? Scott and I consulted the kids.

"We're still a family," Matt said. "Take the photo. Plus Katie would not want to be the one responsible for wrecking the tradition."

We took the photo, our lips smiling but our eyes unable to mask the pain. We did our best—with limited success—not to let our sorrow have the final say.

~❧~

On Christmas morning before the kids awoke, Scott and I followed our usual routine: We started a pot of coffee, built a fire in the fireplace, made our traditional Christmas pastry—a peach flip—and set out a Santa gift for each kid, a tradition we'd kept going long past the age when they knew about Santa. I filled the stockings and slipped the six scrolls into Katie's, which gave it a pleasing plumpness and left me feeling clever and satisfied.

Then, as we do every year, Scott took the stockings down from the mantel and placed them in front of each Santa gift—our way of marking which gift belonged to which person. But of course there was no Santa gift for Katie. Her stocking now hung all alone on the mantel, like the kid chosen last in PE or the person standing alone at the dance.

Neither Scott nor I had prepared for this sight. We stood there staring, and then we turned to each other, and we hugged and we cried.

"I just hate this," he said at last. "I will never not hate it."

"Yep. This is not how life should be."

"Ever."

"Ever."

The kids were still asleep, so we took some time to be sad and to collect ourselves. I sat down to write. Scott sat in his rocking chair, eyes closed, rocking, rocking. Then he got his camera out of the hall closet and snapped a poignant photo of Katie's stocking hanging there, all alone.

Our early morning moments for grieving worked. When the kids awoke, Scott and I were in good shape, and we all enjoyed a tender but beautiful Christmas morning.

After the kids had unpacked their stockings, I took Katie's down from the mantel and handed out the scrolls inside. Each person opened theirs and read aloud what had been given on their sister's behalf. It wasn't a heavy ceremony, though a bit awkward to be sure. Still the kids went along with my stocking plan, and it gave us a moment to acknowledge our girl and give voice to her absence—but in a positive way that didn't tank our morning. Another step forward.

And in Seattle that morning, in his nursing home room, my brother, Greg, opened the gift card given in Katie's honor.

"You should have seen the proud look on his face," my mom told me later on the phone. "He stopped everything and wheeled his way down the hall to find the social director and hand him the card. 'Buy some good Bingo prizes with this,' he had said. 'It's from my niece. She really loved me.'"

One bright spot from that first Christmas deserves some backstory. Tember was still having a rough time sleeping at night—even in Katie's big bed. The piles of spent Kleenex on her nightstand each morning had continued unabated. Bethany, too, had been struggling to sleep since Katie's death. Her roommates had gotten her a kitten to help her sleep at night—and it had worked.

Tember had wanted a cat for years. But Scott is not a cat person. ("If a cat pees in the house, we'll have to burn the whole house down to get rid of the smell.") Never one to miss an opportunity, Tember saw a glimmer of hope in her long-standing quest for a cat. She began dropping strategic hints. She'd bat her big brown eyes at her dad and say, "If only I had a cat like Bethany's to keep me company in bed at night . . ."

Well, shoot. Scott knew he was sunk. He loved Tember more than he hated cats. So on Christmas morning, ol' softy Santa gave Tember a tiny grey kitten of her very own—"to comfort you at night," he smirked.

Lo and behold, it worked. Felipé "Phil" the cat fell in love with Tember from day one, and he snuggled up around her neck in bed each night. The Kleenex piles disappeared. For Tember and Bethany, a cat turned out to be just the trick.

38

A FEW WEEKS INTO THE NEW YEAR, I dreamed about Katie. My dreams of her were growing increasingly rare, so I was thankful for the scene that unfolded in my mind as I slept.

Katie showed up at my bedroom door. She'd been granted a day pass from heaven to spend with me! And she wanted to spend it working on a piece of interactive art together—a black wooden board with a pillow built into the middle of it.

"The pillow is for people to punch, to help them express painful emotions," she explained. "It's not good to leave your feelings bottled up, Mom."

As we sat together on my bedroom floor stuffing the pillow, large clumps of my hair began falling out and landing on my lap.

I felt embarrassed. "It's just from the grief," I said.

"It's all right, Mom," she said. "We can use it for the pillow! Your hair will help soften the blow for people." She scooped up the clumps of my hair and pushed them into the pillow, and I was glad she thought they could be helpful.

"What is it like in heaven?" I asked. "Can you see us down here?"

"Yes," she said. "There is a panel, sort of like a trapdoor, that we can pull open and look down into if we want to." She said this hesitantly, as though she didn't want to hurt my feelings, but why would anyone from heaven want to look down?

Then I awoke. How sweet it was to be "with" Katie! The dream had been so vivid that I gave my hair a tug to be sure it was just a dream, but nothing fell out.

Katie's twentieth birthday rolled around a couple of weeks later, on February 4—another Awful First I had been dreading. I had planned some events to remember our girl: a grief date with Kaye for lunch and then Katie's favorite birthday meal (tater tot casserole) for dinner with the kids, and afterward Katie's birthday dessert of choice, my homemade chocolate cheesecake.

But all through the day, I kept thinking about the dream. *Is there really a trapdoor in heaven? Is she peeking down at me? What is her heavenly birthday like? Does it involve chocolate cheesecake?* How I wished I could open that door and peer into heaven just to see her one more time.

A month or so after my lost hair/trapdoor dream, I discovered something that really triggered my "weird meter." When I put my hair into a ponytail one morning, the elastic holder easily looped three times around my hair. Normally, I can barely loop it twice because my hair is thick. *Bizarre.* I pulled out the ponytail holder, parted my hair on the opposite side, and looked in the mirror. Lo and behold, hundreds of new baby hairs were sticking out all over my head, each about a half-inch long, creating a halo effect, like a baby chick. *Unbelievable! I've actually lost a ton of hair!* Not in clumps like in the dream, but a little at a time, undetected. And now it was starting to grow back. The grief had taken its toll—in ways I hadn't even noticed.

Grief took a physical toll in other ways as well. Early on, Scott and

I both lost a lot of weight. (It eventually came back, of course!) We also developed deep indentations in our thumbnails. I'd heard that this could result from severe trauma. It took months for these indentations to grow out—and then wave after wave of new indentations would follow as the aftershocks of our trauma continued. We both bear ridges on our thumbnails to this day.

The physical exhaustion, too, was surprising. No matter how much sleep I got on any given night, that entire first year was marked by a deep, bone-tired fatigue.

How intricately entwined we are—minds, bodies, and souls.

Friends found creative ways to show their love. My friend Sandy BeLow invited me over for a surprise outing one sunny spring day.

"Meet me at my house at nine," she said. "And wear shoes that can get dirty." She had piqued my curiosity.

At nine o'clock sharp, I entered Sandy's kitchen, where she was packing an ice chest.

"We're going on a picnic," she said, a gleam in her eyes. The ice chest had a greater ratio of carrots to regular food—which gave me a hopeful hint. Sandy knew I was a horse lover.

Sure enough, she was taking me to the ranch where her daughter took riding lessons.

"It's springtime," she said, "and you simply must see the new foals!"

And so on a sunny Saturday, we ate our picnic lunches and used our carrots to bribe several broodmares close to the fence so we could properly ogle their adorable, gangly, fuzz-coated babies. We told stories and laughed hard, as we always do. And we took long walks in the field. Then in the barn, leaning on the gate as a warm breeze blew in from the pasture, Sandy asked me about Katie and listened with soulful eyes as I talked and laughed and cried.

Laughter and tears. Both/and. They make for good friends.

As spring unfolded, we planned a family trip to California for Bethany's college graduation on May 9. Mother's Day was May 10—my first without Katie. I was adamant that this Awful First not interfere with our celebration of Bethany. I was so proud of all she had accomplished, especially after this horrid year. I made plans to pre-grieve the Katie part of my Mother's Day at the crash site before we flew to California.

The last time I'd visited the site, I had noticed that the laminated photo of Katie hadn't weathered its first Chicago winter very well. I went to FedEx to laminate a new eight-by-ten-inch print of Katie.

On the day before our family flew out to California, my friend Kaye accompanied me to the crash site. We met at my house, and she helped me load a shovel and some potted flowers into my minivan. I tucked the photo into my purse, and off we drove.

But when we arrived at the site, I discovered that the original photo was just a five-by-seven—much smaller than my freshly laminated replacement. I removed the weather-beaten photo and thumbtacked the new one onto the small wooden cross. It looked huge! It reminded me of a campaign poster, as if Katie's head were popping out of the grass, saying, "Vote for me!" Kaye and I burst out laughing.

It was the perfect joke for a girl who had loved being in photos, whose thinly veiled attempt at being "caught" on film had led to her classic quote, "Are you *filming* me?" I could almost hear Katie giggling at the inside joke of the campaign poster planted on the side of the road for all to see.

The photo smiled up at us as we planted pink petunias and some orange tiger lilies around Katie's crosses. They mingled with the yellow dandelions and tiny purple violets nestled in the wild grasses.

When we were done, Kaye took a Mother's Day photo.

Then we drove to a nearby forest preserve, hiked a loop of trails, and came across a solitary picnic bench, where we stopped to pray.

"Father, we are surviving, and I think we will live," I said, "but I hate that Katie is gone. This side of heaven, I will never understand how her death was a good plan. I just want her back.

"You are the God of time and space. You see the landscape of eternity. I am asking You, one final time, for Mother's Day: *Turn back the clock.* Give Katie a symptom, a sign of her aneurysm. We will rush her to the hospital, and she will be saved, and no one will be the wiser. Please, please, I am begging You. Turn back the clock!"

I waited.

"And if You don't turn back the clock, as I think You will not," I said, "help me let go of the life I wish I had, the life I loved so deeply. Help me embrace this uninvited life You offer me, the life that is still mine to live."

❧

Three days later at APU, as the setting sun cast its rosy-gold rays on the San Gabriel Mountains behind APU's Cougar Stadium, our Bethany walked across the stage in cap and gown to receive her diploma. In spite of just having lost her sister, she had carried a huge academic load, worked long hours at two jobs, and still graduated summa cum laude. Bethany had prevailed. What a warrior she had been.

The pre-grieving had done its healing work. On Sunday—Mother's Day—I rose early and stepped outside. I knew my friends Lynne and Kaye were praying for me back in Chicago on this day. And I knew Sandy and my mom were praying too. Once again I was being carried. I felt their prayers.

The perfume of the tropical flowers blooming in the hotel courtyard hung in the sultry morning air. The sun was just appearing above the horizon, casting a vacant purple glow and chasing away the last of the stars. The sting of this "first" was already behind me.

Thank You, Father, for the gift of being a mom to these five kids of mine. Thank You for each one. And thank You for nineteen years with Katie.

I stepped back inside, ready to share another Mother's Day as a family—and to celebrate my firstborn daughter, the lovely Miss Bethany Paige.

39

ON MEMORIAL DAY—just six days ahead of the one-year mark of Katie's death—our doorbell rang. Outside on our sidewalk stood two landscape workers bookending a huge tree in a giant pot. The tree towered over their heads, and white lilac blossoms hung heavy from its upper branches.

"Mrs. Vaudrey?" one of them asked, extending a card and receiving slip toward me. "This is for you. Can you sign here, please?"

I signed the slip. *Who is this from?*

"Where would you like us to put it?" he asked. I directed them to our back deck and thanked them.

Scott, Sam, and Tember gathered around as I opened the card and read it aloud:

Dear Vaudrey Family,
This time of year reminds us all of losing Katie just one year ago. I have spent a lot of time thinking about your family and praying for you in this season. Our heavenly Father knows and sees all you are going through. You are deeply loved.

The painting of Katie's I remember the most is the one Scott mentioned she had been painting in the backyard—The Bleeding Tree. *Your APU family thought you might plant this smaller tree in your backyard to remember and celebrate again how deeply your amazing daughter, sister, and friend impacted our lives for the better. One year later, we continue to remember, continue to miss, and continue to hope in life bigger than just the here and now. We hope this flowering Japanese lilac tree will remind you of your daughter, who brought beauty and joy into every space she entered.*

Grace and peace from all of APU,

Woody Morwood
Campus Pastor, Azusa Pacific University

We were deeply moved. Our girl was not forgotten. And clearly trees were a theme for our family.

Matt, Andrea, and Bethany were coming to town to commemorate with us the first anniversary of Katie's death. To distract myself from the pain of this looming landmark, I'd been doing some spring cleaning. On the morning of May 30—the day the kids were to arrive and the eve of the one-year mark—I took a load of stuff to Goodwill. On my way home, something on the side of the road caught my eye. At first I thought it was a squirrel—but the rings on its tail made me do a double take. A baby raccoon was wandering alone on the edge of the busy street.

All my life, I have been a lover of animals. I grew up on a farm, and as an adult, my obsession with animals has not waned. I brought all manner of pets into our home over the years "for the kids"—seven dogs, seven cats, innumerable guinea pigs, a lizard, a rabbit, tropical fish, exotic birds, and even a pygmy hedgehog. Not all at once, mind you. But still . . .

So when I spotted a baby raccoon in harm's way, maternal instinct trumped reason. All thoughts of Katie-sadness shoved aside, I pulled over, parked on the side of the road, and hurried toward the little one, who screamed like a banshee when I picked her up. Once I took off my sweatshirt and wrapped her in it, she settled down.

I know "technically" you're supposed to leave orphaned wild animals alone, but right away I noticed that this tiny raccoon was dehydrated and skinny. Her nose was dry, her eyes dull, her belly sunken, and her gait unsteady. My guess was she'd probably lost her mother a few days prior and had finally left her nest in search of water or food. I scoured the woods beside the road, listening carefully for any rustling of leaves, but there was no sign of brothers, sisters, or mom. If I left the baby there, she'd be roadkill by dusk. So I did what any sane person would do.

I brought home a wild raccoon.

Suffice it to say this wasn't my first such adventure with wild critters. It seems I have a slight reputation in my family for bringing home strays. My children are convinced that this habit of mine will be the end of me someday—that I will either live to be 105 or I will be mauled by a wild animal that I thought was my new friend.

Scott and the kids feigned shock when I showed them my tiny new acquisition. I pulled out our old rabbit cage (I knew it would come in handy again someday!) and set it up.

When I unwrapped the raccoon from my sweatshirt, she was ticked off—frightened beyond words, no doubt, and crazed with hunger. I wrapped her in a towel and placed her in the cage with a bowl of water; then I drove to Petco and picked up some cans of kitten milk and a teeny bottle. When I returned home, the baby sucked down the warmed formula in a heartbeat and fell fast asleep in my lap. I did a quick examination of my fuzzy little ward. She was indeed a girl, and I determined by her emerging teeth and a quick Google search that she was about five weeks old. Within an hour, she was awake again and hungry, her nose cold and wet like a dog's, her eyes bright, her gait more steady, and her rage transformed to affection for her favorite new bottle holder—me.

That afternoon, when the California kids arrived from O'Hare, I introduced them to my new charge. "It's Gloria!" Bethany declared, recalling illustrations of the baby badger with the black mask in her favorite childhood book, *Bread and Jam for Frances*. Gloria she became.

Thus began my summer as Gloria's mother. And Petco's "raccoon lady."

The next morning—the one-year mark of Katie's death—I was not drowning in sorrow as I'd feared but excited to be bottle-feeding a hungry, curious, masked furry baby, cuter than words, which gazed at me with adoring eyes from behind her little bottle and patted my fingers with her tiny hands.

The gift of Gloria did not escape me. From the outside, it might have appeared that I was caring for her, providing her with what she needed to survive. But really—on that particular day and for a woman who had loved animals her entire life—who was caring for whom? God's fingerprints were all over this gift.

When Gloria finished her morning bottle, I carried her into the backyard and sat down in the grass to let her play. The scent of the earth and the freshly cut lawn drew me back to just over a year ago, to my first morning home from the hospital and my 4 a.m. rantings to God. I had wanted to throw myself facedown in the dew-soaked grass, grab God by the ankles, and have it out with Him. But I had resisted. *Undignified. Wet grass . . .*

I felt drawn again to lay myself before Him, though not to rail. Over the past twelve months, I had worn myself ragged with the sobbing. No angry or heartbroken words had gone unspoken, no agony unexpressed. And I was grateful for the many gifts God had tucked into the folds of this past year, one of which now nipped and gnawed on my ankle.

But not everything was resolved between God and me. I felt Him calling—calling me to . . . well, I wasn't sure to what.

God, You have been so amazingly good and kind at every turn of this year. But I am still shocked that Katie is gone. You could have prevented this, but You didn't! You allowed it, and can I just say that, from my vantage point, it was a stupid plan. I hate that this is our reality.

I'm not pulling away from You; but nor am I ready to roll over, to resign, to surrender to this new life that lies before me.

Not now, not yet.

∼◎∽

That night Scott and I laid our heads on our pillows.

"We're one year out," I said. "How can I still be shocked that this is real?"

"I wonder if we will always be shocked," Scott said. "This will never feel normal."

"Never. I'm so raw. I'm still horrified that she's gone."

"Yep. There are no words."

"But looking back over this past year, my heart feels warm and full, too. Every time I thought I couldn't survive this, God showed up in some way. He kept trumping our pain with His goodness. People's kindnesses toward us, the tree we received last fall on the very day Katie's petunias froze, Gloria showing up yesterday . . ."

"It's the paradox," Scott said. "It's the both/and. So awful that I will never understand, and so beautiful that I am shocked."

The "new normal" wasn't new anymore. Nor did it yet feel normal. I was still resisting. I could not yet bring myself to surrender, to let go of my girl—whatever that actually meant. But I felt more certain than ever that God, endlessly patient and good, would not let go of me.

Holding on, letting go . . .

"We have this hope as an anchor for the soul, firm and secure."[3]

It felt good to fall asleep with hope.

---

[3]Hebrews 6:19

cadmium green light

['kad-mee-uhm green lahyt] / a bright
light green with warm yellow undertones

Neon brushstrokes against skeletal bark,

the first leaf buds of spring cannot help but draw our eyes.

That which appears long dead isn't dead at all.

It simply waits, poised,

ready to erupt in a cacophony of color.

Grief . . . cultivates the soil for the seeds of joy.

ANN VOSKAMP

A broken heart is not the end of anything. It's the
beginning of everything. Find the beautiful, right in
the middle of the mess. March into the mess.

GLENNON DOYLE MELTON

40

ON THE FIRST MORNING OF YEAR TWO, I stepped onto the back deck. Before me, a blizzard of cottonwood seeds drifted through the air like miniature angels, their tufts of white stark against the backdrop of towering trees and a cerulean blue sky. "I am good . . ." I had sensed God say a year ago as I stood on that ambulance bay staggering under the weight of what we were facing.

He had been good. What a year it had been. Our hearts were broken, but we had survived. I stared into year two with a healthy dollop of curiosity—and some respectable caution.

Two things troubled me about entering year two. First, I didn't like that it was now more than a year since Katie had died. For the past twelve months, if someone asked me, "When did your daughter pass away?" I had found comfort in being able to answer them in months: "Four months ago" or "Seven months ago." Their stunned reactions matched the degree of shock I felt inside. But now I would be answering, "A year and a half ago," which made Katie's death seem like a thing of the past—a part of history—when it was still shocking news to me.

Second, my very identity had been rattled. Who was I in this new day? I used to be Mother of Five. I'd taken a little pride in that, to be honest. "Five" generated raised eyebrows, a few jokes about birth control, and some "How do you manage?" incredulity. Frankly, I had enjoyed the attention, and I was so proud of our lively, well-behaved gaggle of kids.

But now people viewed me not as Mother of Five but as Mother Whose Child Died, and this generally freaked them out. I was living their worst fears. I frightened them.

Over the past year, I had met a few people who had lost a loved one and seemed to wear that loss proudly, like a purple heart. It was as if their tragedy had become their new identity. They bent every conversation back to their pain and compared their experiences to everyone else's. I saw hints of this propensity in myself, and it alarmed me.

But I had also met plenty of other people who'd lost loved ones and responded just the opposite. They grieved wholeheartedly and allowed the fertile soil of sorrow to grow a depth of character in their souls that I admired. At work I met a young woman whose sister had committed suicide three years before by drowning herself in Lake Michigan—in winter. My friend had gone to the morgue with her cousin and siblings to identify her sister's body. I can only imagine the horror this must have been for her. She and I shared occasional conversations about our losses. Even though she was twenty years my junior, I found she possessed an "old soul" wisdom, a joyful countenance, and a tender peace that gave me hope. Her loss had not ruined her. It had grown her.

I began to notice that the people I looked up to most had this in common: Life had dealt them deep pain or disappointment, from the death of a loved one or from divorce or a significant illness or the demands of raising a special-needs child—any type of life-altering loss. But rather than becoming stalled in their grief or letting it drive them to bitterness, over time they became more alive, more joyful, and wiser than might have been possible before they became acquainted with heartache. They had allowed their sorrow to do its transforming work in their souls. They had stewarded their pain well. I wanted to be like those people.

I was Mother of Five. I was also Mother Whose Child Died. But neither of these roles, frankly, was adequate as an identity. Each was just a title determined by circumstances. Who was I beyond these circumstances? I had no clue. Clearly I had work to do in year two.

Standing on the deck, I reached out and caught one of the cottonwood seeds as it floated by. Just a tiny seed, shorter than a grain of rice and half as fat, surrounded by the snowy down that gave it flight. The cottonwood seed had no control whatsoever over its circumstances; the wind simply shook it free from the tree, then blew it around until, if lucky, it landed on good soil and sprouted and grew. Yet this unassuming little seed carried the potential to be transformed into something that far surpassed its current state. It had everything necessary to become one of the most resilient, thriving trees in North America.

I felt like this drifting cottonwood seed, with no control over the circumstances that had shaken me from the beautiful life I had known. But unlike this tiny seed, I wasn't dependent upon luck to provide me good soil. My circumstances themselves had planted me in soil that held the most growth-producing potential of all: pain. Could I, like the seed, be transformed by the soil of Katie's death? Could I be that resilient? Could I actually thrive?

I lifted the tiny tuft of down and blew it from my fingertips. It rose over the lawn and mingled with its angel neighbors. A gentle breeze carried it up and out of sight.

◦◦◦

My girlfriend Lynne invited Kaye, Bethany, and me over for an intimate "Welcome to Year Two" lunch. (Tember would have joined us, but she was in school.) After we ate, Lynne slid a small ice-blue box my way. I untied the white silk ribbon and lifted the lid. Nestled inside was a sterling silver anchor hanging from a silver chain.

"'An anchor for the soul,'" Lynne said, "from your girlfriends and me."

My eyes filled. "Thank you. God truly has been our Anchor. And you guys have been His tangible way of showing up throughout this mess. I am so grateful." I hugged Lynne and Kaye and clasped the necklace around my neck.

Then Lynne asked a good question: "As you enter this next year, what is it you want?"

I thought of the cottonwood seed. I thought of the grief heroes I knew who had let their loss transform them. While I didn't have a clue about how to let my grief transform me, I knew two practical things I needed for the journey that lay ahead.

"I want to sleep. I feel like I've been running on adrenaline for a year. I am bone-tired. I could sleep for a month. And I want to laugh. I need to laugh. I have overdosed on sorrow. I want to throw back my head and belly laugh until I can't breathe. I am just aching to laugh."

❧

My grief tide began to ebb for longer periods of time, making life more bearable and allowing me to catch my breath in between days of deep sorrow. Sleep brought greater rest. Laughter felt less out of place and became more reflexive. And the number of days in which I cried off my mascara before lunchtime decreased!

But stepping into year two was a bit like coming out of surgical anesthesia. As the fog-like numbness of year one lifted, the hazy protection that it had offered disappeared as well. In some ways, I felt my sorrow more acutely, and my relationship with joy remained unresolved, like a shadow slipping through my fingers.

"*Your* joy is one of the main ingredients to this home's climate," Katie had written in my Mother's Day card just twenty days before she died. "Don't underestimate your contribution!"

What irony. My joy had been leveled by the loss of the very girl who had touted its merits. Was it gone for good? Was I permanently joy disabled?

Since childhood, I had hidden behind "happy" whenever life got painful, but in recent years, I had begun facing some of my own areas of brokenness head-on. To my surprise, I realized that as my capacity to face pain had increased, my capacity for joy had grown deeper too. While I still had far to go, I had begun experiencing life more intensely by saying yes to all that it means to be human: joy, pain, sorrow, love, anger, laughter—a full painter's palette of emotions.

But the death of a child is an enormous buzzkill. How would I fill the gaping wound in my soul that Katie's death had created?

Bitterness would fill it nicely. Anger at God, too. Self-pity—wow, I could fill it to the rim in a heartbeat if I turned to self-pity. Is that what I'd choose?

❧

One balmy night in August, my fear that I might be permanently joy disabled was rebuffed in a small but significant way. I had experienced a couple of good weeks in a row—I'd had a stronger ability to focus, fewer debilitating bouts of tears, and fewer moments when I caught myself reliving some of the more graphic hospital images. As I walked to my car after a fantastic worship service at church and a fun conversation with Kaye, a foreign feeling swept over me—the butterflies-in-your-stomach feeling that comes upon you when the world is good and beautiful and you are so filled with gratitude that you might burst.

I stopped in my tracks. I knew this feeling. There in the muggy haze of a Midwest sunset, I remembered it.

Joy.

Perhaps—just perhaps—the scales in my life were beginning to tip. Perhaps, despite all that had happened, my life was beginning to hold more joy than pain. Not a lot more, mind you. But more.

I climbed into my minivan and lay my forehead on the steering wheel. For the first time in more than fifteen months, the tears I wept were tears of joy.

41

BETHANY FLEW HOME for a few weeks' vacation late that summer. One evening around bedtime, she knocked on our bedroom door. I opened it, and there stood our girl, her eyes sunken, her face white.

"My head is killing me," she said. "This is the worst headache I've ever had."

Scott and I exchanged glances. I'd often heard him say that, in the

ER, whenever someone describes a headache as "the worst in my life," right away doctors think aneurysm.

"I'm taking her in," I said to Scott. He knows I like to be the one who brings the kids to the doctor, and he obliges me.

"It is likely just a regular headache—aneurysms are almost never hereditary. But yes, take her in. I'll keep my cell phone on."

"I'll call you once I know more."

<hr />

As soon as the admitting nurse in the ER learned about Bethany's family history, everyone began to scurry. A tech whisked her back to see the doctor, who quickly ran a few tests, ordered an IV line, and then performed a spinal tap to check for any signs of blood in her spinal fluid.

When the results of the tap were back, the doctor approached. "We found trace samples of blood in your spinal fluid," she said. "We're admitting you to determine the cause."

I knew what one cause could be: a leaking cerebral aneurysm.

Bethany and I looked at each other. "This is like a sick déjà vu," she said.

Lightning had already struck our family once; why wouldn't it strike us twice?

They wheeled Bethany away to CT, and I called Scott.

<hr />

Seven days of hospitalization and myriad tests and procedures later, this story had a happy ending. They determined that the blood in Bethany's spinal fluid was caused by the ER spinal tap itself, as sometimes occurs, and was easily remedied with a simple procedure. Once the leak healed, Bethany's headache—just a really bad headache made worse by the leaky tap—abated, and we brought her home. But it had been a scary week, and it uncovered an ugly little something in me—a resistance to prayer.

One of the tests they had run, an angiogram, is a procedure with some degree of risk. I wanted to pray for Bethany's safety, but this setting—a daughter in a hospital with a crisis related to her head—felt like a rerun of Katie's ordeal, and it brought back memories of my futile begging for God to heal my middle child. God hadn't healed Katie. What was wrong with my prayers? Were they jinxed? Was God impotent? This time around, I couldn't bring myself to pray.

Kaye and Chris had come to the hospital to be with us during Bethany's angiogram, and Kaye sat with me as they wheeled our daughter away.

"My track record for praying for a hospitalized daughter with head pain isn't so great," I told her. "Will you pray?"

"Absolutely," she said. "But just so you know, God isn't offended by your resistance. It makes sense. And we don't just pray for the sake of others—for Katie or for Bethany. We pray for our own sakes, too, because He invites us to trust Him with every part of our lives, regardless of the outcome."

Kaye prayed for Bethany. When she was through, I added timidly, "Father, help me surrender this daughter of mine into Your care. And I ask You, heal her."

When you lose one kid, it becomes very tempting to try to control the world, when in reality you can't. Sitting in that waiting room, I didn't pray out of a certainty that it would change Bethany's outcome. I prayed out of a desire to stay openhanded toward God and toward life.

Today when I pray, I sometimes still beg. God invites us to be honest about what we want, after all. But my experiences with both Bethany (who got better) and Katie (who didn't) broadened my understanding of prayer. God is not a celestial gum-ball machine—insert your request in the slot, get your guaranteed answer out of the magical little metal door. Sometimes the answer we receive isn't a yes. It's a no. And the no can break our hearts.

But the yes or the no isn't the point.

As much as I hate the answer I got when I prayed for Katie, I can't call foul. God never guaranteed me a lifetime with her. He never promised me *any* of the blessings I get to treasure every day. He promises us comfort in sorrow, strength when our own fails, inexplicable peace, His presence in storms, and life in all its fullness for those who follow Him—but not a pain-free life. And the things He promises, He delivers.

I am slowly becoming open to the possibility that God promised me something better than what I had begged Him for. It will never feel "better than" to me this side of eternity. I suspect I will always wish He had just given me my dang yes, and I will always hate the no I received. What mama wouldn't? But I am learning to rest in knowing that some-day beyond this life, I will receive a satisfying answer for each no I have been given. Even the Katie no. Until then, for me, prayer will be about surrender—accepting the answers I get—and then watching for the un-expected ways God shows up, creating beauty even in the worst situations.

42

I MADE REGULAR TREKS to the crash site during year two—sometimes with friends or family, but often alone. Each time, I brought flowers, but I never knew what else I should do. Was there a right way to mark my visits? A ritual I should be following? The setting—with cars whipping by at fifty-five miles per hour—didn't exactly lend itself to moments of serenity. Nonetheless I liked having a place to make an official—though awkward—attempt at ceremony in honoring my daughter.

When I visited the site in early fall, I found that the utilities company was expanding its underground wires along the ditch in front of the crash site, and someone had moved the crosses farther back from the road. When I returned again a month later, the iron cross was knocked down, and a piece of it had broken off. The white cross and its campaign-poster photo of my daughter were gone altogether. Construction was beginning in the field behind the site, and the harsh clanging of bulldozers and dump trucks added to the less-than-serene setting of speeding cars, old beer cans, and stray plastic grocery sacks. It was too much. I lingered only long enough to push the iron cross back into the dirt, arrange my flowers around its base, and say a quick prayer.

❧

"What should we do with Katie's Christmas stocking this year?" I asked Scott one evening in early December. "Maybe we could do a variation of the scrolls. We could let each of the kids pick out which World Vision gift to give on Katie's behalf. What do you think?"

Scott listened intently, then chose his words carefully before he spoke. "This year, hon, I'm wondering if it's the right thing to fill her stocking at all. We can still designate that money to some good causes if you'd like, but is there a chance that filling her stocking is hindering you from facing the full reality that Katie is gone? Perhaps this year, we should let it hang empty."

His words surprised me and triggered my usual defensiveness. *Who, me? Avoiding our reality?* But as I caught my breath, I rummaged around inside my soul, and something in his words rang true. *Dang. He was right.*

I had worked so hard to lean into the pain of losing a child, to not stuff or anesthetize, to pre-grieve before Mother's Day, and all that. I had tried to be so purposeful in my grief. But sometimes even purposefulness can be blind.

Last Christmas, an empty stocking was too much. The clever scrolls had been just the thing to help me through. But a year later, I was in better shape. Was repeating the scrolls my way of avoiding? Sure, it might look like a beautiful little tradition on the outside, but down deep, was I now using it as a crutch? A centerpiece?

Scott's gentle words exposed that I was not impervious to creating the beginnings of an unhelpful shrine. I knew in my gut he was right. *Curses!*

This year, for the health of my own grief journey, I needed to let the stocking go empty.

So on Christmas morning when the kids awoke, Katie's stocking hung in its rightful place on our mantel, but with no scrolls masking its emptiness. I explained why to the kids, and they understood—and maybe looked a little relieved that their mama was trying to move toward acceptance rather than settling for distraction or denial. We would pick up the scrolls again next year, and the year after that. They were a good tradition. But for this year, it felt painfully right to let Katie's stocking hang empty on the mantel.

The thermometer on the back deck registered single digits. Fresh snowflakes were falling, covering the blanket of old snow that had already staked its claim in our yard. Scott and the kids were at work and at school, but I had taken the day off. It was February 4, Katie's birthday.

I built a fire in the fireplace, poured a fresh cup of coffee, and snuggled under a quilt on the family room sofa, feeling drenched with gratitude for all our years with Katie.

She would have turned twenty-one today. She'd been looking forward to this particular birthday since she was in her teens, and no doubt she would have celebrated it with abandon. Matt, Andrea, and Bethany likely would have taken her out for her first drink in a bar—probably some fruity pink concoction with a little paper umbrella and a maraschino cherry. There would have been plenty of laughter, lots of selfies with friends posted to Facebook, and gifts—the girl loved presents. And had I flown to California for her big day, I would have made her our traditional birthday dessert—chocolate cheesecake with granola crust. A milestone birthday from which she would have launched into full-fledged adulthood.

I felt tender but also curious. I wasn't as sad as I thought I might be. Last September, when both Kati Harkin and Dan had turned twenty-one, it sideswiped me. My daughter would have loved to be there, celebrating each of them. Today, I simply felt a quiet pleasure in thinking about my girl.

Last August, when that first surge of joy had swept over me in the church parking lot, I had felt such hope. I was getting my game on—or so I thought. But subsequent flashes of joy had been fleeting, and my days had remained pretty dark. Was I stuck? What was wrong with me? How would joy possibly find a recurring role in my new normal?

This struggle wasn't unique to me. Heartbreak comes in many colors—death, divorce, job loss, poverty, relational fractures, abuse. Pain is the great equalizer, and it spares no one. So where did joy fit?

I stood and stoked the fire. I refilled my coffee and looked out the window. *Such beauty.* Then I snuggled back under my quilt.

Life is hard, and tragedy strikes. Also, life is stunningly beautiful. Both/and. But our circumstances do not have the power to steal our joy without our permission. If our purpose, our identity, our sense of God's direction hinged upon a pain-free life, how precarious the world would be. How weak God would be. How few would ever find true joy.

I thought about the lyrics from one of the songs we'd sung during

Katie's funeral, lyrics taken from the book of Job (a man in the Bible who lost *all* his children): "You give and take away. . . . Blessed be Your name."[4] The words held deeper meaning today than they had when I sung them in a shocked stupor just a week after Katie died. I now knew from personal experience that the same God who allows pain to enter our lives also sends us comfort, His presence, and more strength than we thought we possessed. And with the sorrow, He extends an invitation for the transformation of our character and a richer, wiser appreciation of life. These were all gifts I never asked for—I would have rather had Katie—but slowly embraced.

The logs burned low in the fireplace. I carried my empty coffee cup to the sink and looked out the kitchen window. The backyard was now buried under a heavy blanket of fresh snow. At the far edge of our lawn, fairylike snowflakes drifted around the cottonwood tree, every branch and twig coated in white. *God is good.*

Even on the darkest of days, tiny embers of joy had been glowing undetected beneath the ashes of my soul. There they waited for an invitation to flicker into flame.

43

BETHANY FLEW HOME for a visit that spring, and she gave me an opportunity to both laugh and cringe at my own expense.

We were shopping together at Costco, and I was wearing my silver anchor necklace. The guy bagging our groceries seemed kind but a bit socially awkward.

"Cool anchor," he said, pointing. "Got a boat?"

Bethany sensed where this could lead. Fearing I would launch into telling this complete stranger the full significance of my anchor, she shot me a look and shook her head. *No, Mom . . . please, no. Let it go.* Seems the lollipop story and others like it had earned me a reputation for sharing too much information with complete strangers.

"Uh, no," I said to the bagger. "Actually, I don't own a boat. I, uh . . ."

I looked at Bethany, who raised her eyebrows and gave me the stink eye.

But my hunger to talk about Katie was winning. *Maybe, just maybe,* I rationalized, *this guy's question is a divinely inspired prompt for me to engage him in a meaningful conversation about God—and about my daughter.*

"The anchor was a gift from . . ." I glanced over at Bethany and got a final look that said, *I swear I'll leave you all alone in this Costco.*

Too late.

"Actually, some girlfriends gave this necklace to me to symbolize what a steady anchor God has been for us since my nineteen-year-old daughter died a couple of summers back."

The man stopped loading our groceries and stared, slack-jawed, his mental wheels spinning as he grappled for some sort of response to this woman whose six-pack of canned corn he held in his hand.

Bethany rolled her eyes and smirked at me. *Here it comes, Mom—and you deserve it. I tried to warn you.*

His face brightened as the perfect segue popped into mind.

"Oooooooo. Dead people," he said. "That reminds me, did you hear about those guys from the funeral home in Burr Oak who got arrested for digging up dead people and reselling the graves? I guess they dropped some body parts, and that's how they got caught. Dead people . . . now that's creepy."

Priceless!

I paid the cashier—who politely pretended not to hear my exchange with her bagger—and Bethany and I hurried off with our cart, laughing as soon as we got outside.

"That's what you get, Mom, for baring your soul to Awkward Grocery Bagger!" Bethany said.

But behind her laugher, I could tell she was ticked. I had embarrassed her. And worse, I had put that bagger in a horribly awkward position.

In the car, Bethany let me have it. "Mom, you ambushed that poor guy!" she said. "He didn't deserve that. What did you expect him to say?"

She was right. I had said too much—not because it might serve that guy in some way, as I'd tried to rationalize to myself, but because it had served me. *My* need to tell. *My* need to talk about Katie.

The truth was, I wanted people to know about Katie. If someone asked me how many kids I had, I was quick to tell them five. If they asked their ages, I listed each one—and included a few sentences about what had happened to my middle daughter. I resented the fact that it weirded people out when I mentioned that my child had died, and I bucked against it. Today I had used the bagger's innocent question as an unsolicited launching point. It was a selfish thing to do.

I ached to talk about Katie in the same way I could talk freely about any of my other kids. Plus I wanted people to hear that although I'd lost a child, her death was not the end of our story. I genuinely wanted to give them a glimpse of how good and faithful God had been for us in the midst of this horror. If someday they, too, would have to navigate horrors of their own, perhaps they would remember our story, and it might give them hope.

But my habit of oversharing had come with a price tag I had been choosing to ignore.

Scott and the kids were the opposite of me in how they responded to people with regard to Katie. To them, her death was so significant and personal that they discussed it *only* with those they were close to—not with strangers. Our conflicting styles of grief were mutually exclusive, as Bethany tried to explain to me in the car at Costco.

"Your style of grief trumps ours, Mom," she said. "Once you tell, we can't untell."

But I was a slow learner. A week later, I slipped up again. I overshared. Tember and I were driving in a car with a new girlfriend of hers—and her mother. I managed to slip Katie's passing into the conversation as her friend listened in, sneaking uncomfortable glances at my daughter. Tember was furious with me.

That night at the kitchen table, she and Bethany sat me down and laid it out plain. "Mom, it's one thing when you ambush Awkward Costco Bagger," Bethany said, her eyes flashing. "But when you tell someone I know—or someone Tember knows—you are telling *our* story as well as your own! We can't untell those people. And it's so unfair!"

"We don't have the luxury of doing what works best for us in those situations," Tember added, "because you have already left us exposed.

My sister's death feels too sacred to just mention casually. I feel I am devaluing all she meant to me if I talk about it with people I don't know, who don't know me."

The tension at the kitchen table was high. Both girls were angry. All three of us were crying. It was awful. At first I was defensive, but what they said made such perfect sense I could find no excuse for myself. *How could I have been so blind?*

"You're so right," I told them.

They weren't through.

"Mom, I know sometimes you worry that we hold our grief inside to an unhealthy degree," Bethany continued. "I disagree. It feels right for us."

"But regardless—and this is hard to say because we don't want to hurt your feelings," Tember said, "have you really stopped to consider how healthy it is for you to be leaking on people to the degree you do?"

Ouch. Me? Me, the mother who has psychoanalyzed every word, every glance, every facial expression of my kids these past many months? Me, who has worried so much about how they are doing inside? Had I failed to look at myself with the same rigor?

Yes. Yes, I had.

"Mom," Tember continued, her lashes wet. "It's fine if you're talking to someone who is primarily your friend, or if you're teaching or writing a blog or something. That's totally appropriate because we don't know those people. But when it's someone who's primarily in *our* lives, let us decide who we share our story with."

I couldn't argue. It was one thing for me to talk about our family's story while teaching a grief class, as I'd done a few times—or when writing a blog, or even this memoir. Those were "anonymous" audiences as far as the kids were concerned. But when I was having a personal conversation with the mother of one of their friends, or a new teacher, I was forcing their hand, trumping their style of grieving with my own. (For the record, each of the kids gave invaluable input and their blessing on this manuscript!)

That night at the kitchen table, I finally permitted a spotlight to shine on a part of my grief that desperately needed realignment.

"I am truly sorry," I said. "I've tried so hard not to make Katie's death the centerpiece of my world. How could I not have seen?"

"Mama, to a certain degree, Katie *is* the centerpiece of our family," Bethany said. "And that's okay. Her death has changed everything for all of us. How could it not? I'm not suggesting you go build an official Katie shrine in the living room! But maybe you would do well to accept that because of her death, Katie does hold a different place in our family—and just try to manage that reality rather than fight it."

"Wow," I said. "What you're describing sure would be easier than what I've been trying to do! I am so sorry, you guys."

"We forgive you, Mom," Tember said, patting my knee. "This isn't easy for any of us, and we know we don't always get it right either."

❧

This conversation was a game changer for me. Not that I don't still fail. I do. But as a result of my daughters' challenging but truthful words, I began to implement a new filter into my life: Before sharing, I would simply ask myself, *Is this my story to tell?*

And I began to cut myself—and others!—more slack regarding our propensity to "centerpiece" the loved ones we had lost. Finding that delicate balance between honoring the one who has died and celebrating the ones who still live—it's super hard. I am susceptible to centerpiecing, and rather than fighting this truth, I now try to focus my energies around managing it.

In situations where it won't adversely affect the kids, I definitely err more toward the side of telling people about Katie. And the kids and I agree on one caveat to my new filter: When asked how many children I have, I will always tell people five, not four. No matter the current head count around our kitchen table, Katie's space will forever be kept in my heart.

44

SUFFICE IT TO SAY, my introvert husband has never been lectured for *over*sharing. He chooses carefully when to talk about Katie, and with whom. We are wired so differently that of course our grief has looked very different, too. He is highly sensitive inside but more outwardly stoic. His tears have been rare, but also more piercing and poignant. He has spent countless hours sitting alone just thinking, praying, meditating, or reading. Yet he has never hesitated to listen to me verbally process, and he assures me it is no burden. I adore this about him. Because how can it not be a burden to hear someone talk about the death of your daughter?

I, on the other hand, am rather sturdy inside, but frequently a bit of a mess on the outside. My eyes leak at country ballads, reruns of *Little House on the Prairie*, pretty much anything written by Dickens, Austen, or a Brontë, and the final episode of *The Office*. (Also the "Casino Night" episode, when Jim finally kisses Pam.) So it makes sense that large volumes of tears would be involved when I had lost a child. I also felt compelled to work out my loss in tangible ways, like staying with Katie in the hospital, doing her makeup in the funeral home, visiting the wrecking yard and crash site, and attending the coroner's inquest. And I have needed to put words to my loss. I have written myriad pages and have found comfort in conversations with willing friends, especially Scott, who has let me talk—and talk—and talk. My process has been costly for him. And likewise, his quiet way of grieving has at times been a challenge for me. But for both of us, embracing each other's unique style of surviving has been an honor as well.

Despite our differences, sometimes our grief aligns. Sometimes we lock eyes across the room and read each other's thoughts: *Did this really happen? Is she really gone?* Scott's gentle eyes grow moist. A quiver crosses his lips, and he looks like a little boy. Scott's sorrow is deep and soul shattering. He is digesting it in small, purposeful bites. And I have taken big, messy bites, which fits my personality. Each of the kids falls somewhere in between this spectrum—though closer to Scott. Except Andrea, who is my grief twin.

Each of us is on a solitary journey that fits our God-given temperament. What might look like ignoring, stuffing, or avoiding for one person might be just the right pace or season or style for another.

"There's no wrong way to grieve, so long as you grieve," family friend Chrissie told our kids.

"Mom, when you went back to work a couple of months after Katie died," Bethany told me one day, "it helped you avoid a depression. The work helped your grief. But for me, work and school became places that distracted me from my sorrow, making it harder to grieve."

Same actions, different people, different results.

I wish I had a grief thermometer I could just stick under my kids' tongues to get an accurate read on how they are doing inside. But the reality is, neither Scott nor I can force them to share their grief process on our schedule. (Trust me, I've tried!) Finding the balance between inviting and invading has not come easy to me. I worry. I get panicky. I want to fix their hurt, and I barge in. I drive myself (and my family) a little crazy with my attempts to assess their grief or force an expression of it.

If I discipline myself to ask a simple, straightforward question and then leave space for the kids to share, I am sometimes rewarded with glimpses of their inner journeys. But when I use invasive questions or unspoken expectations to try to force my way inside, they close up, protecting those tender places from my uninvited prying.

It's hard for me to be that disciplined and self-controlled when I am hurting too. When a whole family is deep in grief, the entire home team is on injured reserve, which makes it even harder for me to ask for what *I* need. I don't want to ask anything of the kids when I know they are suffering. And besides, as parents, our job is to do what's best for *them*, right? We sacrifice. We moms in particular are the broken-cookie eaters of the world. But I have found that the healthiest thing for the whole family is simply to be direct. Even if others cannot meet my needs, there is something healthy about me stating those needs without the demand that they be met. No passive-aggressive innuendos, no lingering expectations. Just an honest request.

When I am unable to just come out and say what I need, here's how it usually goes:

Me: Gee, I see Katie's birthday is coming up next Thursday . . .
I wonder if we should do something . . .

Kids: [crickets]

Andrea: Matt and I will host a family dinner! [She always rescues me.]

Kids: We will eat the family dinner.

My kids are not dum-dums. They smell my manipulation, and understandably they resent it. So these days I'm practicing speaking my needs more directly, like an actual grown-up. Here's how it goes when I am being a big girl:

Me: Would any of you be up for marking Katie's birthday with a family dinner?

Kids: Sounds great, Mom!

Andrea: Matt and I will host the family dinner!

Kids: We will eat the family dinner.

Okay, to be fair, the kids all pitch in with the dinner. But that's not my point. Being straightforward is much more effective than being (not very) sneaky. When I am direct, the kids are almost always receptive. If they cannot meet my specific request, that's okay. I might feel disappointed, but I don't feel hurt because I get so fed by the mere honesty of our adult-to-adult exchange. And I can turn to a girlfriend or to Scott—or even just be alone—to get my needs met.

I'm getting better—a little. My interactions with the kids are becoming more straightforward, grown-up to grown-up, with each passing year.

One more thought: In grief—and in life—family is great, but it's not enough. Even with an amazing family to walk alongside me in this season, I have desperately needed my posse of girlfriends. We all need a posse of our own—people who have our backs, who can be there for us when the pain is too great to bear alone, and who are not drowning in their own grief. Therapists make great paid posse members, but friends, too, are vital for the journey ahead. My posse—Kaye, Lynne, Sandy,

Tammy, Lynette, Margaret, and a handful of others—has ridden alongside me over some rough patches of road. I don't know how I might have survived without them. And their investment in me has left me better equipped to ride alongside others as well.

45

It had been almost two years since Katie's death, and I had heard from only one recipient of her organ donation—a thirty-nine-year-old man who had received bone and soft tissue, which had been used to rebuild his knee. His letter moved me deeply. "My favorite things to do include rock climbing, mountain biking, and telemark skiing," he wrote. He'd had multiple knee surgeries, and after his latest sports injury, he'd required yet another operation—this time with a tissue donation. "Because of the gift from your loved one, I will again be able to climb, bike, ski, and enjoy life!" This man is a nurse who cares for critically ill patients, so he often talks with families who have lost a loved one. "I see firsthand what a difficult time this can be for you, and I have experienced firsthand now what a life-changing gift tissue donation is for me. Thank you so very much."

As happy as it made me to think of this man enjoying the outdoors on his freshly repaired knee, I still ached to hear from any of the organ recipients who carried a *living organ* of my daughter inside their bodies. I especially hoped to hear from the girl who'd received Katie's lungs. *What must it have felt like for her on that first morning to wake up from surgery and take a deep breath of air? She and I probably awoke around the same time that morning—me at home, my head foggy with shock and grief, and this young woman in the ICU, her head foggy with anesthesia. I awoke, went outside, and railed at God. Perhaps she awoke and thanked Him.* I secretly hoped to meet her someday—and to see my daughter's lungs in action.

My mailbox had continued to disappoint for almost two years when one day a Gift of Hope envelope appeared. I ripped it open (sorry, Scott and kids, for not waiting till you got home!), and into my hands fell a letter from the woman who had received Katie's liver. Her letter capti-vated me. She had begun writing it in 2008, but it had taken her until now to finish and send it.

"I was three days away from dying when Katie's liver became avail-able for me." The woman explained that she suffered from a chronic illness that had silently destroyed her liver. She also told me that she was the caretaker of her visually impaired husband, served as a deacon in her church, and was a grandmother. "I was sixty-nine when I had the transplant and am now seventy, so a definite senior but with work to accomplish and a family to support. Thank you so much for seeing that Katie could give the gift of life. She surely is still helping to do good in our world. Many people do not understand that others are dying every day because there is no organ for them. You gave me the incredible chance to live days of service and joy to others, just as Katie would have. Thank you—thank you. Hope to hear from you soon."

I want to leave ripples in the lives I leave behind . . . With one simple signature on the back of her driver's license, Katie had done just that.

This woman and I soon talked on the phone, and it was fascinating to hear the voice of someone in whom Katie's liver was busy doing its work. She had a great sense of humor, and I confessed that in our house we referred to her as "The Liver Lady." She laughed out loud. We agreed it would be wonderful to meet face-to-face. She wanted to come to our house and see Katie's art.

The rest of our family had hesitations about meeting her, however. It freaked the kids out, and for Scott it just triggered overwhelming sad-ness. Once again the differences in how we grieved came to bear. For the time being, I set aside our plans to meet. The Liver Lady understood. When the time was right, we could revisit it.

Spring arrived, and with it the approach of the two-year mark. Sights and sounds once again triggered my "body memory" of this time of year—the smell of loam, freshly cut grass, and hawthorn blossoms; the symphony of Midwest songbirds; and the rustle of new leaves on the cottonwood trees. All these brought me back to that fateful weekend when Katie had died. I braced myself for the milestone that was fast approaching.

Sam's high school graduation happened to fall around that second anniversary of Katie's death, and Matt, Andrea, and Bethany flew to town. With all my chicks in the nest, the house was filled with stories, laughter, rich conversation, good food—and plenty of games. Bethany made a giant score chart to keep track of who won which games throughout the week so we could crown an ultimate victor at the end. Sam dubbed the tournament the "Graduational Invitational." Points were awarded in Speed Scrabble, Settlers of Catan, Hearts, Wii Tetris, Mario Kart, and Shanghai. I enjoyed cooking for everyone as much as I enjoyed playing games, so Bethany awarded me points for meals prepared. It kept me on the board.

On the morning of May 31—two years after Katie's accident—my dad called. We chatted about his vegetable garden and mine, and about his latest salmon-fishing trips in Puget Sound. My dad has a wide assortment of fishing buddies—some guys he's been fishing with since I was a kid and some younger guys just starting out. I always enjoy hearing about his adventures.

After a few minutes, Dad grew quiet. "September, I want to tell you about a new fishing buddy of mine," he said. "His name is Dave, and he went with us on a trip up north of Vancouver. After the first day of fishing, he struck up a conversation with me privately at the back of the boat and told me he was sorry to hear about my granddaughter—he'd heard about Katie's death. Then he told me he, too, had lost a child—his six-year-old son had died of cancer. We talked about his son and Katie for quite a while, and he cried, and it was so nice to talk with someone who understands."

It's harder for my dad's generation to discuss matters of the heart, and I was happy he had found a friend with whom he could talk.

"We went out again a couple of weeks ago," my dad continued, "and again Dave made it a point to pull me aside and talk about Katie and his little boy. Whenever he talks about his son, he gets a far-off look on his face, and his eyes well up. You can tell his loss is still very raw, very painful."

My dad paused. When he spoke again, his voice cracked. "Honey, Dave is eighty years old. His son died in 1965, when you were two."

I was speechless. I had envisioned Dave as a guy in his thirties. His boy had died nearly fifty years ago, but to this father, it was like yesterday.

My dad cleared his throat. "I know today is a hard day, hon. I hope it's okay that I told you Dave's story. I thought it might be helpful for you and Scott in the long run."

"Absolutely, Dad," I said. "It's super helpful. And Dave's experience affirms what Scott and I have been suspecting. We will still be crying in forty years, I have no doubt. You just don't get over something like this. At best, you learn to live within it. You embrace the life you still have. While I am hoping I will feel a little better a year from now—or five—I am also convinced that when I'm Dave's age, I will still be heartbroken."

"I love you, babe."

"I love you, too, Daddy."

◦◦◦

Later that day Tember offered to make a Costco run with me to restock the ever-depleting fridge. When we returned home a couple of hours later, the house was spotlessly clean. Bethany and Andrea had commandeered the kitchen, and wonderful aromas wafted from the oven. Sam had vacuumed and was setting the table for dinner. Matt stood at the sink, trimming fresh halibut, tuna, and salmon steaks for the grill. Scott had filled an ice chest with beer and Mike's Hard Lemonade for the twenty-one-and-older crowd, and sodas for Sam, eighteen, and Tember, sixteen. He now sat in the Bug Room, programming a playlist of summer tunes into his iPod.

"Wow!" I said. "You guys sure have been industrious! Thanks!" Even for my normally helpful family, this seemed above and beyond.

I should have suspected something was up.

Thirty minutes later, the doorbell rang. Everyone seemed absorbed in their tasks, so I went to open it. Through the sidelight window, I spotted an RV parked on the road and a woman standing on our front porch with a laundry basket. *What?*

When I opened the door, there stood my dear auntie Brenda and uncle Vic—all the way from Massachusetts!

"Hello, miss," Brenda said, a gleam in her eye. "We're just camping in your neighborhood, and we have some laundry to do. Can we borrow your washer and dryer?"

Behind them stood Scott, filming the whole surprise, which, as it turns out, was only a surprise to me.

"What? What? What!" I couldn't believe my eyes, and my brain could not connect the dots. Leaving my aunt and uncle standing on the front porch, I ran back inside the house, raced halfway up the stairs, then ran back down again before throwing my arms around Brenda's neck, hugging and crying and laughing.

Brenda and Vic are two of the dearest people to our family. Though they live one thousand miles away in New England, they have never let the distance keep them from being a vital part of our lives. They were at our wedding twenty-six years before, at Matt and Andrea's wedding three years ago, and at Katie's memorial two years ago. Now here they stood on my front porch, grinning at the tremendous joke: a surprise visit to help us pass the two-year mark.

"Gotcha," said Uncle Vic, proud as punch.

Everyone piled into the kitchen, and the story began to unroll. Brenda and Vic were taking their fifth-wheel camper on a cross-country road trip, and they had timed their itinerary so they could be here on our doorstep on May 31. Tember's trip to Costco had been part of the ploy to get me out of the house. The rapid housecleaning and amazing dinner prep had all been timed for Brenda and Vic's arrival, which added an air of jubilation to this milestone day.

Once again, God had dreamed up a wildly creative way to help trump our pain. Last year it had been a baby raccoon—now grown and gone. This year it was Brenda and Vic, whose warmth and laughter enriched our lives once again.

God is good.

❦

Two nights later—the two-year mark of Katie's donation surgery (and leave it to Katie to have her "two-year mark" span three days!)—I was feeling restless when I climbed into bed. I really wanted to mark the exact moment of my daughter's final heartbeat—2:18 a.m. I considered setting my alarm but decided against it because it would wake Scott. *It's silly anyway. There was nothing magical about that exact moment.* I closed my eyes and eventually fell asleep.

Some time later, a solitary, deafening thunderclap jolted me awake. A summer storm had rolled in, and lightning illuminated our bedroom. Scott's steady breathing told me he had slept through the thunder. I rolled over and looked at my digital alarm clock—2:18 a.m.

Of course! In His good nature, God had given me a tiny gift: He had awakened me with precisely timed thunder so I could honor this moment in memory of my daughter.

I peered into the darkness as my mind's eyes strained to peek into heaven and envision Katie there. What was she doing at this exact moment?

I miss you, Katie. I miss you. I love you, my sweet girl. You are not forgotten. You are never far from my heart.

God had given me a wake-up call I hadn't even prayed for. I don't understand why the bigger things I've prayed for—Katie's very life, for example—were not given. It will never make sense to me, but I rest in knowing that my human pea brain cannot see the full landscape of eternity as He does.

I straightened my pillow, closed my eyes, and accepted the small blessing He had sent my way.

❦

The overnight storm lingered the next morning, the air thick and humid. I awoke at dawn, dressed, and opened the slider to the back deck. Solitary raindrops plunked to the ground, flicking individual blades of grass. In the distance, thunder rolled like an afterthought, nearly spent. Year two was officially behind us. It was the dawn of year three.

I inhaled the earthy scent of the rain-soaked morning, recalling how I had wandered the yard at dawn a year ago—and the year before that—sensing but resisting God's invitation of surrender. Again, now, I felt His pull—but not toward a surrender where two opponents have battled and someone has finally won. Rather, He was drawing me toward the surrender of a brokenhearted child who finally stops trying to be brave in the face of adversity, lifts up her hands, and runs for comfort into her parent's outstretched arms.

At some point, I needed to let go of my daughter. I needed to say—and accept—"*This* is my life." The stronger play in that moment—the right move—would be to meet God out there in my backyard, storm and all, and have it out with Him, to settle this standoff, to wrestle it to the ground.

But I couldn't do it. I wasn't that strong. I wasn't ready for such surrender.

Surely not now—it's raining, I rationalized. *Only a fool would be caught strolling in her yard in this kind of weather. Maybe later, if the weather breaks . . .*

I stepped back inside, closed the sliding glass door, and turned to make the coffee.

cerulean blue

[suh-'roo-lee-'uhn bloo] / a pure, clear,
sky-blue tincture

The cool bite of spring draws goose bumps from our skin,

but the azure-blue sky overhead declares the approach of summer.

Silhouetting an array of clouds, birds, and

tufts of cottonwood down,

the blue holds promise of warm and gentle days to come.

Life is a balance of holding on and letting go.

ATTRIBUTED TO RUMI

Stop complaining, stop comparing. Pack lightly.

KATIE VAUDREY, 19, FINAL JOURNAL ENTRY

46

Sam planned to start as a freshman at Azusa Pacific that fall, just as Katie had—and Bethany and Matt before her.

"I want to be near my siblings," he had said when it came time to pick a school the previous October. "Plus Matt and Andrea will probably start a family soon, and the baby will need Uncle Sam."

The summer between high school and college had always brought a mixture of joy and sadness for me as a parent—joy for the future each child was stepping into and sadness because I knew how much I would miss him or her. But this summer felt different. It was more unsettling. Why?

One afternoon as Sam played the piano in the living room, I stood in the doorway soaking in the music, and it hit me: *Katie graduated from Fremd. Katie went off to APU. And sometimes when you send a child off for their first year of college, it is also their last year of life. Sometimes they leave the nest and they don't come back.*

My psyche had memorized a pattern of one. These last days at home with Sam felt just like Katie's last days before college. He had graduated from Fremd. He was heading to APU. I had printed Sam the exact same "College Shopping List" that I'd created for Katie, replacing her "decorative wall hanging, cutie throw pillow, teacups, and plates" with "longboard, guitar, electric razor" for her brother. I had taken him to the doctor for the same freshman immunizations, purchased the same plane ticket (probably on the same airline), and witnessed the same closing landmarks of his childhood—the last high school summer camp, the last family getaway, the final packing up of his childhood bedroom. I was repeating the pattern. Would this child's death be part of the pattern too?

I was ashamed to acknowledge these morbid thoughts, but they made sense to me. I no longer assumed bad things wouldn't happen to us. They did. They do. Could they happen twice? To the same family? Absolutely they could.

The odds were astronomically in my favor that Sam would finish his freshman year, complete all four years of college, and live a long and fruitful life. But my irrationality would not be so easily soothed. As I stood there listening to Sam play the piano that day—and every day until I said goodbye to him in California three weeks later—I heard fear's tiny, cruel whisper: *Are these his last days? Are you savoring them fully? Are you making every moment count?* And then, *Will he be taken from you too?* My fears were irrational, I knew, but I couldn't stop the thoughts from coming.

Sam and I flew to California over Labor Day weekend, where he began life as a college freshman. Everywhere we went, feelings of déjà vu kept surfacing from just three years ago, when I'd helped Katie move into college. But the fresh memories Sam and I made on that campus mingled with the old—not just of Katie, but of Matt and Bethany as freshmen as well. And on Sunday afternoon when I said goodbye to Sam, I was glad I'd managed to keep my crazy fears to myself. ("Until you got to the airport!" Scott is quick to remind me. Evidently I was a bit of a blubbering mess when I called my husband from the gate, but Sam was none the wiser.)

As my plane took off for Chicago, I looked out my window. Below I could see the giant "A" for Azusa painted onto the mountainside just above the campus. Somewhere down there was an eighteen-year-old young man whom I loved beyond all measure. With one hand, I held a lifetime of memories with him—and with the other, I let him go.

Once fall was in full swing, I planned another visit to the crash site. Lynne came along, and we stopped at Jewel-Osco to pick up flowers.

"This is the one," I said, lifting a robust bouquet of miniature sunflowers, blue statice, sage-green thistle, and some waxy burgundy berries I'd never seen before. Rich autumn textures and colors.

"My treat," Lynne said, taking the flowers from my hand and heading to the checkout.

As we made the short drive to the site, I filled Lynne in on a recent conversation I'd had with Katie's old boyfriend, Dan, who was now a senior at APU and doing well. Over the past few years he had called or stopped by occasionally to talk about his loss. I gently encouraged him to be open to dating again.

He had called me a few weeks ago to tell me he'd met a girl. "She is joyful and compassionate, and she loves God and loves people," he said. "She stands up for the underdog, just like Katie always did. I think I might want to date her. And I . . . wanted to know what you think."

I suspected his phone call was his way of giving me a heads up that he was ready at last to move on. I sensed it was a goodbye.

"Ask her out!" I told him. And he did.

Navigating where Dan fit into my post-Katie life had been a challenge. I truly wanted him to move on and find the happiness he so deserved—and would need to find apart from my daughter. But letting him go meant grieving one more lost connection to Katie.

Lynne listened as I recounted my conversation with Dan, then probed in her quiet, gentle way. "How were you feeling inside?"

My throat grew tight. "I was quaking," I said. "I was genuinely happy for him, *really*."

"But . . ."

"*But* . . . it is another turning of the page." I wiped my nose on the sleeve of my sweatshirt. "A new chapter in his life is beginning—and without my daughter."

"You're right, it is another turning of the page," she said. "How can this *not* be hard for you?"

"But I have been too slow to accept that his place in our family would inevitably fade. I've clung to these rainbows-and-unicorns hopes that maybe someday he and his future wife would stop by and introduce me to their first baby—as if I were a spare grandma. But how silly that now seems."

"Perhaps your hopes have not been . . . realistic," Lynne said tactfully.

I laughed with affection at her gentle critique. "Perhaps," I said. "Another 'letting go.' I am happy for him, truly, and a bit envious: Though he cannot replace Katie as a person, he can replace the role she played in his life. He can find someone he loves just as much, or even more. I, however, cannot find another middle daughter."

⌒⟨℘⟩⌒

At the crash site, Lynne and I discovered that the area had changed even more since my last visit. The entire property was now a huge, earth-torn construction site. The rental house near where she had crashed had been demolished. Even the driveway that marked the spot was gone.

We parked down the road in the lot of a little church and walked to the site. The iron cross was nowhere to be seen. We began toeing around in the overgrown grasses, looking for it.

"Whenever I'm here, I never quite know what I should do," I confessed as we searched. "I like having a 'place,' but it's always a little awkward, sitting here by the side of the road. And now everything has changed. Even the cross is gone. There's nothing left."

"Maybe it's right that the cross is gone," Lynne said. "Maybe this, too, is another turning of the page."

With no marker to lay her flowers beneath, Lynne walked over to an oak tree at the edge of the field, now under excavation. A weathered vine wrapped around its trunk, and she tucked her flowers between the tree and the vine—perfect. My sweet friend has such an artistic eye for flowers. Katie would have loved the dramatic contrast between the rugged bark and the vivid colors of the bouquet. And she would have liked that the flowers were elevated and thus visible from the road. I took a photo of Lynne next to the tree, and then we walked back to the van.

"Is there someplace nearby where we can get a cup of coffee?" she asked.

"I know just the place!"

⤜⧽

Moments later, we pulled up to Bandito Barney's, the restaurant where Katie would have worked the summer she died. I had wanted to pay this place a visit ever since.

Housed in a refurbished Victorian home and painted a brilliant purple with lime-green trim, I could see right away that the vintage yet whimsical feel of the restaurant would have appealed to my artsy daughter. Inside, worn oak floorboards creaked underfoot, and a crackling fire in a massive yellow-brick fireplace cast flickering light across a dimly lit bar. Its heat chased the briskness of the fall air from our cheeks.

"I'm just warning you," I said to Lynne as we stepped inside, "I'm going to ask them about Katie."

"I wouldn't have it any other way," she said.

We took a booth next to windows that overlooked a labyrinth of decks and porticos in back of the old building. The outdoor seating was closed for the season, but it was easy to envision the lively, high-spirited atmosphere this place was known for on a hot July day. Katie would have had a ball working here.

"What can I get you ladies to drink?" asked a perky waitress with spiky pink hair. A diamond nose piercing caught the sunlight as she spoke. "Daily special: Three-dollar Miller Lite!"

"Can we get coffee—do you sell coffee?" Lynne asked.

"Sure! I can make you coffee," she said. "Wanna add some Baileys and Frangelico?" She winked.

"Sounds delicious," Lynne said.

She turned to place our order, but I stopped her. "Uh, do you mind if I ask—how long have you worked here?"

"About five years."

"My daughter was going to work here, too, two summers ago. Her name was Katie Vaudrey. Do you remember the girl who died on her way to her first day of work?"

"Oh my gosh! I totally remember!" she said, covering her mouth with her hands. "That was so sad! I am so, so sorry!" She studied my face, looking for a cue. I was accustomed to this—people mirroring their responses to match mine. Would I burst out crying? Was I a wreck?

"Thank you. Yes, it is pretty awful," I said, smiling to reassure her I was okay. "I've been wanting to visit here ever since she died, just to see this place that Katie had been so excited about."

Our waitress was relieved that I was not going to fall apart. "I'm so glad you came. It is a really fun place to work. We have a creek and a fountain out back—it's beautiful. In the summer it gets hopping here. We bring in local bands to play rock and roll on Friday and Saturday nights. But I love working Sunday afternoons. We bring in jazz musicians, and the music is wonderful."

I'd figured our pink-haired waitress for a Friday-night girl. But she loved Sundays. Her pride in this place was endearing.

She disappeared with our order. Soon we smelled fresh coffee brewing, and she returned with two steaming mugs.

"How is it?" she asked, watching as we sipped.

"Perfect," I said.

"Extra Frangelico—that's the secret," she said. "Can I add some chocolate syrup?"

We willingly accepted. She fetched chocolate syrup from the fridge. No fancy drizzle, no whip, just a heavy stream of chocolate that sank to the bottoms of our mugs.

"How's that?" she asked.

"Even more perfect!" Lynne said.

She smiled and left us to enjoy our drinks.

The afternoon sun dipped low on the horizon, and a chill began to creep through the old windowpanes, but the fireplace and our coffee kept us warm. Shadows drifted across the outdoor tables, creating dapples of fading sunlight that danced across the deck. I could just picture my girl waiting tables out there, chatting with customers, working her magic as she made people feel valued over their Coronas and burgers. I could hear her laughter, envision her quick steps, her flashing smile.

This was one of those moments—the conversation, the atmosphere, the drinks, the friendship—everything was perfect.

"I love this place," I said. "It feels so . . . right."

"Me too," Lynne said. "You know, there is something about having a place. In the Bible, people built markers—piles of stones—to remember what God had done for them at different times in their lives. And the crash site has served as such a place for you. But you never did feel at home visiting that spot. You never knew quite what to do there. And now the cross is gone . . ." She paused, letting her words sink in before continuing. "Perhaps today was another turning of the page. Perhaps moving forward, Bandito Barney's could become that place for you. A place to gather with family or friends and remember the joy and fun that was Katie."

I let her words ruminate in my mind. "You're right," I said. "It's time to retire the crash site."

As we retraced our route toward home that afternoon, we passed that spot one more time. Lynne's bright bouquet of flowers suspended against the oak tree caught my eye. They were all that remained to mark the spot where Katie had died. Perhaps there was a new tradition for the days ahead—a better one—filled with friends and laughter and good food.

That fall, I sensed we were entering an easier era. We were approaching the third holiday season since Katie had died, and the slap of her absence was not as raw, though we still felt its sting. In many ways, Thanksgiving and Christmas held a richer poignancy now because of Katie's death. How deeply we treasured one another around the Thanksgiving table. How vividly aware we were of the blessings that had come our way in the past twelve months—and of the benevolent Hand that had delivered each one.

As we decorated our Christmas tree, I lingered a little longer over each ornament, recalling its origin and the story it told. I hung Scott's med school ID badge and the dog tags from our farm dog, Lloyd, who'd long since passed. I hung the melted plastic measuring cup I'd accidentally ruined while making hot chocolate one Christmas Eve when the kids were little. I had set the cup on a still-hot burner, and when I lifted it, dozens of clear, shimmering strings pulled from its bottom. This set the kids to giggling—and the cup found its way onto our tree as an ornament that year (thank you, Scott) and every year since. I had tried to throw the cup away numerous times, but it kept coming back from the dead like some sort of relentless Christmas zombie. Every December, it would mysteriously claim a place of prominence on our tree. One year I found it hanging from a branch on a spinning mechanism, spotlighted for all to see. Another year, Sam had taped the cup to the top of the tree in lieu of the Christmas star. Such was our family. Memories like these filled me with irrepressible warmth.

I hung Katie's ornaments, one by one, finishing with her little sterling cradle. There was no hanging that ornament without a few tears. But this year, I found her ornaments—and Christmas as a whole—to be less of reminders of our loss and more of welcomed triggers for cherished memories to be savored and replayed in our minds once again.

The new normal will always be this for us: undaunted joy seasoned by irreversible loss. Both/and. Holding on and letting go.

47

EARLY FEBRUARY brought our first true blizzard since moving to the Midwest—and the third-biggest snowfall in Chicago's history. School was canceled for Tember, and we hunkered down at home, watching for the snowplows that would come unbury our street.

I had been waiting nine years for a real blizzard, and at last the wait was over. I marveled at the beauty outside—each fir branch bowing under weighty blankets of white. The house across the street looked like a Currier & Ives print, the angles of its roofline softened by the snow and its mailbox at the end of the drive wearing a snowy top hat.

I'd always loved a good snow. When I was growing up on our Issaquah farm in the mild, maritime Pacific Northwest, snow was rare. Waiting for snow each winter was practically a career for my brother and me. Anytime the red line on the thermometer dipped into the thirties, we crossed our fingers and raised our eyes skyward, asking each other,

"Do you think it will snow?" And if flakes began to fall, we would worry and ask, "Do you think it will stick?"

One snowfall in particular stands out in my memory, circa 1974, when I was eleven. Greg and I awoke the day after Christmas to find snow falling heavily across the valley, blanketing twigs and fence posts, cedar shakes on the barn roofs, and winter-deadened blackberry brambles along the creek. Even the twisted barbed wire fence lines that crosscut our pastures had become tightropes for precariously balanced blades of snow. The wait was over! A real snowstorm!

Still in my pajamas, I yanked my rubber boots over bare feet, grabbed my brown barn coat, and ran outside. My boots sank ankle-deep in the snow, and the rapidly falling flakes showed no sign of letting up.

By noon, the snow stood nine inches deep. The horses stayed in our barn, munching contentedly on their morning pads of hay, but our cows lived outdoors year-round, and the snow was no fun for them. We'd given them extra rations at breakfast and broken the shell of ice that coated their water trough. They now huddled, hind ends to the wind, beneath an ample cluster of firs at the far side of the pasture, their sweet, steamy breath creating a foggy haze under the snow-laden shelter of the trees.

The kids in the valley—my brother and me, neighbors Kathy and John, and Chris and Tim, whose parents boarded horses at our farm—spent the morning grooming the sledding hill in the back pasture, taking run after run on aluminum discs to flatten down the dry thistles that peppered the steep hillside. Kathy and John owned a real wooden toboggan that could hold three of us at a whack. And my brother's Radio Flyer, a Christmas gift from two years back, was christened on that hill and did not disappoint.

By the time our parents joined us in the afternoon, the run was lightning fast, curving around old stumps and taking full advantage of every rise in the sod that could constitute a jump. My dad sized up the scene, then meandered back toward the house, returning with his GMC pickup. He pulled up next to us at the end of the run. "Want a ride back up the hill?"

"Awesome!" we said. (Or maybe "Far out!" It was the seventies, after all.) We scrambled into the back of the pickup. Dad threw it into four-wheel drive, and up the hill we rumbled—our own private chairlift, country style!

Around dusk, the dads scavenged the woods for downfalls and built a huge bonfire from their dry, dead limbs. My mom took the truck back to the house for food. We kids cut sapling branches for marshmallow sticks. I pulled out my Swiss Army knife—these were the days when pocketknives were tools, not weapons—and sharpened my stick, as well as a few spares for the grown-ups. I popped the caps off their Rainier beer bottles, too, proud to have the right tool for the job.

My mom arrived from the house with a kettle of beef stew, a giant pan of fresh corn bread, and a pot of steaming black coffee. For the kids, she produced a jug of Tang ("the drink of astronauts!"). We served up dinner from the tailgate of Dad's pickup, then ate together, warming ourselves around the fire. We gorged on roasted marshmallows that tasted faintly of fresh maple branch.

The heavy snowfall had laden the maples, alders, and cedars with a winter burden they hadn't carried in years. Old, dead branches began snapping under the heavy weight of the snow, and we heard their repeated shotgun cracks ricocheting across the valley. And just as the sun winked its goodnight and dipped behind Cougar Mountain, the sky lit up with a brilliant explosion—red and blue and pink and green—followed by a thunderous boom. Every farm in the valley went black.

"Transformer blew," Dad said, pointing down the valley.

"The power's out!" We kids cheered. Candles and woodstoves would be our light and heat at bedtime. Could this day get any cooler? Exhausted but exhilarated, we headed for home.

Inside our tiny farmhouse, Mom tucked us in bed by candlelight, piling on extra blankets to ward off the cold. I drifted off to sleep, knowing more sledding awaited tomorrow. The snow had been well worth the wait.

As I looked out my kitchen window at the slowing flurries of this Midwest blizzard, I realized it wasn't just the snow that had created such a memorable experience in my childhood; it was the waiting. If I'd grown up in Fargo, North Dakota, that snowy memory would have been just another winter day. But a sled-worthy snowfall was so rare in Issaquah that when it finally came, we were overjoyed. It was the wait—the longing and anticipation—that made the day so unforgettable.

Farm kids have lots of experience with "wait." Waiting for eggs to hatch, barn cats to have their litters, cows to calve, and horses to deliver their lanky foals. Waiting for bread to rise, for summer blackberries to turn from green to red to sweet purple-black, for hay to cure for baling—hopefully before the next rainfall. Waiting for Christmas—and for snow.

Adulthood, too, holds its fair share of wait. The endless counting of months—and then days—for the arrival of my own five babies had far outstripped my childhood anticipation of foals or kittens or snow. But nine months of pregnancy and the work and pain of delivery became a mere distant memory once each long-awaited babe was in my arms. Some events are simply worth the wait.

We cannot rush kittens, foals, or babies. We can't force blizzards. By waiting, kids and grown-ups alike learn that there are things we cannot shoehorn into our time frame. But the waiting—though uncomfortable—is indeed survivable. And the anticipation actually heightens our eventual joy.

As I stood at the window, I realized that three years earlier, I had entered an endless season of waiting—waiting to see my girl again some-day. In faith, I believe this life on earth is not the end of us, that those who have passed will be seen again on the other side. I must wait for that day—and it is taking forever.

The pain of separation feels unbearable at times—but it is not. These days of waiting will be nothing but a distant memory once my long-awaited girl is in my arms.

Subconsciously, I was also waiting for our tragedy to be done. I was waiting for some sort of resolution to the mess. *I want my old life back.* This turn of events had barged through the front door of my life uninvited—this was not the life I signed up for. I loved my big, full, family-of-seven life! One child missing changed everything.

When the kids were little and one of them would go to a friend's house for the afternoon, the entire dynamic in the house changed. Even with four other lively, creative kids at home, everything felt off-kilter when one child was away. The siblings interacted differently. They insisted we put any special plans on hold until their absent brother or sister got home and could join in the fun. Our levels of energy and joy were more muted, as if we were all just . . . well, waiting. Waiting for the fifth child to come home so we could be whole once again and life could resume.

I was still waiting for my fifth child to come home.

I couldn't seem to convince my psyche that this Katie-less life was it. This *was* whole. My missing child wasn't coming back.

At some point, I needed to let go of the life I had so loved and learn to fall in love with the life I now had, which was broken and yet still beautiful in its own way.

I turned from the waning snowfall outside my kitchen window.

She's not coming back.

I needed to stop waiting.

48

ON EASTER MORNING, Scott, Tember, and I headed for church. The theme of the service was how life can change in an instant, and before the message, a few people on stage shared their personal experiences of sudden change.

The first woman's story was strikingly similar to our own. Her husband had suffered a ruptured brain aneurysm that left him on life support with little hope of recovery. For two weeks at his bedside, she prayed—begged—and then, *ta-da*! Her husband awoke from his coma.

"But God was merciful," the woman said. "He healed my husband." And there he stood, next to her on the stage, completely recovered.

But God was merciful. Just four simple words—yet how they pierced. I fumed silently in my seat.

I understood what the woman meant—and I was happy for her, glad that her life had worked out so well. I was guessing she didn't mean to imply that God's mercy was somehow measured by the outcome of our circumstances. But that's how it sounded to me, and I cried foul.

The God who had so lovingly embraced our family in every moment of this horror was not a flippant god who healed when he felt merciful but allowed your child to die on a gurney when he was not.

God was merciful, period. It was part of His very character. Yet I couldn't deny the paradox. If God was merciful, then why did Katie die? Was He helpless to stop it? I didn't believe Katie had been snatched unwillingly from His grasp. I believed He could heal, and did heal, sometimes. Yet Katie had died.

I had heard people utter sappy-happy words about their loved ones' deaths—and we Christians could be the worst at this. We said things like this: "All things work together for good!" (a misuse of Paul's teaching in Romans 8:28). Or this: "I just count it a privilege that her passing helped so many people find Jesus"—as if their loved one's death were some sort of payment that was worth it because of how God used this tragedy for good. For me, that kind of spiritual commerce was thievery. Those types of responses smacked of emotional disconnect or blatant denial.

I wanted God to bring something good from our tragedy, absolutely. I was glad that lots of people had been moved and marked by Katie's death. Some connected with God in new ways, which was great. But I was selfish enough to want both/and. I wanted people to find Jesus, *and* I wanted my daughter not to die at age nineteen. I refused to force our tragedy into some sort of beautiful blessing without giving nod to our lacerating loss.

No amount of positive outcomes made the loss of Katie worth it to me. It just didn't add up in this mother's heart. It was bad math. I'd have traded them all in a heartbeat for life with my daughter again. God had scooped her into His arms—but out of mine. And I hated it.

"But God was merciful"? Yes, He is merciful. And this is His mercy— not that your loved one was healed (when mine wasn't), but that this world is not the end of us. The years given us, be they nineteen or ninety, are but a blink, the mere welcome mat to eternity—a place where there will be no more tears, where God's transcendent love illuminates both the day and the night, and where death, at last, will lose its sting.[5]

---

[5]Revelation 21; 1 Corinthians 15:55

I take comfort in accepting that my vantage point is limited to my handful of experiences in this life and to what I can see with my own eyes. But God sees the whole sweep of eternity, from beginning to end. I have found Him to be a relentlessly good and loving God. Because of my confidence in His character, I can rest in knowing that someday, *someday*, Katie's short life and premature death will make sense to me. Someday God will scoop me, too, into His arms, and I will step into a world that until that moment I could only sense and never see. I will finally get it. And I will see Him face-to-face.

And you know who else I will see face-to-face on that day?

I will see Katie.

Yes, God is merciful.

49

"Hey, September," said a familiar voice on the other end of my phone earlier that spring. "It's me, Terry Franson."

Terry, APU's dean of students, had stayed in touch with our family since Katie's death, when he and Woody, the campus pastor, had flown out for Katie's memorial. They'd been purposeful about checking in with our kids ever since.

"Hi, Terry!" I said. "Good to hear from you." We chatted a few minutes, and then he cut to the chase.

"I'm calling on behalf of Jon Wallace, APU's president," he said. "As you know, this May is the commencement ceremony when Katie would have graduated."

"Yes, I'm . . . aware. We all are aware. It's another one of those hard milestones."

"I can only imagine. September, I know your daughter attended here just one year, but she had such a profound influence on the student body during that time, and she continues to transform this place through the people whose lives she marked, many of whom are now in student leadership positions."

"Wow, thank you, Terry. That's so good to hear. Katie would love to know that her life left such a ripple."

"Absolutely it did. We want to honor her contribution to Azusa Pacific. Could we fly you and your family down here in May? We'd like you and Scott to receive her diploma on her behalf during the commencement ceremony."

His words caught me by complete surprise. "Wow . . . I am deeply honored. But what about the other students graduating that day? This is *their* celebration. Won't it detract from their big day?"

"Trust me, we've talked it through, and we are doing this for our students as much as for you guys. So many of these graduates knew and loved Katie, and she will be in the back of their minds on gradua-tion day, whether or not we mention her. We want to offer them some closure. And Jon will make sure it won't detract from the celebration. You'll just accept her diploma and then step off the stage. No need to decide right away. Talk to Scott. But get back to me either way, so we can book tickets."

We exchanged goodbyes and I hung up. Then I put my hands to my face, stunned and deeply grateful for APU's generous offer. But mostly I just felt so stinking proud of my daughter. "I want to leave ripples in the lives I leave behind," she had written at fifteen. Indeed, God had used this one person's life, which she had stewarded with purpose and fervor, to leave such ripples. I took a moment and gave myself permis-sion to acknowledge that Katie had been a remarkable human being. *Too good to be true.*

～◎～

I told Scott about the phone call. After being reassured that Jon Wallace would not let it become "the Katie show" at the expense of the other graduates, he agreed it could be very cool. We checked with the kids and got a thumbs-up all the way around.

"Terry's right," Andrea told me. "This will help the other students. A girl in my class died when we were freshmen. And it was really hard on us. She was in the back of our minds on graduation day. This is a good plan, Mom, not just for our family but also for the school."

Bethany added a poignant observation. "This graduation cere-mony will be the final point in time where our family can say, 'At this moment, on this day, Katie would have been right here, in this exact place, doing *this*.'"

The school had offered us the sweetest of gifts, and we were all aware it would be yet another heavy turning of the page.

~◎~

I called Sandy in Spokane to tell her about the school's offer.

"That's incredible!" she said. "How would you feel about our family flying down for the ceremony? Because, well, we are flying down." Once again the McConkeys would be at our side.

The weekend was shaping up to be quite the event. Our whole family would be together, plus the McConkeys and my mom (Dad would be on a prescheduled fishing trip in northern Canada). Matt and Andrea invited everyone to bunk at their house—thirteen of us! Air mattresses, camping mats, sofas, and beds—I love that Matt and Andrea love a mob.

~◎~

As graduation drew near, I began thinking this weekend might provide the sort of communal grief moment I'd been longing for with the kids. Katie had been gone almost three years now, and although she came up in conversations all the time and we did unofficial grief check-ins periodically with one another, rarely had we let ourselves grieve together as a family-minus-one. And I longed for that.

Scott knew my propensity for prying uninvited, and he could see where this was heading.

"Let the weekend unfold naturally," he reminded me. "Losing a sibling is not the same as losing a child. The kids' needs are different from yours and mine. What do *you* want? What would serve *your* process?"

His question gave me pause. What did I want?

For one thing, I wanted a check-in. I wanted assurance that my kids were moving along healthily in their grief—that they were healing in their own unique ways. I hoped this event might give me a peek into their journeys and put my worrisome mama heart at ease. That's one thing I wanted, to be sure.

Also, I wanted this to be over. Psychologically, I was still waiting—waiting for what? May 31, 2008, was the left-sided bookend on this era in my life, and I was still waiting for some magical right-sided bookend to arrive and close out this mess so I could get my old life back. As I pondered Scott's question, I realized I was hoping that this graduation ceremony would be that right-sided bookend—an unrealistic expectation that I would need to set aside.

"Just let the weekend be what it's meant to be," Scott kept reminding me, "and be grateful for whatever that is."

50

"I want to have a talk with the kids about how they are grieving," Tember told me as we sat side by side on our flight to California. "Bethany and I talk about Katie, but the boys don't ever seem to talk about her—at least to me. I don't know how they are doing inside. It's weird that we don't talk about it more together, you know?"

"Agreed," I said, very cool-like. *Woo-hoo! Has she been reading my mind?*

"I want to talk about the fact that we don't talk about it," she said. "I think we should have a family meeting and just check in with everyone and talk about why it's so hard to grieve as a group. And I'll lead the meeting."

"Sounds great, Tem," I said. She sounded more like a sage mom than the sixteen-year-old baby of the family. This kid amazed me, and of course I loved her plan.

Once all the Vaudreys and McConkeys and my mom had arrived in California, we headed to a quaint little diner near Bethany's apartment for dinner. Laughter and good food dominated the night as we caught up on one another's lives.

The next day was the graduation. Bethany's Facebook status that morning articulated our sentiments perfectly:

Today I will be grateful for what was, instead of longing for what should have been.

The poignancy of this event was striking deeper than anyone had anticipated. By midmorning, the laughter had subsided, and a gentle pall hung in the air. In the back of our minds was the reality that Katie, the girl who had delighted in family and fun and pomp and circumstance, was missing her big day. By two in the afternoon, the emotional fragility of our group was beginning to show. We were getting ragged around the edges.

The original plan was to stay for the whole commencement, but Scott pulled me aside and said, "There is no way we can make it through the entire ceremony. We're all on the bubble as it is. I know you want to stay for the whole thing, and I'll stay with you if you want. But after Katie's diploma, we need to release the kids."

Scott was right. He called an audible and told the kids they could slip out as soon as Katie's diploma was in hand.

Blue sky, sunshine, and palm trees waving in a light breeze gave Azusa Pacific's campus a postcard-like beauty as we arrived. Kati Harkin, who had taken a year off from college and wouldn't be graduating that day, joined us. An electric sense of celebration reverberated in the air as parents and families scurried about with bouquets of roses or flower leis for their graduates. Terry Franson met us in the parking lot and ushered us to a bank of reserved seats near the back of the stadium so the kids could slip out easily afterward.

"I've got seats up front for you two," Terry said to Scott and me, "so you can access the stage easily. Stay here for now. I'll come get you when it's time."

As the first notes of "Pomp and Circumstance" floated through the afternoon air, a parade of black caps and gowns—APU's class of 2011— began filing into the stadium.

I recalled what Katie said at her high school commencement just four years ago: "My girlfriends have all been shopping for new graduation dresses," she had told us after an afternoon of thrifting. "But who's gonna see a new dress under those giant muumuu graduation gowns we have to wear? I'm placing my money on the shoes!"

She reached into a shopping bag and pulled out a pair of hot-pink pumps with four-inch heels. She would choose that same color for my petunias a year later.

And sure enough, among the sea of Fremd High School green caps and gowns filing into the stadium that day, those hot-pink pumps stood out like a beacon, making Katie easy to spot from any seat in the house.

What shoes would she have chosen for today? No black flats, I guarantee! As the APU graduates continued filing in, I thought of the graduate who was missing—a radiant brunette in brightly colored heels—waving happily at her family as she walked by. "Are you *filming* me?" she might have called out. And afterward, she would have squealed with delight when she found us, jumping into our arms, filled with joy and gratitude and the kind of self-pride that makes for a healthy person.

⁓☙⁓

Once the class was seated, Terry motioned to Scott and me, and we followed him to our chairs up front. "Just step up to the stage when Jon calls you," he said.

After a Scripture reading, prayer, and the commencement speeches, Dr. Jon Wallace approached the podium.

"Could I invite Scott and September Vaudrey to the platform, please?" he said. An eerie hush fell over the stadium. We rose and walked up the stairs. Jon shook our hands warmly, then turned to the microphone.

"Katie Vaudrey began her freshman year at Azusa Pacific in the fall of 2007. She spent her year in Trinity Hall. She was a vibrant, motivated freshman who inspired other Chicagoland students to come to the West Coast. Katie was strong and a faithful follower of Jesus Christ. Her love for God was evident to everybody who met her. She was a masterful artist, full of joy, and she had a continual hunger to help others."

As I listened to Jon's words, I was reminded yet again of what a treasure Katie was. My eyes stung. I bit my trembling lip. *Don't cry. Don't cry. Don't draw attention.* I stole a glance at stoic Scott and saw large tears rolling down his cheeks. *Well, heck. So much for keeping our emotions in check.*

Jon continued. "Tragically, while she was home for the summer after her freshman year, Katie passed from a ruptured cerebral aneurysm. Katie's presence in our community has been missed. On behalf of this community, it is my privilege to remember Katie and celebrate her remarkable life among us by presenting a diploma to her mother and father—and by extension to her classmates and her friends and her community. Would you please stand and recognize Katie Vaudrey with me?"

The stadium stood to its feet, and the crowd began clapping for our daughter. Jon stepped back from the mic and wrapped us in his arms.

"Thank you for coming here and doing this for our students," he said. "It's an important part of their healing process."

Scott wiped his eyes with the palms of his hands. "Thank you so much for all you've done for us. We love this school and we love you."

"It's our honor," Jon said, handing us her diploma. "We framed a copy of this, and it waits for you in my office. You may pick it up at any time."

We exited the platform and ducked behind the stage's backdrop. The swell of applause continued long and loud in our ears. Even after the people in the grandstands stopped clapping, Katie's graduating class on the field kept up their applause, honoring the girl they knew and loved and lost.

She mattered. Not just to us, but to Terry Franson, to Dr. Wallace, and to this stadium of kids who would not sit down. She made a difference in this world, and she will not be forgotten.

～⊘～

Sandy, her husband, Bobby, and my mom met us at the back of the stadium, and we were all pretty much a blubbery mess. But today's tears felt different. They were tears of relief—a healing salve.

"Where are the kids?" I asked. Their chairs sat empty.

"As soon as you were off the stage, they bolted," Sandy said. "This hit them very hard, especially Bethany and September. They just clung to one another, sobbing. It was pretty heartbreaking. They all headed for Starbucks down the road, just to be together and talk."

The ceremony moved on, and Jon Wallace began calling students' names and handing out diplomas. The crowd quickly regained its jubilance, as was fitting for this day. We slipped out.

At Starbucks, we found Matt, Andrea, Kati Harkin, and the McConkey boys standing together in the parking lot, red-eyed and soft-spoken. Matt led us to Bethany, Sam, and Tember, who were crammed into the backseat of Bethany's Honda Civic—the older two flanking Tember, their arms around her, weeping. Matt climbed into the passenger's seat, reaching his big-brother arm around to Bethany and resting his hand on her shoulder. Scott opened the back passenger door, and we bent down, eye level with the kids.

"Hey, you guys," he said. "We are so sorry. This is so very hard." There was nothing else to say. We just knelt there, crying together, remembering our missing sister and daughter on her graduation day. Katie's absence—and maybe her presence?—felt tangible and concrete to me as we mourned the loss of our family of seven, the Vaudreys we once had been.

That day was healing and productive and right. Those moments in a Starbucks parking lot were exactly what our family needed and what my soul had been aching for—what I had tried to force on my own terms, in my own timing over these past three years. Yet once I let go of trying to make it happen, it happened on its own. The environment here had done its work; Tember had risen to the occasion; and there inside a Honda Civic on a warm spring evening, a beautiful-horrible scene of familial grief had unfolded organically, in a way none of us could have predicted but all of us desperately needed.

When it was time to caravan back to Matt and Andrea's for dinner, Scott worried about Bethany driving her car. "She's too shaken to get behind the wheel," he said.

"I'll drive," Matt said, crossing over to the driver's seat. "We'll meet you at home."

And so in the privacy of Bethany's car, at sixty-five miles an hour on Interstate 10, the four sibs had their grief conversation. The bonds between them deepened through the sharing of their common loss.

Tember—and her mama—got their wish.

❧

The graduation ceremony had released three years of pent-up grief. It was as if we had all been holding our breath and finally exhaled together. It wasn't the bookend I'd hoped for—there could be no such bookend, really; it wasn't possible—but those days brought a degree of resolution that exceeded my expectations, especially with the kids. I had received what my soul had been longing for—a shared moment, an event, a stake in the ground that said, *Yes, we lost someone who meant the world to us, and we are heartbroken. Our lives will never be the same. And yes, we have survived. Our lives had once been beautiful, and our lives are beautiful still.*

Over the next few days with the McConkeys and my mom, between meals and laughter and movies and a day at Universal Studios, the conversations drifted back to Katie and the trauma our families had experienced together, to what each of us had lost, and to how much we had appreciated one another along the way.

On our last morning together, Sam was lounging on the sofa next to Sandy and me, listening as we talked. He seemed pensive and low.

"Sam," I said, "people often mention how hard this has been for Tember, that Katie was her best friend—which is true."

"Yep," he said. "No doubt. And Tember has done really well. I'm proud of her."

"Me too. But Sam, sometimes I wonder if perhaps you've felt like you are in the shadows of Tember's loss, just a bit. Not many people realize how close *you* and Katie were too." His dark-brown eyes filled immediately. I laid my hand on his shoulder, and large tears began rolling down his cheeks, one after the other. "Katie adored you, Sam. The two of you had such a great relationship, son. I can't imagine how hard this has been on you, how deep your loss must go."

He draped his arm across his face, and his chest heaved. I waited.

"Yeah," he said from somewhere beneath his elbow. "We loved each other a lot. She was just . . . she was just great." More tears. I kissed his arm lightly.

"Katie would be so proud of you, Sam, so proud of the man you are becoming. I am so very sorry for how much you have lost."

⟨∾⊙∾⟩

Before we flew home to Chicago, Scott and Sam picked up Katie's diploma from Jon Wallace's office. The school had indeed framed it— and wrapped it with a crimson bow.

Our girl had left ripples.

51

WHEN WE ARRIVED HOME IN CHICAGO, spring was cresting and the earthy aroma of gardens and freshly mowed lawns once again triggered my body memory of the heartache we had incurred at this time of year. Each spring, I had felt the impending arrival of another anniversary of Katie's accident—and its familiar tug toward God. I felt it again now. He was calling.

The three-year mark fell on a Tuesday. I awoke early, dressed, and stepped outside. The energetic serenade of songbirds fell silent at my intrusion, then slowly and bravely they resumed their chatter. Pale-pink petals from our hawthorn tree blossoms—the tree featured in Katie's last work of art—fluttered onto the deck like confetti. A morning breeze sent wisps of thin-white clouds speeding across the sky, rustling the new leaves of the cottonwoods just beyond our fence line. The Midwest humidity had not yet made its summer descent, and the air was warm but without the sticky.

I walked to my vegetable garden at the far side of our yard and said good morning to the snow peas and lettuce. Then I sat down on the lawn and let the rising sun warm my skin. Our dogs, Henry and Alice, trotted over, happy to find me at ground level. I scratched behind their respective ears until, satisfied, they romped off to explore the yard.

Three years ago and every spring since, I had resisted a primal urge to lie down, bury my face in this sod, and rant at God, or cling to Him, or both. These past few months, the urge had grown stronger. I had sensed a showdown coming, and today I was braced for a fight. I lay back, rolled onto my belly, and stretched out my arms. I ran my hands over the lawn and pressed my forehead to the ground. My fingers tightened around fistfuls of grass. I drew my breath. *Bring it on.*

But in that moment, I felt no urge to cry or to shake God by the ankles or to rail at Him in protest. *Why? Where is my fight?*

To my utter shock, I discovered that the fight in me had faded. In its place, the sorrow that had been my constant companion these past three years mingled with an inexplicable sense of peace and unapologetic sparks of joy.

I lay there baffled and a little annoyed by this unforeseen turn of events. *How can this be? My circumstances are the same—my daughter is gone; my heart is broken! Nothing has changed.*

Or had it?

As I lay there with the grass getting scratchy and warm upon my face, it dawned on me: Perhaps what had changed was me. Perhaps over these three years, in tiny, indiscernible increments, I had grown. I had not thought of it as growth at the time. It had felt more like survival. But I couldn't deny that I was not the same person I had been three years ago, or two, or one. These annual backyard struggles—like pencil lines against a kitchen doorway that mark a child's growth—had marked my inner growth as well.

God, always the gentleman, had not rushed me or demanded I accept this life whose story line still horrified me, and perhaps always would. He had simply continued to invite and to fan little embers of joy beneath the ashes as consistent reminders of His love for me. He had not forgotten me or my family or our pain. Not once. *I am good,* I had sensed Him whispering to me as I stood on that ambulance bay a lifetime ago. *This tragedy doesn't change My character. It doesn't change who I am. I am good.*

Through the unfailing partnership of my pain and God's goodness, we had settled things, He and I. Slowly over these past 1,095 days, surrender had been sidling up alongside me, unobserved. My grieving was far from over—it's a lifelong journey, I believe—but I had come to accept the beautiful-tragic life that is mine. It wasn't a story I had ever envisioned before Katie died, but I had found it to be a story of soulful beauty made possible as a result of her death.

In baby steps, I had accepted this uninvited life. I had surrendered.

And this is surrender: inviting laugher and sorrow to dance together in our lives, day by day and hand in hand.

Nearby, the hawthorn tree stood silhouetted against the morning sky. Its confetti petals swirled around me, and my daughter's words echoed in my mind.

"I'm calling it *The Bleeding Tree*," Katie had declared, holding up the rough draft of her final work of art.

"*The Bleeding Tree*? Sounds . . . significant."

"Oh, it is! You're going to love it. I can't wait to tell you what it means!"

This side of heaven, I will never know fully what Katie intended to communicate through this painting she was creating for us—but I can take a guess from the clues she left behind.

For followers of Jesus like Katie and me, a tree is the cross—it's suffering and sacrifice, and also forgiveness and redemption. A tree is seasons—autumns of spectacular dying; stark winters; hopeful springs; and lush, opulent summers. Katie had watched Scott and me navigate a barren winter in marriage—and had seen our relationship bloom again, through spring and into summer.

"I am learning never to waste pain, but to experience it fully," she had written in her senior thesis. "I want my work to be indicative of the beauty within struggle."

My guess—and it's only a guess—is our daughter was celebrating that Scott and I had not wasted our season of marital pain. We had tried to steward that season well, and God had grown something beautiful as a result of our struggle. This is what her work means to me.

Today *The Bleeding Tree* hangs incomplete, yet in a place of honor in our home. Although it is but a shadow of the finished piece Katie intended, I cherish it fully for what it is, not for what it might have been. I marvel at its simple beauty.

So it is with my life. This side of heaven, I will never know the full meaning behind the death of my daughter—or even if there is a pre-scripted meaning to such tragedies here on earth. But I am learning to cherish each day for what it is, not what it might have been. And despite my limited vantage point and incomplete understanding, Katie's life and death hang in a place of honor in my soul.

The morning breeze sent a fresh flutter of hawthorn petals cascading around me. An unrestrained swell of release washed over me, and two warm tears slipped down my cheeks, soaking into the earth.

I sat up and grinned, plucked a blade of grass to chew on, and breathed deep lungfuls of the morning air. The breeze picked up, rustling the distant cottonwood leaves with greater vigor, but its buds had not yet blossomed, and no cottony, miniature-angel tufts floated free. *Late this year, I guess.* Not a problem. God is good.

I stood, stretched, and turned toward the house, ready to face the day.

hansa yellow

['han-suh 'yel-oh] / a cool, clean yellow

The soft, unassuming yellow of a tulip bud

is the understudy to bolder, brassier yellows.

But when at last her turn comes, she steps into the spotlight

and unfurls her petals before us without apology.

She lives out each scene wholeheartedly—

and with tremendous joy.

We must be willing to let go of the life we've planned,
so as to have the life that is waiting for us.

JOSEPH CAMPBELL

Joy is the most infallible sign of the presence of God.

PIERRE TEILHARD DE CHARDIN

Epilogue

A FEW MONTHS BEFORE THE FOUR-YEAR MARK, Matt and Andrea called to tell us the best of all news: They were expecting their first baby! We couldn't have been more overjoyed. *A brand-new Vaudrey!* The first addition to the family since Matt had married Andrea almost five years ago—and the first Vaudrey birth since Tember was born in 1993. Woo-hoo! We were becoming grandparents—and at the tender ages of forty-nine and fifty. The baby wasn't due until early October, seven months away (more waiting!), and we began counting the days.

Tember's high school graduation and her senior prom coincided with the four-year mark. We flew everyone home, and Bethany and Andrea came early to fulfill Katie's promise of helping the youngest Vaudrey sister get ready for her dance.

For Tember's junior prom a year prior, Bethany and Andrea also had been in town, and they turned our master bathroom into a beauty salon for their kid sister. They gave her a French manicure and pedicure and applied her makeup with utmost care. They curled and styled her hair and helped her step into her dress. Their sisterly whispers, chatter, and laughter spilled from the bathroom and filled my heart. I snapped photos as they doted on the baby of the family.

This year, Tember had a job at an upscale salon in nearby South Barrington, so she had lined up appointments with professional hair stylists, makeup artists, and nail technicians. Not quite the crescendo moment of Bethany and Andrea filling in for Katie that I had envisioned! But Tember wasn't the same eighth-grade girl who had hinted in her eulogy about being alone on this day. She was eighteen and had grown up—not just physically, but into a level of maturity that was serving her well.

"I realize now that Katie perfectly fulfilled my desires for her pre-dance help on that day of my eighth-grade dance," she told me. "And Bethany and Andrea spoiled me in the best of ways last year. Today I'm going to take advantage of having friends at the spa who want to help me out."

When Tember arrived home from her appointments, time was running short, so her sisters helped her put on her dress—a stunning emerald-green satin gown accented with silver rhinestones—and applied final touches to her hair. When at last the youngest Vaudrey descended our staircase for the dance, she was indeed a vision to behold.

"Tember, I promise you," Katie had said four years ago, "wherever I am, I will fly home for your senior prom and help you get ready. I will be here. I wouldn't miss it for the world!"

Katie's intentions with the promise she couldn't keep had been fulfilled—not once, but twice—by sisters who loved her so. And who knows? Perhaps in a way beyond what my eyes could see, Katie had been here all along.

❧

"Will you paint a mural for our baby's nursery?" Matt asked me over the phone in late June.

"Of course!" I replied.

Katie had planned to paint a mural in Matt and Andrea's first apartment, but it was one of the many goals she didn't get to accomplish in her short life. I have a fraction of my daughter's artistic talents, but this mural was within my skill set—and I knew just the tools I would use.

After I hung up with Matt, I decided to do something I'd been putting off for four years. I headed to the basement to find Katie's art toolbox.

Dusty and a little cobwebby, it sat undisturbed on the shelf where I'd stored it the day it arrived from California. I wiped away the cobwebs, sat down on the cement floor, and opened the lid.

The waft of turpentine and oil paints once again hit my nose, bringing fond remembrances. My throat tightened. I let myself explore.

The top tray of the toolbox held Katie's paintbrushes, and in typical Katie fashion, they were in need of a good cleaning. Her senior year, I had finally boycotted gifting Katie with any new brushes until she began to care properly for the ones she had—and she did show some improvement. But today, gladly, I would clean her brushes well. Fifteen minutes and a little bristle soap would be a small price to pay for welcoming Aunt Katie's brushes back into service on a mural for my grandchild.

In the middle tray, on top of her paints, palette knives, oil pastels, and such, I found a stack of invitations to the various senior exhibits of fellow art students at APU. Katie must have been saving the invitations—each individually designed—as examples for the day she would create an invitation for her own senior exhibit.

Underneath the invitations were a few encouraging notes from friends. Each bore thumbtack holes. Katie must've tacked them to the wall of her studio space. One, from Kati Harkin, closed with, "The world is truly fortunate to get to know your heart. And I am so lucky to be your friend." Katie would say *she* was the lucky one. Perhaps that was part of her secret.

And there in the bottom of her toolbox was her green Starbucks apron, shoved in a bundle just where I'd left it four years ago. I pulled it out, gave it a shake, and held it up. I ran my fingers over the dried paint, and this time I did not cry. Instead, I drew the apron to my face and breathed deeply, taking in its oil-and-acrylic smells. The sturdy canvas fabric felt cool against my cheek. Covered with dried smudges, splatters, smears where Katie had wiped her hands, and the faint fingerprint she had left behind, this apron itself had become a work of art, a canvas that told the story of my girl.

I pulled the apron strap over my head and smoothed out its wrinkles against my chest. I sat for a moment, looking down at it, thinking. *There is no turning back.* I would bring it to California and wear it while I painted my grandchild's mural, adding my own smudges and fingerprints to the story this apron told. I was not hoping to channel Katie's artistic talents through the apron—nothing like that. But I wouldn't complain if I felt a bit of her joy as I painted, joy she would have been sharing with me—perhaps was sharing now—in this pre-auntie, pre-grandma season, which was short-lived and delicious. This was a good plan.

Beneath the apron, under heavy tubes of oil paint, I found two Tazo tea bags—Wild Sweet Orange and Awake. Classic Katie—of course she would store tea along with her art supplies, making it easy for her to engage the savory senses as part of her "artist's life." I turned the tea bags over in my hand and imagined my daughter sipping from a cup and sharing a conversation with a friend in her little studio space at APU, the pungent aroma of the tea mingling with the fumes of paint and turpentine. I imagined how she might have brewed herself a cup of tea late at night as she finished an art project, alone with her joy and her tools and her God. I would bring the tea bags, along with her brushes, paints, and the apron, to paint a mural in California.

In mid-August, Tember and I took a train across the country to California so she could begin her new life as a college freshman at—you guessed it—Azusa Pacific University. We went a week early so I could paint the mural. We crashed at Matt and Andrea's, and the next morning I set to work.

The expectant parents had chosen Nintendo's Baby Mario as the theme. I didn't even know that *baby* Mario was a thing, but it is, and Matt introduced me to Baby Mario, Luigi, Daisy, and Peach, to Yoshi and mushroom toads and flying turtles, to Mario clouds, stars, and trees. I pencil-sketched a Baby Mario scene filled with these characters, spanning the two walls that surrounded the baby's crib. Then I pulled Katie's apron over my neck, tied its strings around my waist, mixed her acrylic paints on her palette, loaded her clean-as-a-whistle Grumbacher half-inch sable brush, and got busy.

I spent the next four days immersed in the mural. I wiped my paint-splattered fingers on Katie's apron, and I rinsed her brushes (thoroughly!). Twice I brewed myself a cup of her tea, steeping the bags that had spent four years nestled alongside Katie's oil paints and art supplies. I would not wholeheartedly recommend a cup of Wild Sweet Orange and turpentine tea for others, but I drank it for myself, and I toasted my middle daughter the artist—the lover of God and beauty and people. And I toasted the yet-to-come grandchild, whose fresh eyes would wake from a nap, and blink, and look upon a mural painted with brushes that could tell countless stories and carried their artist's joy.

~ இ ~

On September 20, I witnessed firsthand the grand entrance of the lovely Cadence Ruth Vaudrey—six pounds, five ounces of delicate perfection! The waiting was over—and this event had certainly been worth the wait! When at long last I held little Cadence in my arms, my eyes were hungry to memorize every bit of her. She was scrumptious to behold—tiny fingernails, a dusting of dark hair, perfect little lips, eyebrows, and ears— and eyes so large she looked a bit like a Nintendo character herself. Yet her entire face was no bigger than a saltine. (I measured with a cracker from Andrea's hospital dinner tray.) My granddaughter was smart, too! When she gave a tiny, baby-birdlike yawn, we all had no choice but to marvel at her brilliance.

And on that day, our family turned a page. We welcomed a delightful new chapter into our lives, a chapter filled with promise. A brand-new family had been formed: Our son became a father and our daughter-in-law a mother. Aunts, uncles, and grandfathers were created that day— and grandmothers, too. You may call me Nana.

~ இ ~

Welcome, little Cadence. What shall your nana tell you about this life you have been given? What promises can I make about this world you have graced?

I, your nana, hereby promise to love you always, to let you add way too many chocolate chips to the cookie dough, and to talk your parents into letting you keep the puppy that "followed us home." I will read you every Laura Ingalls Wilder book once we finish with Junie B. Jones. I will show you how to plant pumpkin seeds, make apricot jam, and determine if a peach is ripe for the picking. I will help you sew a quilt if you'd like, and I'll explain why strong verbs trump adverbs every time. I'll teach you tricks for getting a pony to take her bit, and most certainly I will buy you Levi's instead of Calvin Klein when Levi's is the best choice for the job. We will dig up the potatoes in the fall, climb the tree one branch higher than you think we can, and tame raccoons as needed. We will have grand adventures, you and I. I can hardly wait!

Little Cadence, this world is cradled by the hands of a loving God who always has your best interest at heart—though you may not fully understand His ways this side of eternity. His thumbprints are everywhere if you simply take time to notice. And although someday you—like all of us—will taste heartache, let me share a secret your nana has learned: By inviting heartache to do its transforming work, your life will grow richer, more meaningful, and more marked by both beauty and joy—not in spite of, but *because* of the pain that has seasoned it along the way.

Cadence—"Cady," as they plan to call you, a nice variation on a theme—God willing, for many decades to come you will bless those around you with the talents and gifts He has given you to bring a bit of His Kingdom to this broken world. You will play hard, love deeply, and experience fervently the life you have been given. Your every day will enrich those around you, and you will leave ripples too.

And when you grow old, perhaps with grandchildren of your own, you will scoop them into your arms and kiss their velvet cheeks and necks and toes as I am kissing yours today.

And one day when you step across the threshold into eternity, you'll be welcomed by those who went before you—a mom and a dad, nanas and papas, aunties and uncles, and also a certain brown-eyed beauty, the aunt you never got to meet. When she spots you, no doubt she will squeal with delight, wrap you in her arms, and swing you around, filling your ears with her laughter. Then perhaps she'll take you by the hand—Katie and Cady—and introduce you to the One she loves best of all: the God of all beauty and joy, who has looked after her family with such goodness and tenderness and faithfulness while she has been away.

Katherine Vaudrey, 1989–2008

Gallery

Katie, age 5.
Some dreams she got to fulfill.

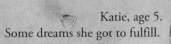

Silly then . . .
(Matt, Katie, Tember,
Bethany, Sam)

. . . silly now.
Our joy is richer today,
and laughter is still allowed.
(Matt, Andrea, Tember, Bethany,
Sam, Scott, me)

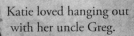

Katie loved hanging out
with her uncle Greg.

Self-Portrait
*Watercolor on
140-lb. cold-press paper
18" x 24" | Age 17*

Saying goodbye
to her dad
("my superhero!")
before she boarded
a plane for college

Our Katies: Kati Harkin
with Katie Vaudrey, who
is wearing the necktie
and shirt from her job
training earlier that
day—the same outfit
she would wear again
three days later

5/28/2008   5:17

Lavender Orchids
Watercolor on 140-lb. cold-press paper, 12" x 21" | Age 19
Employing an alla prima ("first attempt") brush technique reserved mostly for oils, Katie used watercolors to capture the birthday flowers her boyfriend sent. This technique requires speed— which, of course, made it fun for Katie.

I want to leave ripples in the lives i leave behind

—Katie, age 15

Mommy—
    Your joy is one of the main ingredients to this home's climate. Dont underestimate your contribution! I am thrilled to be home with you.
        Happy Mothers Day, Mama.
            I love you!
                Katie

Katie's last Mother's Day card, age 19. Would her words hold true?

On the night of Tember's eighth-grade dance, Katie
told Scott, "I want a picture with just me and Tember!"
This simple request gifted us with our last photo of Katie.

Kisses goodbye . . .

. . . and a goodbye prayer:
our final moments as a
complete family

On the day Gloria showed up, it was unmistakably clear who was really caring for whom.

At the crash site: pre-grieving my first Mother's Day without Katie

McConkeys and Vaudreys, 2011: Life is better with these people at our side. *Front*: Collin, Tember, Bethany, Aaron *Middle*: Brian, Sam, Andrea, Sandy *Back*: Matt, Scott, me, Bobby

Our family today, 2015: Andrea holding Clayton (and carrying baby #3!), Matt, Scott, me, Bethany holding Cadence, Sam, Tember

About the Art

FOR ME, EACH PIECE OF KATIE'S ART tells two distinct stories: the primary story she intended to communicate when she created it, and the secondary story of the work's creative process. It is this secondary story that has left the most vibrant brushstrokes of memory in my mind: what Katie was doing on the day she painted it; what she was wearing at the time; her depth of passion for whatever wrong she was fighting, which drove certain pieces; and always the flash in her eyes and earnest intensity in her voice when she described its meaning. These secondary stories can be summed up in one word: joy. It gave her such joy to create. And it is with joy that I invite you to explore a few of the secondary stories behind my daughter's art—and a few photos as well, which hold stories of their own.

FRONT COVER
The Bleeding Tree
Watercolor on sketch paper, 14" x 21" | Age 19

This rough draft, completed the day before she died, is Katie's final work of art. (Sorry, Katie, for putting one of your rough drafts on the cover of a book!) This final work is a treasure to us, and someday Scott and I will learn what our daughter *really* meant by its cryptic title.

INSIDE FRONT COVER
A Tree Called Life
Watercolor on 140-lb. cold-press paper, 18" x 25" | Age 19

Katie was a lover of contrasts, and perhaps that is what captured her eye when she saw this tree. I can relate to the gnarled, weathered tree trunk—but it is the flourish of new-growth leaves that gives me hope.

OPENING PAGES
My Voice (title page)
Black and white ebony on recycled paper, 28" x 9" | Age 19

My Voice II (contents)
Black and white ebony on recycled paper, 15" x 22" | Age 19

Katie chose ebony to depict her favorite paintbrushes as a freshman at Azusa Pacific University. She wrote, "The subject of this still life is my voice." These works are drawn in the negative on recycled brown paper, using white or black ebony to show highs and lows and allowing the dark paper to show through from underneath.

Katie's Christmas stocking ("But One"): To help ease the pain of our first Katie-less Christmas, I'd planned something clever to fill the emptiness of Katie's stocking. What I had not anticipated was that once we handed the rest of the kids their stockings, the starkness of our new reality would be left hanging tangibly, visibly clear.

Mama and daughter (foreword): Even at thirteen, Katie wasn't beyond a good snuggle.

PART 1: VERMILLION
Thunderclouds (page xiv)
Watercolor on 140-lb. cold-press paper, 13" x 21" | Age 19

We found this painting still attached to a tablet of watercolor paper. It shows Katie's trademark haste—and her powerful use of color and texture.

Vaudrey family, 2007: The original Vaudrey seven in 2007: Katie (18), Matt (22), Scott, me, Sam (15), Bethany (20), Tember (13), and our toy Australian shepherds, Henry and Alice.

PART 2: PAYNE'S GREY
Masquerade (page 46)
Colored pencil and graphite on paper, 17" x 21" | Age 16

This piece hung in the school district office for a year and now hangs in Scott's office. We love its intrigue—and the level of detail created with colored pencils.

PART 3: INDIGO
It Needed Yellow (page 102)
Acrylic on stretched canvas, 36" x 48" | Age 17 (yellow added at age 19)

Two years after completing this piece in red, black, grey, and white, Katie whipped out her brushes as we chatted in her room. She mixed up a wash of cadmium yellow and began adding fresh brushstrokes to the piece—as it hung on her bedroom wall. "It needed yellow," she explained.

PART 4: BURNT SIENNA
Lighthouse III (page 164)
Oil pastels on paper, 18" x 24" | Age 16

During her sophomore year, Katie had a penchant for drawing and painting lighthouses. This one—my favorite—hangs in her sister Tember's room at college.

PART 5: CADMIUM GREEN LIGHT
Sharpening her skills . . . (page 214)
Watercolor with her sumi-e brushes on watercolor paper, 9" x 12" | Age 19

PART 6: CERULEAN BLUE
The Siblings (page 242)
India ink wash with sumi-e brushes on torn watercolor paper, 12" x 36" | Age 19

It gave Katie great joy to capture the childhood years of all five of our kids. This is one of the few paintings she was satisfied with—and a family favorite.

EPILOGUE: HANSA YELLOW

Cadence's mural (page 272): My grandchild's nursery, Katie's brushes and apron, and a cup of Sweet Wild Orange and turpentine—the perfect blend.

Nana and Cadence: I'm a nana! A joyful turning of the page.

INSIDE BACK COVER

Katie painting at a wedding: Katie completed a twenty-four-by-forty-six-inch watercolor during the twenty-minute prelude to the wedding of friends Eric and Sue (photo by Brian Kammerzelt).

Discussion Questions

1. Despite the chaos and overwhelming uncertainty September and Scott faced when they arrived at the hospital following Katie's accident, September describes a brief moment in the ambulance bay when she sensed God's voice, which filled her with peace and a calm that went beyond her understanding. Have you ever had a similar experience in the midst of trials or loss? Spend time remembering and sharing what occurred.

2. Throughout the book, September talks about the importance of having a community and a strong support system during seasons of deep loss. In times like these, who are the people who walk alongside you? How can you be more purposeful about supporting your loved ones when they experience loss or pain?

3. Upon hearing the news that a witness had seen Katie unconscious behind the wheel of her car before the crash, September realized that an aneurysm—not a broken neck or a cracked skull—caused her daughter's bleed. Even though this news didn't bring her daughter back, she was relieved to know that the accident hadn't been caused by reckless driving and could not have been prevented. Have you ever celebrated unusual news or information in the midst of sorrow? Explain.

4. When stress or emotional pain becomes too much, it helps to have a place to hide away and give yourself a break or an opportunity to breathe. Where is your "safe place" to get away from everything and give yourself a minute of peace or a chance to let yourself fall apart?

5. Going through Katie's things, September struggled to find the balance between viewing her daughter's belongings and artwork as treasured mementos and turning them into a shrine. What kinds of things do you hold on to for the sake of a memory? How do you keep them from becoming a barrier to healthy healing from loss?

6. Throughout the book, September mentions times when she discovered God's "thumbprints" showing up through the care and concern of others. When has a simple act of kindness or a small encouragement made all the difference and lifted your spirits? Describe your experience.

7. The Vaudreys had to accept life without Katie as their "new normal." Have you ever experienced a new normal, when everything was different from before? Describe your experience—your before and your after.

8. Each member of the Vaudrey family handled his or her loss very differently. How do you deal with your emotions during seasons of loss? In what ways does your style of grief differ from your loved ones' styles? How can you be more accepting of these differences and help family members through painful seasons?

9. As you look back at some difficult situations you have faced, can you see how God carried you through them? Explain.

10. A few months into year two, September felt butterflies in her stomach, which she recognized as unexpected flickers of joy. When has this happened to you after a season of hardship? Was it a fleeting moment, or did it linger?

11. Bandito Barney's became a place of remembrance, joy, and laughter for September and her family in honor of Katie. Do you or your family have a special place that gives you solace and peace? How did you discover this sanctuary?

12. September powerfully describes the different "colors" of grief she experienced as she mourned the loss of Katie. Do you see these colors reflected in your own experience? Which do you relate to most today, or what color has been added to your palette?

13. After reading about September's journey through grief, what are the key takeaways for you? How might they equip you to navigate your own seasons of pain, or to support others through theirs?

September's Selected Resources
on Grief and Loss

I've read a lot of grief books, and the list below contains some of my favorites. These authors write from a variety of perspectives. Some are people of faith; all speak honestly of their raw, human experience. Grief is an individual process, but pain is pain, and we can learn from one another's experiences. We can engage with one another's stories, absorb that which rings true for us, and let the rest sift through our fingers. (I trust you have done so with *Colors of Goodbye*!) Continue your journey. Read on.

Memoirs on Grief and Loss
- *A Grace Disguised: How the Soul Grows Through Loss*, by Jerry Sittser
- *A Grief Observed*, by C. S. Lewis
- *A Three Dog Life*, by Abigail Thomas
- *And Life Comes Back: A Wife's Story of Love, Loss, and Hope Reclaimed*, by Tricia Lott Williford
- *Choosing to See: A Journey of Struggle and Hope*, by Mary Beth Chapman
- *I Will Carry You: The Sacred Dance of Grief and Joy*, by Angie Smith
- *Let's Pretend We're Normal: Adventures in Rediscovering How to Be a Family*, by Tricia Lott Williford

- *One Thousand Gifts: A Dare to Live Fully Right Where You Are*, by Ann Voskamp
- *Rare Bird: A Memoir of Loss and Love*, by Anna Whiston-Donaldson
- *Swimming with Maya: A Mother's Story*, by Eleanor Vincent
- *The Hardest Peace: Expecting Grace in the Midst of Life's Hard*, by Kara Tippetts
- *The Year of Magical Thinking*, by Joan Didion

Books on Loss, Change, Faith, and Growth
- *Bittersweet: Thoughts on Change, Grace, and Learning the Hard Way*, by Shauna Niequist
- *Carry On, Warrior: The Power of Embracing Your Messy, Beautiful Life*, by Glennon Doyle Melton
- *Healing after Loss: Daily Meditations for Working through Grief*, by Martha Whitmore Hickman
- *Lose, Love, Live: The Spiritual Gifts of Loss and Change*, by Dan Moseley
- *Shattered Dreams: God's Unexpected Path to Joy*, by Larry Crabb
- *The Grief Club: The Secret to Getting Through All Kinds of Change*, by Melody Beattie
- *The Healing Path: How the Hurts in Your Past Can Lead You to a More Abundant Life*, by Dan B. Allender
- *When Your Family's Lost a Loved One: Finding Hope Together*, by David and Nancy Guthrie
- *Where Is God When It Hurts?*, by Philip Yancey

Leave Ripples

Two Ways to Give Life

Give through Compassion

In Memory of Trifonia
Watercolor on 140-lb. cold-press paper, 18" x 26" | Age 17

Visible Anjelin
Watercolor on 140-lb. cold-press paper, 18" x 26" | Age 19

Trifonia was a beautiful little girl from Rwanda—Katie's age—whom our family got to know through sponsorship with Compassion International. In the aftermath of the 1994 Rwanda genocide, Trifonia disappeared. During college, Katie began corresponding with a child she sponsored on her own: "This is a portrait of my Compassion child, Anjelin, from Indonesia, who just turned five, who is real, alive, and irreplaceable." If Katie's story has moved you to explore sponsoring a child in need through Compassion, you can learn more at compassion.com.

Give the Gift of Life

You can give the gift of life by registering to be an organ donor. Find your state's organ donation registry here:

organdonor.gov/becomingdonor/stateregistries.html

Acknowledgments

When I first sat down with Chris Ferebee and his wife, Christy, I offered them this promising trifecta in the publishing industry: (1) unknown author, (2) wrote a memoir, and (3) about grief. Woo-hoo! But luckily for me, in Chris I found not only a fantastic agent but also a lover of books who cares about beautiful language and believes *Colors of Goodbye* holds a story worth sharing. Thank you, Chris, for your gentle wisdom and keen guidance in our first project together.

A special thanks to Shauna Niequist, who nudged me to turn my loss journey into a book and has coached me each step of the way. Shauna, I am forever grateful for how generously you have spent your own remarkable influence as a gifted speaker and author to help *Colors* reach its audience.

Thank you to Sarah Atkinson, my acquisitions editor, who championed this book from beginning to end. Thanks to Jan Long Harris and my Tyndale Momentum team—Jillian VandeWege, Sharon Leavitt, Nancy Clausen, Cassidy Gage, Rachel Lance, Mark Lane, Dean Renninger, Anisa Baker, Alison Shurtz, Todd Starowitz, Katie Dodillet, and Maggie Rowe—for your remarkable skill, commitment to excellence, and encouragement. Special thanks to my editor, Kimberly Miller, for doggedly engaging with each round of edits until we landed just the right words.

Thank you to early readers of the manuscript, including many mentioned elsewhere, as well as Sarah Springer, Heather Larson, Katie Kulchar, Lisa Hartman, Lori Hall, and my entire family (including Mom and Andrea—at least twice!). The book is so much stronger for your insightful, invaluable input.

These dear friends carried us with their presence and help in the days and weeks after Katie's death: the McConkeys (Bobby, Sandy, Aaron, Brian, and Collin); Galen, Brenda, Kristin, Greg, Brett, Jenny and PJ, Dave, and Garry; Kim, Jim, and Linda; Liz; Brooks; Ute; Brenda and Wayne; Sandy and Steve; Clarence, Elizabeth, and Steve; Jimmy, Leanne, Ester, Bizzy, and Davy; Bill and Gail; Brooke and Deanna; Tom and Anna; Wally and Kaleen, Patti and Kerry, Craig, Bryan, Chrissie, Darren, Pat and Dave, Dave and Vicki, Bryan, Deirdre, Greg and Beth, Jay, John and Heather, Kristy, Ryan, Shane and Wendy, Steve, Sue and Eric, Tyler, Sarah, and Hannah; Jeremiah; Kevin and Meg; Heather; and Joe and Shawna.

To those integrally involved in Katie's Willow Creek memorial, our deepest thanks: Bill, Brandon, Leanne, Jon P., Jon K., Phil, Chris, Nate, Ken, Matt, Deanna, and Bowman. A special thanks to those who created the Life Exhibit—the art show of my daughter's dreams: Susan, Sibyl, and Dawn and Greg; Katie's Impact friends; and the Willow Creek staff.

Thanks to Grandma Gerali, who opened her Vegas condo as a space for us to grieve—and stocked the fridge with her famous Italian cooking; to Steve and Jan for shipping Katie's art to Chicago—and for raising the daughter-in-law of our dreams; to our extended family—Janice and Bob Vaudrey; Russell and Jody; Tamaren and Clay; Brenda and Vic, Gail and George, Linda, Connie, Tuny, and Judy and Bud; Rod and Sammie; and our wonderful cousins—for grieving alongside us.

Thanks to Jon, Terry, Woody, and the Azusa Pacific community for walking with us and creating a university environment where our children could thrive.

On behalf of Katie, a joyful thank you to the friends who made her nineteen years so rich, including Kati, Dan, and Whitney; Michelle, Kara, and Molly; Casey, Melissa, Darla, Ester, Marie, Laura, and Caitlin; Chris, Dave, Mark, Steve, Nate, and Jenna; Marissa, Amber, Courtney, Red, Brooke, Troy, Leighton, Chase, and CJ; Kanani, Kelisha, and Heather.

Thanks to Jill Landback and Leigh Wilson, my high school drama and English teachers. You heaped value onto the fragile scales of my adolescence, and your influence still marks me today. (Leigh, I did as you instructed: "Never stop writing!")

A special thanks to the Hot Moms—a group of remarkably gifted, young Willow women who met monthly at my house during the writing of these pages: Under the guise of learning about parenting from me, you taught me buckets about how to be a better mom and a better human being.

Grief is a solitary journey we dare not take alone. Deep thanks to my posse of girlfriends who walk shoulder to shoulder with me each step of the way: Sandy, Lynne, Kaye, Tammy, Margaret, and Lynette. Special thanks to Chris and Scott, who, with their wives, share conversation, laughter, and tears with my husband and me in the Bug Room. Those conversations are holy ground, and we are grateful.

The gratitude I feel for my parents, Greg and Teda Voss, grows deeper with each passing year. You have been a faithful safety net for our family through every crisis—and especially through losing your granddaughter. Your relentless support and encouragement have shaped our family in ways you may never know. We thank you. We love you. I love you.

A heartfelt thanks to my wonderful brother, Greg, who is a loving uncle to our kids. You hold a special place in Katie's heart—and mine.

"Acknowledgments" is an inadequate title to contain the level of gratitude I hold for my husband and kids . . .

To Matt, the funniest meme writer and most grace-filled firstborn I know: Thank you for gentle exhortations to be kinder to myself and for being the type of big brother who dons a yellow rain slicker and hops on his Vesper in a downpour to go help his kid sister hang pictures in her new dorm room. People tease you and me for "seeing something shiny," but when they say we are alike, it's the best compliment I could receive.

To Andrea, the gold standard daughter-in-law and my grief twin: Thank you for holding in your heart the words of loss I could not share elsewhere, for enfolding our family as your own, and for loving our son and grandkids so well. Had Matt not chosen you for a wife, I would still choose you for a friend.

To Bethany, the perfect balance of wisdom and kindness: How I have admired your grief journey! You lost not only a kid sister but also an entire adulthood of sisterly memories, which were just beginning to bloom. From toddlerhood to today, you have been a faithful deliverer of love, laughter, and truth in my life. Dad was right—you make a terrific grown-up.

To Katie, who continues to influence my life through the example of how she lived hers: Not a sunset passes when I don't ache for your presence, Katie. I count the days until I can hold you in my arms once again—and until that day, I carry you in my heart.

To Sam, the lover of all things family: Witnessing your quiet, tender grief at the loss of the sister who "loved you more!" has expanded my understanding of how to love an introvert—for which Dad thanks you (and I do too!). You consistently counter our decade of familial sorrow with your ability to bring value and laughter to every conversation.

To Tember, our grand finale: The bravery you exhibit despite losing your best friend/sister never ceases to amaze me. You've maintained your goofball humor, tenacious drive against injustice, and burgeoning intellect—qualities that make you a fascinating, delightful, and dangerous adult. You fill this mama's heart, and I am so grateful for you.

And to Scott, my partner in every sense of the word: Thank you for making a commitment in 1984 to give our kids the best possible story and fulfilling that pledge day after day with such stunning beauty. More so, thank you for being a relentless truth bearer in my life. You help me live a better story with each passing year. You are my favorite human, and I am yours forever.

About the Author

SEPTEMBER AND HER HUSBAND, Scott, have been married for thirty-two years and have five grown children and two grandkids—and counting.

September grew up on an old dairy farm in Issaquah, Washington, and thus prefers Levi's over Calvin Klein. She works in her garden bare-handed at the expense of her nails and finds it life-giving to listen to the stories of others who are navigating seasons of loss. She serves as writer/content developer in the pastoral response department at Willow Creek Community Church, where she also teaches workshops on parenting, grief/loss, and marital restoration.

September finds deep satisfaction in building things from scratch, finding just the right sentence to close the scene, and savoring time with friends until the coffee has long grown cold.

September and Scott live just outside of Chicago.

Explore Katie's art portfolio— and bring life to others.

To explore more of Katie's portfolio—
including prints available for purchase—
go to **septembervaudrey.com**.
Proceeds from your purchase help bring life
to others through select charities that benefit
children in the developing world.